THE OFFICIAL

1989 BLACKBOOK

PRICE GUIDE OF UNITED STATES

PAPER MONEY

TWENTY-FIRST EDITION

BY MARC HUDGEONS, N.L.G.

HOUSE OF COLLECTIBLES
NEW YORK, NEW YORK 10022

©1988 Random House, Inc.

All rights reserved under International and Pan-American Copyright Conventions.

Published by: The House of Collectibles
201 East 50th Street
New York, New York 10022

Distributed by Ballantine Books, a division of Random House, Inc., New York and simultaneously in Canada by Random House of Canada Limited, Toronto.

Manufactured in the United States of America

Library of Congress Catalog Card Number: 80-644107

ISBN: 0-876-37095-4

10 9 8 7 6 5 4 3 2 1

TABLE OF CONTENTS

OFFICIAL BOARD OF CONTRIBUTORS

PUBLISHER'S NOTE

The Official Blackbook Price Guide of United States Paper Money is designed as a reference aid for collectors, dealers, and the general public. Its purpose is to provide historical and collecting data, as well as current values. Prices are as accurate as possible at the time of going to press but no guarantee is made. We are not dealers; persons wishing to buy or sell paper money, or have it appraised, are advised to consult collector magazines or the telephone directory for addresses of dealers. We are not responsible for typographical errors.

NOTE TO READERS

All advertisements appearing in this book have been accepted in good faith, but the publisher assumes no responsibility in any transactions that occur between readers and advertisers.

MARKET REVIEW

Though the market in paper money has generally remained stable, it appears that the value of higher-grade notes, especially in crisp, uncirculated condition, has been making substantial gains in recent months. As indicated by the price increases on certain issues, many new collectors are entering the market. It also seems that the serious, long-time collectors are responding to the market activity by looking for bargains among rare issues, primarily in fine condition, but also in less than crisp, uncirculated condition. New collectors who are now entering the market are concentrating on lesser grades and more common issues. In other words, the influx of new blood in the marketplace is increasing the market's activity. Look for the market to strengthen in the coming year.

Evidently, the celebrations of the bicentennial of the Constitution, the Statue of Liberty, the release of the newly minted bullion coins, and the accompanying promotional and advertising campaigns have contributed to the growth of interest in paper money collecting, and are sparking renewed interest in the large-size classic bills and those issues of large-size paper money whose designs depict important events in our early history. No other collectible shows our American heritage in more interesting and colorful detail as does our early American paper money.

Auction sales of the past year are another indication of the increased interest and activity in the field of large bills, and they confirm the preeminence of the large-size bill in the paper money market. Attractively framed sets of these classic notes are very much in demand these days as decorative and conversation pieces in both the home and the office. Many of these notes are extremely rare, especially in better condition, and the values that were increasing slowly and steadily are now increasing at a greater rate. No doubt, the appearance of new collectors in the field will lead to even more substantial increases in the years to come.

Interest and activity in small-size currency is growing as well, though not as noticeably as with large-size bills. And while the prices have increased over the past year, they remain a great deal more affordable than the older classics. Certain dates, issues, and seals are rarer than others, and these, of course, are commanding relatively higher prices. Consequently, these issues are the ones to look for, as they will appreciate in value more rapidly than the more common notes. As always, though, the small currency area of collecting offers a wonderful introduction to the field, as it involves the new collector in the many aspects of paper money collecting—from the variety of dates and series to the federal districts. And since the prices for these notes are still within the range of those just starting out, this end of paper money collecting offers the new collector a great opportunity to build a collection that will increase in value.

The paper money market has enjoyed a great infusion of new collectors in the past year. The uncertainties of today's economy has encouraged many of those who previously invested elsewhere to investigate new areas of investment opportunity; certainly, one of those is the field of collectibles. The steady growth of this hobby is quite unlike that found in any other field of investment. But other investments do not give the same sense of enjoyment and fulfillment that you can get from handling your collection. You can leisurely spread out your treasures and indulge in the feeling of having created something very special. Indeed, many collectors start finding it hard to part with any piece from their collection—regardless of the price.

Not much is being said about the design changes currently being contemplated for the format of U.S. currency. However, occasional bits of news indicate that major changes are under consideration, coming either as a gradual transformation or a sweeping, across-the-board change. It seems that the main obstacle to introducing any new designs is not in the designs themselves, but the mechanics under which such a change would take place. One change currently being implemented is a device that is expected to be in all new 1987 currency issues from $1 to $100 bills. A single, synthetic thread imbedded in the paper crosses the bills from top to bottom and incorporates microscopic printing, reflecting the bill's denomination. This thread is visible only under special lighting conditions. The idea behind this new feature is to protect the currency from counterfeiters taking advantage of the new and highly sophisticated color copiers. If this new device is successful, it will undoubtedly be used on all future series and issues of paper money. But given the current system and the vast number of bills now in circulation, implementing this and other proposed changes will be a monumental task.

HOW UNITED STATES CURRENCY BEGAN

The present series of United States paper currency had its origins in 1861 and thus is 120 years old. Obviously, modern business could not operate without currency, but very likely its appearance would not even have occurred as early as 1861, without the pressing need brought about by the Civil War. Coinage was in very short supply almost from the war's outset, and both sides, North and South, resorted to printing notes. This was in a sense "emergency money" and at first circulation was disorderly and disorganized. The Union undoubtedly anticipated a return to bullion money as soon as possible upon the war's conclusion. Resumption of regular striking of coins in the mid- to late-1860's fell short of meeting the need for money, however, and paper currency continued in use. It did, in fact, increase and has been increasing since. The earliest U.S. notes (1861) are so-called Demand Notes. In 1862, Legal Tender Notes appeared and subsequently, a variety of notes, some of which were in circulation simultaneously.

COLLECTING PAPER MONEY

Paper money can be a fascinating hobby. Though of more recent origin than coinage, U.S. paper money exists in enormous varieties and can be collected in many ways.

Potential specialties are numerous. The following is not by any means a complete list.

1. Series collecting. Here the collector focuses upon a certain series of notes, such as the $5 1863-75 National Bank Notes, and attempts to collect specimens showing each of the different signature combinations, points of issue, seal colors, or whatever varieties happen to exist in the series. This may sound restrictive but, as an examination of the listings in this book will show, most series are comprised of many varieties. Generally, the older the series, the more difficult or expensive will be its completion, while certain series include great rarities beyond the budget range of most collectors. The cost can be brought down somewhat if one does not demand the finest condition but is content to own an example of the note in whatever condition he can reasonably afford. It should be pointed out, though, that in reselling paper money there is generally a greater loss—or smaller profit—on notes whose condition is less than Very Fine.

2. Set collecting. Sets are groups of notes of different denominations, issued at the same time (or approximately the same time), which were in current circulation together.

3. Place or origin collecting. Collecting notes by the city whose Federal Reserve Bank issued them.

4. Signature collecting. Collecting one specimen of every note bearing the signature of a certain Secretary of the Treasury.

5. Confederate currency collecting. The notes issued for use within the Confederate States of America during the Civil War.

6. Portrait collecting. By the individual or individuals depicted on the note. This is sometimes known as topical collecting.

7. Freak and oddity collecting.

8. Fractional currency collecting.

Imagination, especially if placed into use in a coin-shop well stocked with paper money, will suggest further possibilities. All is fair; there are no strict rules on what makes a worthwhile collection, so long as the material included is not seriously defective or of questionable authenticity.

Don't expect to build a large collection rapidly. Paper money is not comparable to stamps, where a beginner can buy a packet of 1,000 different stamps and instantly have a sizable collection. Nor should the size of a collection be regarded as a mark of its desirability or worth. Many prizewinning collections contain fewer than a hundred pieces; some consist of only two or three dozen. Direction and quality count much more in this hobby than weight of numbers. Collectors seeking to own a large collection generally end up with one whose only recommendation is its size. It may impress beginners but is not likely to be regarded highly by more experienced collectors.

RECOGNIZING THE VALUABLE NOTES

Every note ever issued by the United States government is worth, at minimum, face value. This applies even to notes of which one-third is missing. Whether a note is worth *more* than its face value—to collectors and dealers in paper currency —depends chiefly upon its age, condition, scarcity, and popularity among hobbyists.

All obsolete notes (such as Silver Certificates) are worth more than face value when the condition is "crisp uncirculated" (or CU as it is called by collectors). Many notes, hundreds in fact, have premium value even in lower grades of condition due to their scarcity. The premium on a collectible note may be double or triple face value or more. There are early 1.00 notes worth more than one thousand times face value. While 19th century notes tend to be more valuable, as fewer were printed and saved, notes of considerable value did occur among those of the 20th century.

A note may be valuable as the result of belonging to a series in which all had limited printings, such as the historic 1862 United States Note. This type of valuable note is of course the easiest for a beginner to recognize, as the notes look very different compared to those of the present day.

Conveniently, notes have dates on them, and an early date is yet another indicator of possible value. But even without dates and size differences there would be little difficulty in distinguishing an early note. The earlier the note, the more it will differ in design, color, and other details from later currency. It may picture an individual no longer shown on notes, such as Robert Fulton, Samuel Morse or James Garfield. It may have the portrait on the back instead of the front. The portrait may be to one side rather than centered. The serial numbers may not be where they are normally found. Such notes are instantly recognizable as being very old. They, in fact, look so unlike modern currency that some non-collectors take them for stocks or bonds or something other than legal tender.

A non-collector often believes that the value of old paper money is linked to its serial numbers. While a serial number can contribute to value, it is well down the list of ingredients for valuable notes. Among specimens of very high value, the serial number is hardly ever of consequence.

What is? Quite often the signatures. The signatures on a note play a very considerable role in the collector's world. If notes did not carry signatures, or if the signatures were never changed, the paper money hobby would be a mere shadow of what it is today. To cite just one example, the 1902 series of 10.00 National Bank Notes without dates yielded fifteen different varieties for the hobbyist to collect. Every one of them is a signature variety! Take away the signatures and all would be identical. Nothing changed but the signatures, yet they changed fifteen times. A rarity was created, too: the Jones-Woods combination is worth about three times as much as any of the other fourteen. If you did not look at the signatures and were unaware of the rarity of this particular combination, you would surely fail to pick this note out of a batch of 1902 10.00 National Bank Notes. There is absolutely nothing remarkable by which to notice it.

There are many other notes in which the signatures are vitally important. The 1875 Bruce-Jordan combination on the 5.00 National Bank Note is so rare that pricing it is difficult. The other eight signature combinations from this series, while definitely of value, are not in that class.

The color of the seal, which has varied on notes in the 19th and 20th centuries, is seldom a major factor in value. In most cases where it appears to be a factor, some other element is in fact responsible for the note's value. An example of this is the 2.00 United States Note of 1878 with red seal and signatures of Scofield and Gilfillan. It is quite a bit more valuable than any 2.00 U.S. Note with a brown seal, leading many people to think that the seal color is a factor in its value. The rarity of this note derives from the signature combination. Another was issued with the same date and same red seal, but with signatures of Allison and Gilfillan. Its value is less than one-tenth as much.

However there are a few cases in which the seal color makes a great difference in value, so it should not be totally dismissed. The 1.00 United States Note of 1878 with a maroon seal is valuable, while the same note with a red seal—identical in all other respects—is worth sharply less.

The date appearing on a note can be a value factor, not just by indicating the note's age. There may be two or more variations of the note that are distinguished by the date. In the case of Federal Reserve Notes (the only notes still being printed), the district of origin can influence their value. In some series there were not as many printed for Kansas City or Dallas as for New York or Chicago, and the scarcer ones have gained an edge in collector appeal and value. This applies to an even greater extent among National Bank Notes, which involved literally thousands of local banks across the country.

It's safe to say that paper money should be carefully examined. When examined by a person who knows what he's looking for, there is little chance of a rarity slipping by undetected.

BUYING PAPER MONEY

Browsing in coin shops is the usual way in which beginners start buying paper money. Just about every coin dealer—and many stamp dealers—stock paper money to one degree or another, from a single display album with elementary material to vaults filled with literally millions of dollars worth of specimens. Be observant of condition when shopping from dealers' stocks. There is really no excuse for unsatisfactory purchases from shops—the buyer has ample opportunity for inspection. Don't buy in a rush. Get to know the dealer and become familiar with his grading practices. Some dealers will grade a specimen higher than another dealer, but this may be offset by the fact that they charge a lower price.

Bargains. Is it possible to get bargains in buying paper money? To the extent that prices vary somewhat from dealer to dealer, yes. But if you're talking about finding a note worth 100.00 selling at 50.00 this is unlikely to happen. The dealers are well aware of market values and the slight price differences that do occur are merely the result of some dealers being overstocked on certain notes or, possibly, having made a very good "buy" from the public. What may appear to be a bargain will generally prove, on closer examination, to be a specimen in undesirable condition, such as a washed bill on which the color has faded.

Auction sales. Many coin auctions feature selections of paper money, and there are occasional sales (mostly of the postal-bid variety) devoted exclusively to it. There is much to be said for auction buying if you have some experience and know how to read an auction catalog.

Shows and conventions. Paper money is offered for sale at every coin show and exposition. These present excellent opportunities to buy, as the dealers exhibiting at such shows are generally out-of-towners whose stock you would not otherwise have a chance to examine. As many sellers are likely to be offering the same type of material, you have the opportunity to make price and condition comparisons before buying.

CARING FOR YOUR COLLECTION

Paper money is not at all difficult to care for, store and display attractively. It consumes little space and, unlike many other collectors' items, runs no risk of breakage. Nevertheless, it is important that the hobbyist give some attention to maintenance, as a poorly kept collection soon becomes aimless clutter and provides little enjoyment.

There is not much question that albums are the favorite storage method of nearly all paper money enthusiasts. In the days before specially made albums with vinyl pocket-pages, collectors used ordinary scrapbooks and mounted their specimens with philatelic hinges or photo-corners. This, of course, may still be done, but such collections do not have the advantage of displaying both sides of the notes. Furthermore, the use of gummed hinges may leave marks upon removal, whereas specimens may be removed and reinserted into vinyl-page albums without causing the slightest blemish. We especially recommend the albums and "currency wallet" sold by Anco Coin & Stamp Supply, P. O. Box 782, Florence, Alabama 35630.

Faded color. There is no known restorative for faded color.

Holes. It is suggested that no effort be undertaken to repair holes, as this will almost certainly result in a further reduction in value.

Missing corners. Missing corners can seldom be restored in a manner that is totally satisfactory. The best that can be done is to secure some paper of approximately the same color and texture, trim a small piece to the proper size, and glue it in place as described below. If a portion of printed matter is missing, this can be hand-drawn, in ink, after restoration. Obviously, this kind of repair is not carried out to "fool" anybody, but simply to give a damaged specimen a less objectionable appearance.

Repairs to paper money. Repair work on damaged or defaced paper money is carried out strictly for cosmetic purposes; to improve its physical appearance. Repairs, even if skillfully executed, will not enhance the value of a specimen, as it will still be classified as defective. Amateurish repair efforts can very possibly make matters worse.

Tears. Tears can be closed by brushing a very small quantity of clear-drying glue to both sides of the tear, placing the note between sheets of waxed kitchen paper and setting it under a weight to dry. A dictionary of moderate size serves this function well. Allow plenty of drying time and handle gently thereafter.

Wrinkles. Wrinkles, creases and the like can sometimes be improved by wetting the note (in plain water) and drying it between sheets of waxed paper beneath a reasonably heavy weight—five pounds or more. This should not be done with a modern or recent specimen if there is danger of losing crispness.

Many ills to which paper money falls prey result from not being housed in a suitable album, or any album at all. Framing and mounting present some risk, as the item may then be exposed to long periods of direct sunlight, almost sure to cause fading or "bleaching" of its color.

SELLING YOUR COLLECTION

Selling to a dealer. All dealers in paper money buy from the public, but not all buy every collection offered to them. Some are specialists and are interested only in collections within their fields of specialization. Some will not purchase (or even examine) collections worth under $100, or $500, or whatever their line of demarcation happens to be. Obviously, a valuable collection containing many hard-to-get notes in VF or UNC condition is easier to interest a dealer in than a beginner-type collection. If a dealer is interested enough to make an offer, this is no guarantee that another dealer would not offer more. In the case of a collection worth $50,000, offers from several dealers might vary by as much as $5,000. This is not an indication that the dealer making the lowest offer is unscrupulous. Dealers will pay as much as the material is worth to them, and one dealer may be overstocked on items that another badly needs. Or one dealer may have customers for certain material that another doesn't. For this reason it makes good sense, if you choose to sell to a dealer, to obtain several offers before accepting any. But should you sell to a dealer at all? The chief advantage is quick payment and reduced risk. The price may not be as high as would be obtained at auction, however, depending on the property's nature and pure luck.

Selling by auction. Auction selling presents uncertainties but at the same time offers the possibility of gaining a much better return than could be had by selling to a dealer. It is no easy matter deciding which route to follow. If your collection is better than average, you may be better advised to sell by auction. This will involve a waiting period of, generally, four to six months between consigning the collection and receiving settlement; over the summer months it may be longer. However, some auctioneers will give a cash advance, usually about 25 percent of the sum they believe the material is worth. In special circumstances a larger advance may be made, or the usual terms and conditions altered. One auctioneer paid $100,000 under a special contract, stipulating that the money was not to be returned regardless of the sale's outcome or even if no sale took place. But this was on a million-dollar collection. Auctioneers' commissions vary. The normal is 20 percent but some houses take 10 percent from the buyer and 10 percent from the seller. This would appear to work to the seller's advantage, but such a practice may discourage bidding and result in lower sale prices.

Selling to other collectors. Unless the owner is personally acquainted with a large circle of collectors, this will likely involve running ads in periodicals and "playing dealer," which runs into some expense. Unless you offer material at very favorable prices, you are not apt to be as successful with your ads as are the established dealers, who have a reputation and an established clientele.

INVESTING

1. Buy only specimens in V.F. (Very Fine) or better condition.

2. Be sure the notes you buy are properly graded and priced in accordance with their grade.

3. Avoid Federal Reserve Notes of the past thirty years. These have been stockpiled by dealers to such extent that their value is not likely to show dramatic increase.

4. For investment purposes it is usually wise to avoid the very highly specialized types of notes. Investment success depends on continued growth of the hobby, and most new collectors will buy the standard items.

5. Do not seek quick profits. It is rare for an investment profit on paper currency to occur in less than five years. When holding five years or longer the possibility of a profit is much greater.

6. Notes recommended by their sellers as investments are sometimes the worst investments. Learn about the paper money market and make your own selections.

7. Do not invest more than you can afford to. Tying up too much capital in investments of any kind can be hazardous.

GLOSSARY

BROKEN BANK NOTE

Literally, a broken bank note is a note issued by a "broken" bank—a bank that failed and whose obligations could therefore not be redeemed. It may be presumed, by those who recall passing of legislation establishing the Federal Deposit Insurance Corporation, that banks failed only in the financial panic of 1929. During the 19th century, bank failures were common, especially in western and southwestern states. These were generally small organizations set up in frontier towns, which suffered either from mismanagement or a sudden decline in the town's fortunes. Some collectors make a specialty of broken bank notes.

DEMAND NOTES

Demand Notes have the distinction of being the first official circulating paper currency of this country, issued in 1861. There are three denominations: five, ten and twenty dollars, each bearing its own design on front and back. Demand Notes arose out of the coinage shortage brought about by the Civil War. A total of $60,000,000 in Demand Notes was authorized to be printed, amounting to several million individual specimens. Though this was an extraordinary number for the time, it was small compared to modern output and only a fraction of the total survived. These notes were signed not by any specially designated Treasury Department officers but a battery of employees, each of whom was given authority to sign and affix their names by hand in a slow assembly-line process, two signatures to each note. Originally the spaces left blank for signatures were marked "Register of the Treasury" and "Treasurer of the United States." As the persons actually signing occupied neither of these offices they were obliged to perpetually add "for the . . ." to their signatures. In an effort to relieve their tedium, fresh plates were prepared reading "For the Register of the Treasury" and "For the Treasurer of the United States," which required nothing but a signature. This created a rarity status for the earlier specimens, which are now very desirable collectors' items.

ENGRAVING

Engraving is the process by which designs are printed on U.S. paper money. Engraving involves the use of a metal plate, traditionally copper, into which the design is drawn or scraped with sharply bladed instruments. Ink is smeared over the surface and allowed to work into the grooves or lines comprising the design. The ink is then cleaned away from raised portions (intended to show blank in the printing). The engraving is pressed against a sheet of moistened paper and the ink left in these grooves transfers to the paper, resulting in a printed image. When done by modern rotary press, it's a fast-moving process.

FEDERAL RESERVE NOTES

Federal Reserve Notes, the notes in current circulation, were authorized by the Federal Reserve Act of December 23, 1913. Issued under control of the Federal Reserve Board, these notes are released through twelve Federal Reserve Banks in various parts of the country. Originally they were redeemable in gold at the United States Treasury or "lawful money" (coins) at a Federal Reserve Bank. In 1934 the option of redemption for gold was removed.

FEDERAL RESERVE BANK NOTES

Federal Reserve Bank Notes were issued briefly in 1915 and 1918. Like National Bank Notes they were secured by bonds or securities placed on deposit by each Federal Reserve Bank with the U.S. government. While issued and redeemable by the member banks of the Federal Reserve system, these notes are secured by —and are obligations of—the government.

FREAK AND ERROR NOTES

Bills which, by virtue of error or accident, are in some respect different from normal specimens. See the section on Freak and Error Notes.

GOLD CERTIFICATES

When gold coinage became a significant medium of exchange, the government decided to hold aside quantities of it and issue paper notes redeemable by the Treasury Department. The first Gold Certificates for public circulation were released in 1882. The series lasted until the era of small-size currency, ending in 1928. In 1933 all were ordered returned to the Treasury Department for redemption, including those in possession of collectors. A new law in 1964 permitted their ownership by collectors, though they can no longer be redeemed for gold.

LARGE-SIZE CURRENCY

Large-size currency is the term generally used to refer to U.S. notes issued up to 1929, which were somewhat larger in size than those printed subsequently. The increased size permitted more elaborate design, which seldom fails to endear Large-Size Currency to beginners. Some of the earlier examples (especially of the 1870's, 1880's and 1890's) are works of art. Though economic considerations were mainly responsible for the switch to a reduced size, there is no doubting that today's notes are far more convenient to handle and carry. Large-size notes are sometimes referred to as "bedsheet notes."

NATIONAL BANK NOTES

This is the largest group of notes available to the collector. They were issued from 1863 to 1929 and present collecting potential that can only be termed vast. More than 14,000 banks issued notes, in all parts of the country. While the approach to collecting them is usually regional, sets and series can also be built up, virtually without end. The National Banking Act was instituted in 1863, during the Civil War, to permit chartered banks to issue and circulate their own currency.

Printing was done at the U.S. Government Printing Office and the designs were all alike, differing only in names of the banks, state seals, bank signatures and the bank's charter number. Each charter bank was limited to issuing currency up to 90 percent of the value of bonds that it kept on deposit with the government. Charters remained in force for 20 years and could be renewed for an additional 20 years. National Bank Notes circulated in the same fashion as conventional currency and, thanks to the bond-deposit system, gained public confidence. The financial panic of 1929, which brought ruin or near-ruin to many banks, put an end to National Bank Notes.

NATIONAL GOLD BANK NOTES

These notes were issued exclusively by California banks during the 1870's under the same terms as ordinary National Bank Notes, their values backed by bonds deposited with the government. Events surrounding their origins form a unique chapter in the history of American economy. Following the discoveries of substantial quantities of gold in California in the late 1840's, that metal soon became the chief medium of local exchange, largely because it was more readily available in that remote region than coinage. Later, when gold coins and tokens began to circulate heavily in California, banks became so swamped with them that they petitioned Washington for authority to issue Gold Notes that could be substituted for the actual coinage. On July 12, 1870, Congress voted favorably on this measure, giving the right to issue such notes to nine banks in California and one in Boston. The Boston bank, Kidder National Gold Bank, appears not to have exercised its right, as no Gold Notes of this institution have been recorded. The California banks wasted no time in exercising their authority, the result being a series of notes ranging from five- to five-hundred dollars in denomination. All were printed on yellow-toned paper so as to be instantly identifiable. The banks issuing these notes were permitted to redeem them in gold coins.

REFUNDING CERTIFICATES

Refunding Certificates, a sort of hybrid between currency and bonds or securities, were issued under a Congressional Act of February 26, 1879. These were notes with a ten dollar face value which could be spent and exchanged in the fashion of ordinary money but drew interest at the rate of 4 percent per year. The purposes behind Refunding Certificates were several. They were chiefly designed to encourage saving and thereby curb inflation, which even at that time was becoming a problem. Also, they provided a safe means of saving for persons who distrusted banks (safe so long as the certificates were not lost or stolen), and, probably more important, were readily obtainable in areas of the country not well served by banks. In 1907 the interest was halted. Their redemption value today, with interest, is $21.30.

SERIAL NUMBER

The serial number is the control number placed on all U.S. paper bills, appearing below left-center and above right-center. No two bills in the same series bear repetitive serial numbers. The use of serial numbers is not only an aid in counting and sorting bills as printed but a deterrent to counterfeiting.

SIGNATURES

The inclusion of signatures of Treasury Department officials on our paper bills, a practice as old as our currency (1861), was begun as a mark of authorization and a foil to counterfeiters. The belief was that the handwriting would be more difficult to copy than an engraved design. Persons whose signatures appear on notes did not always occupy the same office. From 1862 to 1923, the two signers were the Treasurer and the Register (or Registrar as it appears in old writings) of the Treasury. Subsequently, the Treasurer and Secretary of the Treasury were represented. These signatures are of great importance to collectors as some notes are relatively common with certain combinations of signatures and others are rare. A "series" collection is not considered complete until one obtains every existing combination, even though the specimens may be in other respects identical.

SILVER CERTIFICATES

Silver Certificates were authorized in 1878. America's economy was booming at that time and the demand for silver coinage in day-to-day business transactions outdistanced the supply. Silver Certificates were not intended to replace coinage but to create a convenient medium of exchange, whereby the government held specific quantities of Silver Dollars (later bullion) and agreed to redeem the notes or certificates against them. In 1934 the Treasury Department ceased redemption of these notes in Silver Dollars and on June 24, 1968, redemption in all forms was ended. The notes are still, however, legal tender at their face value. When printing of Silver Certificates was discontinued, a flurry of speculation arose and many persons began hoarding them. This was done not only in hope of eventual redemption for bullion but the belief that such notes would become valuable to collectors. Though Silver Certificates are popular with hobbyists, they have not increased sufficiently in price to yield speculators any great profits—especially since many collectors saved specimens in circulated condition.

STAR NOTES

United States Notes, Silver Certificates, and Gold Certificates sometimes have a star or asterisk in place of the letter in front of the serial number. Federal Reserve Notes and Federal Reserve Bank Notes have it at the end of the serial number. These notes are known as "Star Notes."

When a note is mutilated or otherwise unfit for issue, it must be replaced. To replace it with a note of the same serial numbers would be impractical, and "Star Notes" are therefore substituted. Other than having their own special serial number and a star, these notes are the same as the others. On United States Notes and Silver Certificates, the star is substituted for the prefix letter; on Federal Reserve Notes, for the suffix letter. All defective notes are accounted for and destroyed by burning them in an incinerator.

Large stars after the serial number on the 1869 series of United States notes, and 1890 and 1891 Treasury Notes, do not signify replacement notes as are known in later and present day "Star Notes."

Serial numbers on early large-size notes were preceded by a letter and were ended by various odd characters or symbols. These characters are not known to have any significance, except to show that the number was terminated, and prevented any elimination or addition of digits. The suffix characters were replaced by alphabet letters on later issues of notes.

TREASURY OR COIN NOTES

Treasury Notes were authorized by Congress in 1890. Their official title was Coin Notes, as they could be redeemed for silver or gold coins. The series did not prove popular and was discontinued after the issue of 1891.

TREASURY SEAL

The Treasury Seal is the official emblem of the U.S. Treasury Department, which has appeared on all our currency since 1862. It is missing only from the early Demand Notes, issued in 1861, and some Fractional Currency. Two versions have been employed, distinguished readily by the fact that one (the original) bears a Latin inscription, while the current Treasury Seal is in English. The basic motif is the same, a badge displaying scales and a key. The original Seal, somewhat more decorative, was in use until 1968.

UNITED STATES NOTES

Also known as Legal Tender Notes, this substantial and ambitious series followed Demand Notes and constitutes the second earliest variety of U.S. paper currency. There are five distinct issues, running from 1862 to 1923. Though United States Notes are all "large size" and their designs not very similar to those in present use, they show in their successive stages the evolutionary advance from this nation's first efforts at paper money to its currency of today. The first issue is dated March 10, 1862. Denominations are $1, $2, $5, $10, $20, $50, $100, $500, $1,000, $5,000 and $10,000. Individuals portrayed included not only Presidents but other government officials: Salmon P. Chase (Lincoln's Secretary of the Treasury), Daniel Webster, and Lewis and Clark. Some of the reverse designs are masterpieces of geometrical linework. A number of rarities are to be found among Legal Tender Notes, but in general the lower denominations can be collected without great expense.

WILDCAT NOTES

Wildcat notes are the notes that were issued by so-called "Wildcat Banks," in the era of State Bank Notes before the Civil War. Numerous banks sprang up around the middle part of the 19th century, mostly in the west and southwest, operated by persons of questionable integrity. Some never had capital backing and were instituted purely as a front for confidence swindles. After issuing notes, the bank shut down, its directors disappeared, and owners of the notes were left with worthless paper. As news traveled slowly in those days, the same persons could move from town to town and work the scheme repeatedly. Notes issued by these banks, or any banks that became insolvent, are also called Broken Bank Notes. Apparently the origin of the term "wildcat" derives from public sentiment of the time, which held that owners of such banks had no greater trustworthiness than a wild animal. "Wildcat" may also refer to the rapid movement of swindling bank officials from one locality to another.

CURRENCY TERMS

Check Letter and Quadrant Number · Federal Reserve District Seal · Serial Number · Treasury Seal

District Numbers · District Numbers

Serial Number · Series · Check Letter and Plate Check Number

THE FEDERAL RESERVE BANKS

The Federal Reserve system is divided into 12 Federal Reserve districts, in each of which is a Federal Reserve Bank. There are also 24 branches. Each district is designated by a number and the corresponding letter of the alphabet. The district numbers, the cities in which the 12 banks are located, and the letter symbols are:

1-A—Boston
2-B—New York
3-C—Philadelphia
4-D—Cleveland
5-E—Richmond
6-F—Atlanta
7-G—Chicago
8-H—St. Louis
9-I—Minneapolis
10-J—Kansas City
11-K—Dallas
12-L—San Francisco

O Reserve Bank Cities
• Branch Bank Cities
— District Boundaries
-- Branch Territory Boundaries
★ Board of Governors of the Federal Reserve System

32 SUBJECT SHEET LAYOUT

All United States currency is now printed with 32 subjects (notes) to a large sheet. The first printing is the green back. The second printing is the face of the note, in black. This includes the portrait and border, the series year, the check letter and quadrant number, two signatures and the face plate number. The sheet is then cut in half vertically for the third printing. This includes the black Federal Reserve seal, the four Federal Reserve district numbers, the green Treasury seal and two green serial numbers.

The 32 subject sheet is divided into four quarters called quadrants for numbering and other controls. Each quadrant has its own numbering sequence for the eight notes, with serial numbers advancing by 20,000 to the next note. The quadrant number and check letter in the upper left section indicates the first, second, third or fourth quadrant and the position of the note in the quadrant. In the lower right corner the position letter is shown again with a plate number. On the back of the note the same small number in the lower right is the back plate number.

FIRST QUADRANT				THIRD QUADRANT			
A1		E1		A3		E3	
A00000001A	A100	A00080001A	E100	A00320001A	A100	A00400001A	E100
B1		F1		B3		F3	
A00020001A	B100	A00100001A	F100	A00340001A	B100	A00420001A	F100
C1		G1		C3		G3	
A00040001A	C100	A00120001A	G100	A00360001A	C100	A00440001A	G100
D1		H1		D3		H3	
A00060001A	D100	A00140001A	H100	A00380001A	D100	A004600001A	H100
A2		E2		A4		E4	
A00160001A	A100	A00240001A	E100	A00480001A	A100	A005600001A	E100
B2		F2		B4		F4	
A00180001A	B100	A00260001A	F100	A00500001A	B100	A00580001A	F100
C2		G2		C4		G4	
A00200001A	C100	A00280001A	G100	A0050001A	C100	A00600001A	G100
D2		H2		D4		H4	
A00220001A	D100	A00300001A	H100	A00540001A	D100	A00620001A	H100

SECOND QUADRANT   FOURTH QUADRANT

THE NUMBERING SYSTEM OF
UNITED STATES PAPER CURRENCY

The system of numbering paper money must be adequate to accommodate a large volume of notes. For security and accountability purposes, no two notes of any one class, denomination and series may have the same serial number. The two serial numbers on each note have a full complement of eight digits and an alphabetical prefix and suffix letter. When necessary, ciphers are used at the left of the number to make a total of eight digits.

Whenever a numbering sequence is initiated for United States Notes or Silver Certificates, the first note is numbered A 00 000 001 A; the second A 00 000 002 A; the hundredth A 00 000 100 A; the thousandth A 00 001 000 A; and so on through A 99 999 999 A. The suffix letter A will remain the same until a total of 25 groups, or "blocks" of 99 999 999 notes are numbered, each group having a different prefix letter of the alphabet from A to Z. The letter "O" is omitted, either as a prefix or as a suffix, because of its similarity to zero. The 100 000 000th note in each group will be a Star Note, since eight digits are the maximum in the mechanical operation of numbering machines.

At this point, the suffix letter changes to B for the next 25 groups of 99 999 999 notes, and proceeds in the same manner as the suffix letter A. A total of 62,500,000,000 notes could be numbered before a duplication of serial numbers would occur. However, it has never been required to number that many notes of any one class, denomination and series.

The Federal Reserve Notes printed for the 12 districts are numbered in the same progression as United States Notes and Silver Certificates, except that a specific alphabetical letter identifies a specific Federal Reserve district. The letter identifying each district is used as a prefix letter at the beginning of the serial numbers on all Federal Reserve Notes and does not change. Only the suffix letter changes in the serial numbers on Federal Reserve currency.

PORTRAITS AND BACK DESIGN ON SMALL-SIZE NOTES

DENOMINATION	PORTRAIT	BACK DESIGN
$1.00	Washington	Great Seal of the United States
$2.00	Jefferson	Monticello
$5.00	Lincoln	Lincoln Memorial
$10.00	Hamilton	United States Treasury
$20.00	Jackson	The White House
$50.00	Grant	United States Capitol
$100.00	Franklin	Independence Hall
$500.00	McKinley	"FIVE HUNDRED"
$1000.00	Cleveland	"ONE THOUSAND"
$5000.00	Madison	"FIVE THOUSAND"
$10,000.00	Chase	"TEN THOUSAND"
$100,000.00	Wilson	"ONE HUNDRED THOUSAND"

DATING UNITED STATES CURRENCY

Unlike coins, the date is not changed each year on United States currency.

The date appearing on all notes, large or small, is that of the year in which the design was first approved or issued. For instance, large-size One Dollar United States Notes of the series 1880 were issued with the same date until the new series of 1917 was issued. There was no further date change until the series of 1923.

The same rules apply to small-size notes. However, in this case a letter is added after the date to designate or indicate a minor change in the main design or probably a change in one or both of the signatures. For example: the One Dollar Silver Certificate of 1935 was changed to 1935-A because of a change in the size of the tiny plate numbers appearing in the lower right corners of the face and back of the note. It was changed again from 1935-A to 1935-B in 1945 when the signatures of Julian/Morganthau were changed to Julian/Vinson. Subsequent changes in signatures continued the 1935 series to the year 1963 when the signatures of Smith/Dillon terminated the issue with the series of 1935-H. Therefore, these notes were issued for 28 years bearing the date 1935.

NEW TREASURY SEAL

FORMER DESIGN:
The former design had the Latin inscription:
"Thesaur. Amer. Septent. Sigil.,"
which has several translations. It was the Seal of the North American Treasury.

NEW DESIGN:
This new design drops the Latin and states "The Department of The Treasury, 1789." First used on the $100 Note of the Series of 1966.

GRADES AND CONDITIONS OF PAPER MONEY

CONDITION

The physical condition of a note or bill plays an important role in determining its value. There are many notes that have no premium value beyond face value in ordinary condition but are valuable or moderately valuable when uncirculated. Even in the case of scarce early specimens, the price given for an "average" example is generally much less than that commanded by Fine or Very Fine condition.

Defects encountered in paper money include:

Creases, folds, wrinkles. Generally the characteristic that distinguishes uncirculated notes from those that almost—but not quite—qualify for such designation is a barely noticeable crease running approximately down the center vertically, resulting from the note being folded for insertion into a wallet or billfold. It may be possible, through manipulation or storage beneath a heavy weight, to remove evidence of the crease; but the knowledge that it once existed cannot be obliterated.

Discoloration. Discoloration is not as easy to recognize as most defects but it must be classed as one. A distinction should be made between notes printed from underinked rollers and those that originally were normally colored but became "washed out." Sometimes washing is indeed the cause; a well-intentioned collector will bathe a note, attempting to clean it, with the result that its color is no longer strong. This should not happen if warm water is used, without strong cleanser. Atmospheric conditions may play some part in discoloration.

Foxing. Fox spots may sometimes be observed on old notes, especially those of the pre-1890 era, just as on old paper in general. They seem more common to foreign currency than American, but their presence on our notes is certainly not rare. These are tiny brownish-red dots, caused by an infestation of lice attacking the paper fibres.

Holes. Holes are more likely to be encountered in early paper money than specimens of recent origin. In early years it was customary for federal reserve banks to use wire clips in making up bundles of notes for distribution to banking organizations, and these clips or staples often pierced the bills. Another common occurrence years ago was the practice of shop clerks and cashiers in general to impale notes upon holders consisting of nails mounted on stands.

Missing pieces. Missing pieces are a highly undesirable defect which, except in the case of rare specimens, renders the item valueless to collectors. Even if only a blank unprinted corner is torn away, this is called a missing-piece note and hardly anyone will give it a second glance.

Stains. Notes sometimes become stained with ink or other liquids. If the specimen is commonplace and easily obtainable in VF or Uncirculated condition, it will be worthless with any kind of stain. In a note of moderate value, its price will be hurt to a greater or lesser degree depending on the stain's intensity, size, nature, and the area it touches. A stain in an outer margin or at a corner is not so objectionable as one occurring at the center or across a signature or serial number.

Ink stains, because of their strong color, are generally deemed the worst, but bad staining can also be caused by oil, crayon, "magic marker" and food substances. Pencil markings, which frequently are found on bank notes, will yield to ordinary erasing with a piece of soft "artgum" worked gently over the surface and brushed away with an artist's camel-hair brush. Most other stains cannot be so easily removed. With ink there is no hope, as any caustic sufficiently strong to remove the ink will also injure the printing and possibly eat through the paper as well. Oil stains can sometimes be lightened, though not removed, by sprinkling the note on both sides (even if the stain shows only on one) with talcum powder or other absorbent powder, placing it between sheets of waxed kitchen paper, and leaving it beneath a heavy weight for several days in a room where the humidity is not unduly high.

Tears. Tears in notes are very common defects, which may be minute or run nearly the whole length of the bill. As a rule the paper on which American currency is printed is fairly rugged and will not tear so readily as most ordinary paper, but given careless or hurried handling anything is possible. An old worn note is more apt to tear in handling than a new one. Repaired tears are more common in the world of paper money collecting than may be generally supposed. A clean tear—one which does not involve loss of surface—can be patched up so as to become virtually unnoticed, unless examined against a light or through a strong magnifying glass. X-ray examination will reveal repairs when all else fails.

CONDITION STANDARDS

The following condition standards have been used throughout this book and, with slight variations depending upon individual interpretation, are generally current in the trade.

Uncirculated—UNC. A specimen that for all appearances has not been handled or passed through general circulation; a crisp fresh note in "bank" condition. There may be minor blemishes, such as a finger smudge or pinhole, but if these are in any respect severe the condition merits description as "almost uncirculated." There is not much satisfaction to be taken in a note fresh and crisp that has gaping holes and fingerprints. Obviously, an 1870 "uncirculated" note should not be expected to match a 1970 in appearance or feel.

Almost Uncirculated—A.U. In the case of modern or semi-modern notes, this is generally taken to mean a specimen that shows no evidence of having passed through general circulation but because of some detraction fails to measure up to a rating of "uncirculated." The problem may be finger smudges, counting crinkles, a light crease, a fold along one or more of the corners, or pinholes. But if more than one of these impairments is present, the item would surely not deserve a classification of "almost uncirculated."

Extremely Fine—X.F. A note exhibiting little evidence of wear from handling, but not so perfect or near-perfect as to qualify for a rating of "uncirculated" or "almost uncirculated." On a used note issued before 1900 there may be clear evidence of circulation, but no disfiguring marks.

Very Fine—V.F. A very fine note has experienced some circulation but escaped without "being mangled." It is still clean and crisp and its creases are not offensive.

Fine—F. Here the scale begins sliding down. It is obvious that, being the fifth in rank of condition grades, "fine" notes are quite a good deal removed from "uncirculated." They have been handed around pretty thoroughly and suffered the normal consequences, but still are without serious blemishes such as tears, missing corners, serious stains or holes.

Very Good—V.G. A well-circulated note bearing evidence of much folding, creasing and wrinkling. It may possibly be lightly stained, smudged or pin punctured, but major defects—such as a torn-off corner—would drop it into an even lower category.

Good—G. Heavily circulated, worn notes that are possibly stained or scribbled on, edges could be frayed or "dog-eared." There may be holes larger than pin punctures, but not on the central portion of design. This is the lowest grade of condition acceptable to a collector, and only when nothing better is available. Unless very rare, such specimens are considered space-fillers only.

A.B.P.—Average Buying Prices. The average buying prices given here are the approximate sums paid by retail dealers for specimens in good condition. As selling prices vary, so do buying prices, and in fact they usually vary a bit more.

ABOUT THE PRICES IN THIS BOOK

Prices shown in the *Official Blackbook Price Guide of United States Paper Money* are compiled from offerings made by dealers and from auction sale results. In all cases (except for the Average Buying Price) the prices are retail selling prices. While prices are current at the time of publication, the market can be influenced by buying or selling trends, causing prices to change. All prices, except in the case of seldom offered rarities, are averages, calculated from numerous sales. The actual prices charged by any individual currency dealer may be slightly higher or lower than those indicated in this book. In any given sale various factors play a role, such as whether the seller is overstocked on notes of that type.

HOW TO USE THIS BOOK

The *Official Blackbook Price Guide of United States Paper Money* provides a convenient reference to prices of all standard U.S. currency, old and new, as well as many unusual issues.

Notes are divided into section by denomination. Within each section can be found the various series of notes for that denomination. The series are arranged chronologically and will vary slightly from section to section, as some notes were issued in one series and not in another. An index page is provided at the beginning of each section.

To price a note correctly, it is necessary that it be accurately identified and graded. The illustrations will aid in identification, and a grading guide has been provided. In the case of some notes, particularly very old ones, the value depends upon minor details. In all such cases these details have been clearly noted.

Listings include the following information:

Date. This is the "series date," as it appears on the note, and may bear no relation whatsoever to the year in which the note was actually issued. The date of actual issue is not of importance to collectors. If the series date on the note carries a suffix letter, such as 1935A, it will be so indicated in the listing.

Seal. The color of the Treasury Seal will be noted, along with other information if relevant.

Signatures. All U.S. notes carry two signatures, and the names of each signer are given for every note listed. If different signature combinations exist for your note, be sure you refer to the correct signature combination. The listings will show you whether there is just one set of signatures for that note, or more than one.

Type. In a small minority of cases, notes were issued in more than one type. For example, a slight change was made in the paper or printing. All recorded types are identified in the listings.

Issuing Bank. This information is provided for Federal Reserve Notes and Federal Reserve Bank Notes only. Check the Federal Reserve seal on your note to identify the issuing bank. In some instances there is a difference in value depending on where the note originated. Space prevents us from listing the numerous local banks issuing National Bank Notes.

A.B.P. The first price column is the A.B.P. or Average Buying Price. This is the approximate sum being paid by dealers for a specimen in the lowest listed grade of condition. The lowest listed grade of condition is the column next to the A.B.P. If the next column is headed "Good," the A.B.P. is for a specimen in Good condition. In all cases the A.B.P. includes the face value of the note. This is an important consideration insofar as U.S. notes, regardless of their age or physical condition, can still be spent as legal tender.

Current Selling Prices. The current selling prices are given in two or three different grades of condition, as indicated at the top of each price column. Different groups of notes are priced in different condition grades, owing to market availability. Some are virtually unobtainable in uncirculated condition so it would be pointless to give such a price. Others are of no premium value in less than V.F., hence V.F. is the lowest grade shown.

RECORD KEEPING

For your convenience, we suggest you use the following record-keeping system to note condition of your paper money in the checklist box:

| ◻FAIR | ☒VERY GOOD | ◻VERY FINE | ☒ALMOST UNC |
| ☒GOOD | ◻FINE | ☒EXTREMELY FINE | ■UNCIRCULATED |

ONE DOLLAR NOTES

ORDER OF ISSUE

ONE DOLLAR NOTES (1862) UNITED STATES NOTES
(ALSO KNOWN AS LEGAL TENDER NOTES)

(Large Size)   **NOTE NO. 1**

Face Design: Portrait of Salmon Portland Chase (1808–1873), Secretary of the Treasury under Lincoln, red Treasury Seal, signatures of Chittenden and Spinner, lower right.

Back Design: Large circle center with legal tender obligation.

SERIES SIGNATURES	SEAL	A.B.P.	GOOD	V. FINE	UNC.
1862 Chittenden-Spinner					
☐ Type I-National Bank Note, American Bank Note without Monogram	Red	40.00	70.00	200.00	600.00
☐ Type II-National Bank Note, American Bank Note with Monogram ABNCO	Red	25.00	45.00	160.00	525.00
☐ Type III-National Bank Note, National Bank Note without Monogram	Red	25.00	45.00	160.00	525.00
☐ Type IV-National Bank Note, National Bank Note with Monogram ABNCO	Red	25.00	45.00	180.00	550.00

ONE DOLLAR NOTES (1869) UNITED STATES NOTES
(ALSO KNOWN AS LEGAL TENDER NOTES)

(Large Size)

NOTE NO. 2

Face Design: Portrait of President Washington in the center, large red seal to the right. Scene of Columbus in sight of land to left; also called "Rainbow Note" because of the many colors used in printing. Black ink for main design, red seal and serial numbers, green background for the serial number, green shading in upper-half and blue tint in paper left of portrait to deter counterfeiting.

Back Design: Green, "ONE DOLLAR" and "ONE" over "1" center, letters U.S. interwoven to left. Legal tender obligation to right of center.

SERIES	SIGNATURES	SEAL	A.B.P.	GOOD	V. FINE	UNC.
☐ 1869	Allison-Spinner	Red	30.00	50.00	200.00	825.00

ONE DOLLAR NOTES (1874–1917) UNITED STATES NOTES
(ALSO KNOWN AS LEGAL TENDER NOTES)

(Large Size)

NOTE NO. 3

Back Design: Large green "X" with United States of America in the center. Legal tender obligation and counterfeiting warning to right.

Face Design: No blue or green shading and tinting.

SERIES	SIGNATURES	SEAL		A.B.P.	GOOD	V. FINE	UNC.
☐ 1874	Allison-Spinner	Red	Sm.	15.00	30.00	125.00	475.00
☐ 1875	Allison-New	Red	Sm.	15.00	80.00	70.00	325.00
☐ 1875	Same Series A	Red	Sm.	32.00	60.00	160.00	675.00
☐ 1875	Same Series B	Red	Sm.	20.00	45.00	160.00	640.00
☐ 1875	Same Series C	Red	Sm.	25.00	60.00	190.00	840.00
☐ 1875	Same Series D	Red	Sm.	50.00	80.00	200.00	840.00
☐ 1875	Same Series E	Red	Sm.	75.00	160.00	340.00	1100.00
☐ 1875	Allison-Wyman	Red	Sm.	15.00	30.00	65.00	200.00
☐ 1878	Allison-Gilfillan	Red	Sm.	15.00	35.00	75.00	325.00
☐ 1878	Allison-Gilfillan	Maroon Sm.		—	—	—	1250.00
☐ 1880	Scofield-Gilfillan	Brown	Lg.	15.00	25.00	91.00	280.00
☐ 1880	Bruce-Gilfillan	Brown	Lg.	15.00	25.00	64.00	220.00
☐ 1880	Bruce-Wyman	Brown	Lg.	15.00	25.00	64.00	220.00
☐ 1880	Rosecrans-Huston	Red	Lg.	25.00	42.00	150.00	620.00
☐ 1880	Rosecrans-Huston	Brown	Lg.	25.00	42.00	160.00	680.00
☐ 1880	Rosecrans-Nebeker	Brown	Lg.	25.00	43.00	160.00	700.00
☐ 1880	Rosecrans-Nebeker	Red	Sm.	14.00	22.00	62.00	220.00
☐ 1880	Tillman-Morgan	Red	Sm.	14.00	22.00	62.00	260.00
☐ 1917	Tehee-Burke	Red	Sm.	14.00	22.00	35.00	160.00
☐ 1917	Elliott-Burke	Red	Sm.	12.00	20.00	28.00	150.00
☐ 1917	Burke-Elliott*	Red	Sm.	18.00	32.00	78.00	370.00
☐ 1917	Elliott-White	Red	Sm.	10.00	24.00	35.00	165.00
☐ 1917	Speelman-White	Red	Sm.	10.00	20.00	35.00	165.00

Sm.—Small Seal, Lg.—Large Seal
*This note with signatures of Burke and Elliott is an error issue. The regular procedure was to have the signature of the Register of the Treasury on the left, and that of the Treasurer to the right. The signatures were transposed in this instance.

ONE DOLLAR NOTES (1923) UNITED STATES NOTES
(ALSO KNOWN AS LEGAL TENDER NOTES)

(Large Size)

NOTE NO. 4

Face Design: Portrait of President Washington in center. Red seal to left, red "1" to the right, red serial numbers.

Back Design: "United States of America" and "ONE DOLLAR" in center. Figures "1" to right and left. This was the last issue of large-size "ONE DOLLAR" United States Notes. The last series of large-size notes was kept in use until 1929 when the first issue of small-size notes was released.

SERIES	SIGNATURES	SEAL	A.B.P.	GOOD	V. FINE	UNC.
☐ 1923	Speelman-White	Red	10.00	16.00	40.00	230.00

ONE DOLLAR NOTES (1928) UNITED STATES NOTES
(ALSO KNOWN AS LEGAL TENDER NOTES)

(Small Size)

Face Design: Red seal to left—red serial numbers, large "ONE" to right. This is the only issue of the $1.00 United States Note, small size. At the present time only the $100.00 United States Note is current.

Back Design: Large "ONE" in center with "ONE DOLLAR" overprint, back printed in green.

SERIES SIGNATURES	SEAL	A.B.P.	GOOD	V. FINE	UNC.
☐ 1928 Woods-Woodin	Red	5.00	10.00	25.00	60.00

ONE DOLLAR NOTES (1863–1875) NATIONAL BANK NOTES
FIRST CHARTER PERIOD (Large Size)

NOTE NO. 6

Face Design: Name of National Bank top center, maidens at altar below.

Back Design: Landing of Pilgrims—center, state seal of state issuing bank to left, eagle and flag.

SERIES SIGNATURES	SEAL		A.B.P.	GOOD	V. FINE	UNC.
☐ Original* Colby-Spinner	Red	w/r	35.00	65.00	210.00	925.00
☐ Original* Jeffries-Spinner	Red	w/r	105.00	260.00	1300.00	2900.00
☐ Original* Allison-Spinner	Red	w/r	35.00	65.00	210.00	1100.00
☐ 1875 Allison-New	Red	w/s	35.00	65.00	210.00	725.00
☐ 1875 Allison-Wyman	Red	w/s	35.00	65.00	210.00	725.00
☐ 1875 Allison-Gilfillan	Red	w/s	35.00	65.00	210.00	725.00
☐ 1875 Scofield-Gilfillan	Red	w/s	35.00	65.00	210.00	725.00

w/r—with Rays, w/s—with Scallops
*Early notes of the First Charter Period did not have the series imprinted on them. They are known by the date on the bill which was usually the date of charter or organization, or as the Original Series. These notes had a seal with rays or small notches. In 1875 the series was imprinted in red and the seal was changed to have scallops around the border. The charter number was added to later issues of notes of the original series and to all notes of the 1875 series.

ONE DOLLAR NOTES (1886) SILVER CERTIFICATES

(Large Size)   **NOTE NO. 7**

Face Design:
Portrait of
Martha Washington

Back Design

SERIES SIGNATURES	SEAL	A.B.P.		
☐ 1886 Rosecrans-Jordan	Red Sm	20.00	35.00	110.00	600.00
☐ 1886 Rosecrans-Hyatt	Red Sm	20.00	32.00	200.00	1100.00
☐ 1886 Rosecrans-Hyatt	Red Lg	20.00	35.00	110.00	600.00
☐ 1886 Rosecrans-Huston	Red Lg	21.00	35.00	200.00	975.00
☐ 1886 Rosecrans-Huston	Brown Lg	21.00	38.00	110.00	600.00
☐ 1886 Rosecrans-Nebeker	Brown Lg	21.00	40.00	210.00	1100.00
☐ 1886 Rosecrans-Nebeker	Red Sm	28.00	50.00	210.00	1100.00

ONE DOLLAR NOTES (1891) SILVER CERTIFICATES

(Large Size)

NOTE NO. 8

Back Design

Face Design:
Same as Note
No. 7

SERIES SIGNATURES	SEAL	A.B.P.	GOOD	V. FINE	UNC.
☐ 1891 Rosecrans-Nebeker	Red Sm	25.00	45.00	170.00	550.00
☐ 1891 Tillman-Morgan	Red Sm	35.00	65.00	260.00	950.00

ONE DOLLAR NOTES (1896) SILVER CERTIFICATES
(Large Size)
NOTE NO. 9

The Educational Note

Face Design: History instructing youth. To the right, panoramic view of the Capitol and Washington Monument. Constitution on tablet, names of famous Americans on top and side borders.

Back Design: Portrait of Martha Washington to left and President Washington to right with large numeral "1" in center.

There is a story that when this note was issued people objected to it because they said No "1" (ONE) should stand between George and Martha Washington. The set consists of $1.00, $2.00, and $5.00 denominations. They all have very beautiful engravings, and they are truly the most beautiful notes ever issued by our government. They were first released in 1896 and replaced by a new issue in 1899. They were short-lived because of objections to the unclad female on the $5.00 note.

SERIES SIGNATURES	SEAL	A.B.P.	GOOD	V. FINE	UNC.
☐ 1896 Tillman-Morgan	Red	30.00	55.00	210.00	800.00
☐ 1896 Bruce-Roberts	Red	32.00	65.00	170.00	920.00

ONE DOLLAR NOTES (1899) SILVER CERTIFICATES
(Large Size)   **NOTE NO. 10**

Face Design: Eagle on flag and Capitol background over portraits of Presidents Lincoln and Grant.

Back Design

SERIES	SIGNATURES	SEAL	A.B.P.	GOOD	V. FINE	UNC.
	SERIES OF 1899 is above upper right serial number.					
☐ 1899	Lyons-Roberts	Blue	12.00	25.00	40.00	140.00
	SERIES OF 1899 is below upper right serial number.					
☐ 1899	Lyons-Roberts	Blue	10.00	20.00	30.00	180.00
☐ 1899	Lyons-Treat	Blue	10.00	20.00	30.00	180.00
☐ 1899	Vernon-Treat	Blue	10.00	20.00	30.00	180.00
☐ 1899	Vernon-McClung	Blue	10.00	20.00	30.00	180.00
	SERIES OF 1899 is vertical to right of blue seal on the following notes:					
☐ 1899	Napier-McClung	Blue	10.00	20.00	30.00	160.00
☐ 1899	Napier-Thompson	Blue	17.00	35.00	85.00	600.00
☐ 1899	Parker-Burke	Blue	10.00	20.00	30.00	160.00
☐ 1899	Teehee-Burke	Blue	10.00	20.00	30.00	160.00

SERIES	SIGNATURES	SEAL	A.B.P.	GOOD	V. FINE	UNC.
☐ 1899	Elliott-Burke	Blue	10.00	20.00	30.00	160.00
☐ 1899	Elliott-White	Blue	10.00	20.00	30.00	160.00
☐ 1899	Speelman-White	Blue	10.00	20.00	30.00	160.00

ONE DOLLAR NOTES (1923) SILVER CERTIFICATES

(Large Size)

NOTE NO. 11

Face Design: Portrait of President Washington in center, blue seal left, blue "1 DOLLAR" right, blue numbers.

Back Design: Same as Note No. 4

SERIES	SIGNATURES	SEAL	A.B.P.	GOOD	V. FINE	UNC.
☐ 1923	Speelman-White	Blue	5.00	10.00	20.00	62.00
☐ 1923	Woods-White	Blue	5.00	10.00	20.00	62.00
☐ 1923	Woods-Tate	Blue	10.00	22.00	42.00	230.00

ONE DOLLAR NOTES (1928) SILVER CERTIFICATES
(Small Size)   **NOTE NO. 12**

Face Design: Portrait of President Washington, blue seal to the left, "ONE" to right, blue seal and numbers. "ONE SILVER DOLLAR" under portrait.

Back Design

First issue series of 1928. United States paper money was reduced in 1928 from the old large size to the size presently in use. This was mostly an economy measure. Unlike large-size notes, the small notes have a letter designation after the date to denote a minor change in design or change of one or both signatures.

SERIES SIGNATURES	SEAL	A.B.P.	GOOD	V. FINE	UNC.
☐ 1928 Tate-Mellon	Blue	1.50	3.00	10.00	25.00
☐ 1928A Woods-Mellon	Blue	1.50	3.00	6.00	15.00
☐ 1928B Woods-Mills	Blue	1.50	3.00	6.00	15.00
☐ 1928C Woods-Woodin	Blue	16.00	31.00	105.00	570.00
☐ 1928D Julian-Woodin	Blue	15.00	27.00	78.00	340.00
☐ 1928E Julian-Morgenthau	Blue	60.00	105.00	330.00	1010.00

ONE DOLLAR NOTES (1934) SILVER CERTIFICATES
(Small Size)   **NOTE NO. 13**

Face Design: Portrait of President Washington, blue "1" to left. "ONE" and blue seal to right. "ONE DOLLAR IN SILVER," under portrait.
Back Design: Same as Note No. 12.

SERIES SIGNATURES	SEAL	A.B.P.	GOOD	V. FINE	UNC.
☐ 1934 Julian-Morgenthau	Blue	1.50	3.00	7.00	22.00

ONE DOLLAR NOTES (1935) SILVER CERTIFICATES
(Small Size)   **NOTE NO. 14**

Face Design: Portrait of President Washington in center. Gray "1" to left, blue seal right, and blue numbers. "ONE DOLLAR IN SILVER," under portrait.

The following notes are without "IN GOD WE TRUST" on back.

SERIES SIGNATURES	SEAL	A.B.P.	GOOD	V. FINE	UNC.
☐ 1935 Julian-Morgenthau	Blue	1.50	2.75	4.00	12.00
☐ 1935A Julian-Morgenthau	Blue	1.25	2.50	3.25	6.50
☐ 1935A Julian-Morgenthau	Brown ...	3.00	6.00	9.00	43.00

This note was a special issue for use in war zones in the Pacific area during World War II. Brown serial numbers and HAWAII stamped on front and back.

ONE DOLLAR NOTES (1935) SILVER CERTIFICATES

(Small Size)   **NOTE NO. 14**

SERIES SIGNATURES	SEAL	A.B.P.	GOOD	V. FINE	UNC.
☐ 1935A Julian-Morgenthau	Yellow ...	3.50	6.50	13.00	62.00

The above note was a special issue for use in war zones in the North African and European areas during World War II. Blue serial numbers and yellow seal.

| ☐ 1935A Julian-Morgenthau | Blue ..... | 7.00 | 13.00 | 25.00 | 220.00 |

Red "R" between the Treasury Seal and signatures of Morgenthau. This was an experimental issue to test wearing qualities of differently treated paper.

| ☐ 1935A Julian-Morgenthau | Blue ..... | 6.00 | 11.00 | 21.00 | 180.00 |

Above note with red "S" between Treasury Seal and signature of Morgenthau. Experimental issue "R" was for regular paper, "S" for special paper.

☐ 1935B Julian-Vinson	Blue	1.25	2.50	4.00	7.50
☐ 1935C Julian-Snyder	Blue	1.25	2.00	2.50	7.00
☐ 1935D Clark-Snyder	Blue	1.25	2.00	2.50	7.00

Wide design on back. This and all notes of 1935 prior to this, have the wide design. See Fig I.

| ☐ 1935D Clark-Snyder | Blue ..... | 1.25 | 2.00 | 2.50 | 6.50 |

Narrow design on back. This and all $1.00 notes following have narrow design. See Fig. II.

FIG. I WIDE DESIGN

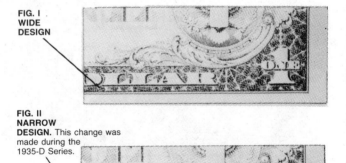

FIG. II NARROW DESIGN. This change was made during the 1935-D Series.

ONE DOLLAR NOTES (1935) SILVER CERTIFICATES

(Small Size)   **NOTE NO. 14**

SERIES SIGNATURES	SEAL	A.B.P.	GOOD	V. FINE	UNC.
☐ 1935E Priest-Humphrey	Blue	1.25	1.75	2.25	5.00
☐ 1935F Priest-Anderson	Blue	1.25	1.75	2.25	5.00
☐ 1935G Smith-Dillon	Blue	1.25	1.75	2.25	5.00

"IN GOD WE TRUST" added. All notes following have the motto.

☐ 1935G Smith-Dillon	Blue	1.25	1.75	2.25	5.00
☐ 1935H Granahan-Dillon	Blue	1.25	1.75	2.25	5.00

ONE DOLLAR NOTES (1957) SILVER CERTIFICATES

(Small Size)   **NOTE NO. 14**

The following three notes are the last issue of the $1.00 Silver Certificates. The reason for the change in series from 1935H to 1957 was due to printing improvements. The 1935 series, up until the issue of Clark and Snyder, was printed in sheets of 12 subjects to a sheet. During the term of Clark and Snyder notes were printed 18 subjects to a sheet. Starting with the series of 1957, new high speed rotary presses were installed and notes were printed 32 subjects to a sheet.

SERIES SIGNATURES	SEAL	A.B.P.	GOOD	V. FINE	UNC.
☐ 1957 Priest-Anderson	Blue	1.10	1.50	2.00	4.00
☐ 1957A Smith-Dillon	Blue	1.10	1.50	2.00	4.00
☐ 1957B Granahan-Dillon	Blue	1.10	1.50	2.00	4.00

The redemption of Silver Certificates by the U.S. Treasury Department ended on June 24, 1968. These notes are now worth only their face value, plus the numismatic value to collectors. Notes in used condition are not regarded as collectors' items.

ONE DOLLAR NOTES (1890) TREASURY OR COIN NOTES
(Large Size)

NOTE NO. 15

Face Design: Portrait of Stanton, Secretary of War during the Civil War.

Back Design: Green large ornate "ONE." Entire back is beautifully engraved.

SERIES	SIGNATURES	SEAL	A.B.P.	GOOD	V. FINE	UNC.
☐ 1890	Rosecrans-Huston	Brown	30.00	55.00	280.00	1250.00
☐ 1890	Rosecrans-Nebeker	Brown	30.00	55.00	290.00	1350.00
☐ 1890	Rosecrans-Nebeker	Red	25.00	45.00	240.00	1200.00

ONE DOLLAR NOTES (1891) TREASURY OR COIN NOTES
(Large Size)

NOTE NO. 16

Face Design: Is similar to Note No. 15.

Back Design: More unengraved area, numerous "ONEs" and "1s."

SERIES	SIGNATURES	SEAL	A.B.P.	GOOD	V. FINE	UNC.
☐ 1891	Rosecrans-Nebeker	Red	25.00	55.00	110.00	575.00
☐ 1891	Tillman-Morgan	Red	25.00	55.00	105.00	510.00
☐ 1891	Bruce-Roberts	Red	25.00	55.00	105.00	510.00

ONE DOLLAR NOTES (1918)
FEDERAL RESERVE BANK NOTES

(Large Size)

NOTE NO. 17

Face Design: Portrait of President Washington, signature to left of center. Bank and city center, blue seal to right. Signatures of government officials above. Signatures of bank officials below. Federal Reserve district letter and numbers in four corners.

Back Design: Flying eagle and flag in center. All are series 1918, and have blue seals and blue numbers.

ONE DOLLAR NOTES (1918)
FEDERAL RESERVE BANK NOTES

(Large Size)   **NOTE NO. 17**

BANK & CITY	GOV'T SIGNATURES	BANK SIGNATURES	A.B.P.	GOOD	V. FINE	UNC.
☐ Boston	Teehee-Burke	Bullen-Morss	9.00	16.00	46.00	180.00
☐ Boston	Teehee-Burke	Willet-Morss	20.00	41.00	80.00	325.00
☐ Boston	Elliot-Burke	Willet-Morss	9.00	16.00	46.00	180.00
☐ New York	Teehee-Burke	Sailer-Strong	9.00	16.00	46.00	180.00
☐ New York	Teehee-Burke	Hendricks-Strong	9.00	16.00	46.00	180.00
☐ New York	Elliott-Burke	Hendricks-Strong	9.00	16.00	46.00	180.00
☐ Philadelphia	Teehee-Burke	Hardt-Passmore ..	9.00	16.00	46.00	180.00
☐ Philadelphia	Teehee-Burke	Dyer-Passmore ...	9.00	16.00	46.00	180.00
☐ Philadelphia	Elliott-Burke	Dyer-Passmore ...	9.00	16.00	46.00	180.00
☐ Philadelphia	Elliott-Burke	Dyer-Norris	9.00	16.00	46.00	180.00
☐ Cleveland	Teehee-Burke	Baxter-Fancher ...	9.00	16.00	46.00	180.00
☐ Cleveland	Teehee-Burke	Davis-Fancher ...	9.00	16.00	46.00	180.00
☐ Cleveland	Elliott-Burke	Davis-Fancher ...	9.00	16.00	46.00	180.00
☐ Richmond	Teehee-Burke	Keesee-Seay	9.00	16.00	46.00	180.00
☐ Richmond	Elliott-Burke	Keesee-Seay	9.00	16.00	46.00	180.00
☐ Atlanta	Teehee-Burke	Pike-McCord	9.00	16.00	46.00	180.00
☐ Atlanta	Teehee-Burke	Bell-McCord	9.00	16.00	46.00	180.00
☐ Atlanta	Teehee-Burke	Bell-Wellborn	9.00	16.00	46.00	180.00
☐ Atlanta	Elliott-Burke	Bell-Wellborn	9.00	16.00	46.00	180.00
☐ Chicago	Teehee-Burke	McCloud-McDougal	9.00	16.00	46.00	180.00
☐ Chicago	Teehee-Burke	Cramer-McDougal	9.00	16.00	46.00	180.00
☐ Chicago	Elliott-Burke	Cramer-McDougal	9.00	16.00	46.00	180.00
☐ St. Louis	Teehee-Burke	Attebery-Wells ...	9.00	16.00	46.00	180.00
☐ St. Louis	Teehee-Burke	Attebery-Biggs ...	9.00	16.00	46.00	180.00
☐ St. Louis	Elliott-Burke	Attebery-Biggs ...	9.00	16.00	46.00	180.00
☐ St. Louis	Elliott-Burke	White-Biggs	9.00	16.00	46.00	180.00
☐ Minneapolis	Teehee-Burke	Cook-Wold	11.00	22.00	55.00	260.00
☐ Minneapolis	Teehee-Burke	Cook-Young	105.00	210.00	510.00	1050.00
☐ Minneapolis	Elliott-Burke	Cook-Young	11.00	22.00	55.00	260.00
☐ Kansas City	Teehee-Burke	Anderson-Miller ..	9.00	16.00	46.00	180.00
☐ Kansas City	Elliott-Burke	Anderson-Miller ..	9.00	16.00	46.00	180.00
☐ Kansas City	Elliott-Burke	Helm-Miller	9.00	16.00	46.00	180.00
☐ Dallas	Teehee-Burke	Talley-VanZandt ..	9.00	16.00	46.00	180.00
☐ Dallas	Elliott-Burke	Talley-VanZandt ..	21.00	41.00	100.00	260.00
☐ Dallas	Elliott-Burke	Lawder-VanZandt	9.00	16.00	46.00	180.00
☐ San Francisco	Teehee-Burke	Clerk-Lynch	9.00	16.00	46.00	180.00
☐ San Francisco	Teehee-Burke	Clerk-Calkins	9.00	16.00	46.00	180.00
☐ San Francisco	Elliott-Burke	Clerk-Calkins	9.00	16.00	46.00	180.00
☐ San Francisco	Elliott-Burke	Ambrose-Calkins	9.00	16.00	46.00	180.00

ONE DOLLAR NOTES (1963) FEDERAL RESERVE NOTES
(Small Size)   **NOTE NO. 18**

Face Design: Portrait of President Washington in center, black Federal
Reserve seal with city and district letter to left, green Treasury Seal to right.
Green serial numbers, Federal Reserve numbers in four corners.
Back Design: Same as all $1.00 Notes from 1935.

SERIES OF 1963 GRANAHAN-DILLON—GREEN SEAL

DISTRICT	A.B.P.	UNC.	DISTRICT	A.B.P.	UNC.
☐ 1A Boston	1.50	3.25	☐ 7G Chicago	1.50	3.25
☐ 2B New York	1.50	3.25	☐ 8H St. Louis	1.50	3.25
☐ 3C Philadelphia	1.50	3.25	☐ 9I Minneapolis	1.50	3.25
☐ 4D Cleveland	1.50	3.25	☐ 10J Kansas City	1.50	3.25
☐ 5E Richmond	1.50	3.25	☐ 11K Dallas	1.50	3.25
☐ 6F Atlanta	1.50	3.25	☐ 12L San Francisco	1.50	3.25

The Dallas note of this series as shown, with the letter "K" in the black seal and
the numbers "11" in the four corners, does not have any more significance or
value than any other notes with their respective district letter and corresponding
number.

A false rumor was circulated several years ago that the "K" was for Kennedy,
the "11" was for November, the month in which he was assassinated, and that
the note was issued by the Dallas bank to commemorate the occasion. The entire
story is apocryphal.

This note is in no way associated with the late President Kennedy. The notes
were authorized by the act of June 4, 1963. This was five months before Kennedy
was assassinated. The Federal Reserve district for Dallas is K-11.

SERIES OF 1963A GRANAHAN-FOWLER—GREEN SEAL

DISTRICT	A.B.P.	UNC.	DISTRICT	A.B.P.	UNC.
☐ 1A Boston	1.50	3.50	☐ 7G Chicago	1.50	3.50
☐ 2B New York	1.50	3.50	☐ 8H St. Louis	1.50	3.50
☐ 3C Philadelphia	1.50	3.50	☐ 9I Minneapolis	1.50	3.50
☐ 4D Cleveland	1.50	3.50	☐ 10J Kansas City	1.50	3.50
☐ 5E Richmond	1.50	3.50	☐ 11K Dallas	1.50	3.50
☐ 6F Atlanta	1.50	3.50	☐ 12L San Francisco	1.50	3.50

ONE DOLLAR NOTES (1963-B) FEDERAL RESERVE
(WITH SIGNATURE OF JOSEPH W. BARR)

(Small Size)

NOTE NO. 18

Joseph W. Barr served as Secretary of the Treasury from December 20, 1968 to January 20, 1969, filling the unexpired term of Henry H. Fowler. His signature appears on the $1.00 Federal Reserve notes of the series of 1963-B only.

During the one month term of Joseph W. Barr about 471 million notes were printed with his signature. These notes were for the following Federal Reserve Banks.

NOTES ISSUED

REGULAR NUMBERS	A.B.P.	UNC.	STAR NUMBERS	A.B.P.	UNC.
☐ 2B New York 123,040,000	2.00	4.50	3,680,000	2.00	4.75
☐ 5E Richmond 93,600,000	2.00	4.50	3,040,000	2.00	4.75
☐ 7G Chicago 91,040,000	2.00	4.50	2,400,000	2.00	4.75
☐ 10J Kansas City 44,800,000	2.00	4.50	None Printed		
☐ 12L San Francisco .. 106,400,000	2.00	4.50	3,040,000	2.00	4.75

ONE DOLLAR NOTES (1969) FEDERAL RESERVE NOTES
(WORDING IN GREEN, TREASURY SEAL CHANGED FROM LATIN TO ENGLISH)

FORMER DESIGN:
The former design had the Latin inscription: *"Thesaur. Amer. Septent. Sigil.,"* which has several translations. It was the Seal of the North American Treasury.

NEW DESIGN:
This new design drops the Latin and states *"The Department of The Treasury, 1789."* First used on the $100 Note of the Series of 1966.

ONE DOLLAR NOTES (1969) FEDERAL RESERVE NOTES
(Small Size)   **NOTE NO. 18A**

SERIES OF 1969—ELSTON-KENNEDY, GREEN SEAL

Boston	2.70	Cleveland	2.70	Chicago	2.70	Kansas City	2.70
New York	2.70	Richmond	3.65	St. Louis	2.70	Dallas	2.70
Philadelphia	2.70	Atlanta	2.70	Minneapolis	2.70	San Francisco	2.70

SERIES OF 1969A—KABIS-KENNEDY, GREEN SEAL

Boston	2.70	Cleveland	2.70	Chicago	2.70	Kansas City	2.70
New York	2.70	Richmond	2.70	St. Louis	2.70	Dallas	2.70
Philadelphia	2.70	Atlanta	2.70	Minneapolis	2.70	San Francisco	2.70

SERIES OF 1969B—KABIS-CONNALLY, GREEN SEAL

Boston	2.70	Cleveland	2.70	Chicago	2.70	Kansas City	2.70
New York	2.70	Richmond	2.70	St. Louis	2.70	Dallas	2.70
Philadelphia	2.70	Atlanta	2.70	Minneapolis	2.70	San Francisco	2.70

SERIES OF 1969C—BANUELOS-CONNALLY, GREEN SEAL

Boston	2.70	Cleveland	2.70	Chicago	2.70	Kansas City	2.70
New York	2.70	Richmond	2.70	St. Louis	2.70	Dallas	2.70
Philadelphia	2.70	Atlanta	2.70	Minneapolis	2.70	San Francisco	2.70

SERIES OF 1969D—BANUELOS-CONNALLY, GREEN SEAL

Boston	2.70	Cleveland	2.70	Chicago	2.70	Kansas City	2.70
New York	2.70	Richmond	2.70	St. Louis	2.70	Dallas	2.70
Philadelphia	2.70	Atlanta	2.70	Minneapolis	2.70	San Francisco	2.70

SERIES OF 1974—NEFF-SIMON, GREEN SEAL

Boston 2.20	Cleveland 2.20	Chicago 2.20	Kansas City .. 2.20
New York 2.20	Richmond 2.20	St. Louis 2.20	Dallas 2.20
Philadelphia .. 2.20	Atlanta 2.20	Minneapolis ... 2.20	San Francisco 2.20

SERIES OF 1977—MORTON-BLUMENTHAL, GREEN SEAL

Boston 2.20	Cleveland 2.20	Chicago 2.20	Kansas City .. 2.20
New York 2.20	Richmond 2.20	St. Louis 2.20	Dallas 2.20
Philadelphia .. 2.20	Atlanta 2.20	Minneapolis ... 2.20	San Francisco 2.20

SERIES OF 1977A—MORTON-MILLER, GREEN SEAL

Boston 2.20	Cleveland 2.20	Chicago 2.20	Kansas City .. 2.20
New York 2.20	Richmond 2.20	St. Louis 2.20	Dallas 2.20
Philadelphia .. 2.20	Atlanta 2.20	Minneapolis ... 2.20	San Francisco 2.20

SERIES OF 1981—BUCHANAN-REGAN, GREEN SEAL

Boston 2.20	Cleveland 2.20	Chicago 2.20	Kansas City .. 2.20
New York 2.20	Richmond 2.20	St. Louis 2.20	Dallas 2.20
Philadelphia .. 2.20	Atlanta 2.20	Minneapolis ... 2.20	San Francisco 2.20

SERIES OF 1981A—ORTEGA-REGAN, GREEN SEAL

Boston 2.20	Cleveland 2.20	Chicago 2.20	Kansas City .. 2.20
New York 2.20	Richmond 2.20	St. Louis 2.20	Dallas 2.20
Philadelphia .. 2.20	Atlanta 2.20	Minneapolis ... 2.20	San Francisco 2.20

SERIES OF 1985—ORTEGA-BAKER, GREEN SEAL

Boston 1.55	Cleveland 1.55	Chicago 1.55	Kansas City .. 1.55
New York 1.55	Richmond 1.55	St. Louis 1.55	Dallas 1.55
Philadelphia .. 1.55	Atlanta 1.55	Minneapolis ... 1.55	San Francisco 1.55

TWO DOLLAR NOTES

ORDER OF ISSUE

TWO DOLLAR NOTES (1862) UNITED STATES NOTES
(ALSO KNOWN AS LEGAL TENDER NOTES)

(Large Size)

NOTE NO. 19

ALEXANDER HAMILTON (1754–1804)

Face Design: Portrait of Hamilton, cloverleaf twos in upper corners, medallion with "11" in lower left, medallion with "1, 2, 3," right of portrait.

Back Design: "2" in each corner, with "2" motif repeated in scallop circles around obligation, back is printed green.

SERIES SIGNATURES	SEAL	A.B.P.	GOOD	V. FINE	UNC.
☐ 1862 Chittenden-Spinner					
TYPE I: American Banknote Company vertical in left border	Red	60.00	85.00	360.00	1300.00
☐ 1862 Chittenden-Spinner					
TYPE II: National Banknote Company vertical in left border	Red	60.00	85.00	360.00	1300.00

TWO DOLLAR NOTES (1869) UNITED STATES NOTES
(ALSO KNOWN AS LEGAL TENDER NOTES)

(Large Size)

NOTE NO. 20

Face Design: Portrait of President Jefferson to left, Capitol in center, large red seal to right.

Back Design: Roman II left, Arabic "2" center, "TWO," right. This is the companion note to the $1.00 "RAINBOW NOTE" (see Note No. 2).

SERIES SIGNATURES	SEAL	A.B.P.	GOOD	V. FINE	UNC.
☐ 1869 Allison-Spinner	Red	60.00	92.00	430.00	1650.00

TWO DOLLAR NOTES (1874) UNITED STATES NOTES
(ALSO KNOWN AS LEGAL TENDER NOTES)

(Large Size)

NOTE NO. 21

Face Design: Portrait of President Jefferson, same as previous Note No. 20.

Back Design: Completely revised.

SERIES	SIGNATURES	SEAL	A.B.P.	GOOD	V. FINE	UNC.
☐ 1874	Allison-Spinner	Red	42.00	73.00	210.00	660.00
☐ 1875	Allison-New	Red	32.00	62.00	160.00	410.00
☐ SERIES A	Allison-New	Red	55.00	105.00	305.00	610.00
☐ SERIES B	Allison-New	Red	55.00	105.00	305.00	610.00
☐ 1875	Allison-Wyman	Red	18.00	40.00	90.00	420.00
☐ 1878	Allison-Gilfillan	Red	21.00	42.00	150.00	610.00
☐ 1878	Scofield-Gilfillan	Red	600.00	1000.00	2600.00	5000.00
☐ 1880	Scofield-Gilfillan	Brown	15.00	26.00	65.00	310.00
☐ 1880	Bruce-Gilfillan	Brown	15.00	26.00	65.00	335.00
☐ 1880	Bruce-Wyman	Brown	15.00	26.00	65.00	335.00
☐ 1880	Rosecrans-Huston	Red	40.00	85.00	205.00	460.00
☐ 1880	Rosecrans-Huston	Brown	40.00	85.00	210.00	460.00
☐ 1880	Rosecrans-Nebeker	Red	14.00	26.00	55.00	280.00
☐ 1880	Tillman-Morgan	Red	21.00	41.00	65.00	335.00
☐ 1917	Teehee-Burke	Red	10.00	20.00	32.00	210.00
☐ 1917	Elliott-Burke	Red	11.00	22.00	30.00	180.00
☐ 1917	Elliott-White	Red	11.00	22.00	31.00	205.00
☐ 1917	Speelman-White	Red	11.00	22.00	31.00	200.00

TWO DOLLAR NOTES (1928) UNITED STATES NOTES
(ALSO KNOWN AS LEGAL TENDER NOTES)
(Small Size)   **NOTE NO. 22**

Face Design: Portrait of President Jefferson, red seal left, "TWO" right, red serial numbers.

Back Design: Jefferson Home—Monticello.

SERIES SIGNATURES	SEAL	A.B.P.	GOOD	V. FINE	UNC.
☐ 1928 Tate-Mellon	Red	5.00	9.00	16.00	42.00
☐ 1928A Woods-Mellon	Red	11.00	19.00	42.00	160.00
☐ 1928B Woods-Mills	Red	32.00	50.00	160.00	410.00
☐ 1928C Julian-Morgenthau	Red	2.50	5.00	10.00	62.00
☐ 1928D Julian-Morgenthau	Red	2.50	5.00	10.00	17.00
☐ 1928E Julian-Vinson	Red	3.25	6.00	19.00	55.00
☐ 1928F Julian-Snyder	Red	2.50	6.00	11.00	21.00
☐ 1928G Clark-Snyder	Red	2.50	5.00	9.00	16.00

TWO DOLLAR NOTES (1953) UNITED STATES NOTES
(ALSO KNOWN AS LEGAL TENDER NOTES)

(Small Size)   **NOTE NO. 23**

Face Design: Portrait of President Jefferson, gray "2" to left, red seal to right over "TWO."

Back Design: Same as Note No. 22.

SERIES SIGNATURES	SEAL	A.B.P.	GOOD	V. FINE	UNC.
☐ 1953 Priest-Humphrey	Red	2.20	3.25	6.00	8.50
☐ 1953A Priest-Anderson	Red	2.20	3.25	4.50	7.00
☐ 1953B Smith-Dillon	Red	2.20	3.25	4.50	7.00
☐ 1953C Granahan-Dillon	Red	2.20	3.25	4.50	7.00

Back Design: "IN GOD WE TRUST" on back.

Face Design: Same as previous note.

SERIES SIGNATURES	SEAL	A.B.P.	GOOD	V. FINE	UNC.
☐ 1963 Granahan-Dillon	Red	2.20	3.25	6.00	7.00
☐ 1963A Granahan-Fowler	Red	2.20	3.25	6.00	7.00

Production of Two Dollar United States Notes was discontinued on Aug. 10, 1966.

TWO DOLLAR NOTES (1875) NATIONAL BANK NOTES
FIRST CHARTER PERIOD (Large Size)
NOTE NO. 24

Face Design: This note is known as "The Lazy Two Note" due to the unusual "lying down" shape of the "2" shown on the face. Liberty with flag and red seal.

Back Design: Sir Walter Raleigh in England, 1585, exhibiting corn and smoking tobacco from America, state seal and eagle.

SERIES SIGNATURES	SEAL	A.B.P.	GOOD	V. FINE	UNC.
☐ Original Colby-Spinner	Red	110.00	210.00	550.00	2500.00
☐ Original Jeffries-Spinner	Red	380.00	780.00	1825.00	5000.00
☐ Original Allison-Spinner	Red	110.00	210.00	525.00	2450.00
☐ 1875 Allison-New	Red	95.00	190.00	405.00	2200.00
☐ 1875 Allison-Wyman	Red	95.00	190.00	405.00	2150.00
☐ 1875 Allison-Gilfillan	Red	95.00	190.00	405.00	2200.00
☐ 1875 Scofield-Gilfillan	Red	95.00	190.00	405.00	2200.00

TWO DOLLAR NOTES (1886) SILVER CERTIFICATES
(Large Size)

Face Design: General Hancock portrait left. Treasury seal to the right of center.

Back Design: "2" left and right, very ornate engraving, obligation in center of note. Note is printed in green.

SERIES SIGNATURES	SEAL	A.B.P.	GOOD	V. FINE	UNC.
☐ 1886 Rosecrans-Jordan	Red	40.00	80.00	310.00	1100.00
☐ 1886 Rosecrans-Hyatt	Red Sm ..	40.00	80.00	210.00	1250.00
☐ 1886 Rosecrans-Hyatt	Red Lg ..	40.00	80.00	310.00	1250.00
☐ 1886 Rosecrans-Huston	Red	40.00	80.00	210.00	1425.00
☐ 1886 Rosecrans-Huston	Brown ...	40.00	80.00	320.00	1225.00

TWO DOLLAR NOTES (1891) SILVER CERTIFICATES

(Large Size)   **NOTE NO. 26**

Face Design: Portrait of William Windom, Secretary of the Treasury 1881–1884 and 1889–1891, red seal right.

Back Design: "2" left and right, scalloped design center with obligation, printed in green.

SERIES SIGNATURES	SEAL	A.B.P.	GOOD	V. FINE	UNC.
☐ 1891 Rosecrans-Nebeker	Red	41.00	82.00	460.00	1550.00
☐ 1891 Tillman-Morgan	Red	41.00	82.00	460.00	1675.00

TWO DOLLAR NOTES (1896) SILVER CERTIFICATES
(Large Size)

NOTE NO. 27

Face Design: Science presenting Steam and Electricity to Industry and Commerce.

Back Design: Portraits of Robert Fulton and Samuel F. B. Morse.

THIS IS THE SECOND NOTE OF THE POPULAR EDUCATIONAL SERIES

SERIES	SIGNATURES	SEAL	A.B.P.	GOOD	V. FINE	UNC.
☐ 1896	Tillman-Morgan	Red	75.00	160.00	610.00	2475.00
☐ 1896	Bruce-Roberts	Red	55.00	105.00	380.00	1650.00

TWO DOLLAR NOTES (1899) SILVER CERTIFICATES
(Large Size)   **NOTE NO. 28**

Face Design: Portrait of President Washington between figures of Trade and Agriculture, blue "2" left, blue seal right.

Back Design

SERIES	SIGNATURES	SEAL	A.B.P.	GOOD	V. FINE	UNC.
☐ 1899	Lyons-Roberts	Blue	9.50	18.50	160.00	610.00
☐ 1899	Lyons-Treat	Blue	9.50	18.50	105.00	480.00
☐ 1899	Vernon-Treat	Blue	9.50	18.50	105.00	480.00
☐ 1899	Vernon-McClung	Blue	9.50	18.50	105.00	505.00
☐ 1899	Napier-McClung	Blue	9.50	18.50	105.00	480.00
☐ 1899	Napier-Thompson	Blue	19.00	35.00	410.00	1410.00
☐ 1899	Parker-Burke	Blue	9.50	18.50	105.00	480.00
☐ 1899	Teehee-Burke	Blue	9.50	18.50	105.00	480.00
☐ 1899	Elliott-Burke	Blue	9.50	18.50	105.00	510.00
☐ 1899	Speelman-White	Blue	9.50	18.50	105.00	510.00

TWO DOLLAR NOTES (1890–1891)
TREASURY OR COIN NOTES

(Large Size)   **NOTE NO. 29**

Face Design: Portrait of General James McPherson.

Back Design: Large "TWO" center, over obligation. Large "2" on engraved background right. Intricate engraving, printed green.

SERIES SIGNATURES	SEAL	A.B.P.	GOOD	V. FINE	UNC.
☐ 1890 Rosecrans-Huston	Brown	70.00	160.00	610.00	2675.00
☐ 1890 Rosecrans-Nebeker	Brown	70.00	160.00	610.00	2675.00
☐ 1890 Rosecrans-Nebeker	Red	78.00	160.00	610.00	2675.00

TWO DOLLAR NOTES (1890–1891)
TREASURY OR COIN NOTES

(Large Size)   **NOTE NO. 30**

Face Design: Similar to Note No. 29
Back Design: Revised.

SERIES SIGNATURES	SEAL	A.B.P.	GOOD	V. FINE	UNC.
☐ 1891 Rosecrans-Nebeker	Red	40.00	82.00	230.00	710.00
☐ 1891 Tillman-Morgan	Red	40.00	82.00	230.00	710.00
☐ 1891 Bruce-Roberts	Red	40.00	82.00	230.00	710.00

TWO DOLLAR NOTES (1918)
FEDERAL RESERVE BANK NOTES

(Large Size)   **NOTE NO. 31**

Face Design: Portrait of President Jefferson to left, name of bank in center, blue seal to the right, blue numbers, Federal Reserve district letter and

Back Design: American battleship of World War I.

TWO DOLLAR NOTES (1918)
FEDERAL RESERVE BANK NOTES

(Large Size)

NOTE NO. 31

BANK & CITY	GOV'T SIGNATURES	BANK SIGNATURES	A.B.P.	GOOD	V. FINE	UNC.
☐ Boston	Teehee-Burke	Bullen-Morss	30.00	55.00	155.00	405.00
☐ Boston	Teehee-Burke	Willet-Morss	30.00	55.00	155.00	405.00
☐ Boston	Elliot-Burke	Willet-Morss	30.00	55.00	155.00	405.00
☐ New York	Teehee-Burke	Sailer-Strong	30.00	55.00	155.00	405.00
☐ New York	Teehee-Burke	Hendricks-Strong	30.00	55.00	155.00	405.00
☐ New York	Elliott-Burke	Hendricks-Strong	30.00	55.00	155.00	405.00
☐ Philadelphia	Teehee-Burke	Hardt-Passmore ..	30.00	55.00	155.00	405.00
☐ Philadelphia	Teehee-Burke	Dyer-Passmore ...	30.00	55.00	155.00	405.00
☐ Philadelphia	Elliott-Burke	Dyer-Passmore ...	30.00	55.00	155.00	405.00
☐ Philadelphia	Elliott-Burke	Dyer-Norris	30.00	55.00	155.00	405.00
☐ Cleveland	Teehee-Burke	Baxter-Fancher ...	30.00	55.00	155.00	405.00
☐ Cleveland	Teehee-Burke	Davis-Fancher ...	30.00	55.00	155.00	405.00
☐ Cleveland	Elliott-Burke	Davis-Fancher ...	30.00	55.00	155.00	405.00
☐ Richmond	Teehee-Burke	Keesee-Seay	30.00	55.00	155.00	405.00
☐ Richmond	Elliott-Burke	Keesee-Seay	30.00	55.00	155.00	405.00
☐ Atlanta	Teehee-Burke	Pike-McCord	30.00	55.00	155.00	405.00
☐ Atlanta	Teehee-Burke	Bell-McCord	30.00	55.00	155.00	405.00
☐ Atlanta	Elliott-Burke	Bell-Wellborn	30.00	55.00	155.00	405.00
☐ Chicago	Teehee-Burke	McCloud-McDougal	30.00	55.00	155.00	405.00
☐ Chicago	Teehee-Burke	Cramer-McDougal	30.00	55.00	155.00	405.00
☐ Chicago	Elliott-Burke	Cramer-McDougal	30.00	55.00	155.00	405.00
☐ St. Louis	Teehee-Burke	Atlebery-Wells	30.00	55.00	155.00	405.00
☐ St. Louis	Teehee-Burke	Atlebery-Biggs ...	30.00	55.00	155.00	405.00
☐ St. Louis	Elliott-Burke	Atlebery-Biggs ...	30.00	55.00	155.00	405.00
☐ St. Louis	Elliott-Burke	White-Biggs	30.00	55.00	155.00	405.00
☐ Minneapolis	Teehee-Burke	Cook-Wold	30.00	55.00	155.00	405.00
☐ Minneapolis	Elliott-Burke	Cook-Young	30.00	55.00	155.00	405.00
☐ Kansas City	Teehee-Burke	Anderson-Miller ..	30.00	55.00	155.00	405.00
☐ Kansas City	Elliott-Burke	Helm-Miller	30.00	55.00	155.00	405.00
☐ Dallas	Teehee-Burke	Talley-VanZandt ..	30.00	55.00	155.00	405.00
☐ Dallas	Elliott-Burke	Talley-VanZandt ..	30.00	55.00	155.00	405.00
☐ San Francisco	Teehee-Burke	Clerk-Lynch	30.00	55.00	155.00	405.00
☐ San Francisco	Elliott-Burke	Clerk-Calkins	30.00	55.00	155.00	405.00
☐ San Francisco	Elliott-Burke	Ambrose-Calkins	30.00	55.00	155.00	405.00

TWO DOLLAR (1976) FEDERAL RESERVE NOTES
(Small Size)   **NOTE NO. 31A**

Face Design: Portrait of President Jefferson.

Back Design: Signing of The Declaration of Independence.
SERIES OF 1976 NEFF-SIMON—GREEN SEAL

DISTRICT	A.B.P.	UNC.	DISTRICT	A.B.P.	UNC.
☐ 1A Boston	2.60	6.00	☐ 7G Chicago	2.60	6.00
☐ 2B New York	2.60	6.00	☐ 8H St. Louis	2.60	6.00
☐ 3C Philadelphia	2.60	6.00	☐ 9I Minneapolis	2.60	6.00
☐ 4D Cleveland	2.60	6.00	☐ 10J Kansas City	2.60	6.00
☐ 5E Richmond	2.60	6.00	☐ 11K Dallas	2.60	6.00
☐ 6F Atlanta	2.60	6.00	☐ 12L San Francisco	2.60	6.00

FIVE DOLLAR NOTES

ORDER OF ISSUE

FIVE DOLLAR NOTES (1861) DEMAND NOTES

(Large Size)

Face Design: Left, Statue of America by Crawford atop United States Capitol. Center, numeral "5" in green. Right, portrait of Alexander Hamilton, statesman, first Secretary of the Treasury.

Back Design: Numerous small "fives" in ovals. This note has no Treasury Seal. The signatures are those of Treasury Department employees who signed for officials.

PAYABLE AT	A.B.P.	GOOD	V. GOOD
☐ Boston (I)	170.00	510.00	880.00
☐ New York (I)	170.00	510.00	880.00
☐ Philadelphia (I)	170.00	510.00	880.00
☐ Cincinnati (I)	370.00	2650.00	4650.00
☐ St. Louis (I)	310.00	1700.00	3600.00
☐ Boston (II)	150.00	350.00	570.00
☐ New York (II)	150.00	350.00	570.00
☐ Philadelphia (II)	150.00	350.00	570.00
☐ Cincinnati (II)	250.00	2450.00	4000.00
☐ St. Louis (II)	210.00	1225.00	2450.00

FIVE DOLLAR NOTES (1875–1907) UNITED STATES NOTES
(ALSO KNOWN AS LEGAL TENDER NOTES)

(Large Size)   **NOTE NO. 35**

Back Design: Note No. 33. First Obligation.

Back Design: Note No. 33A. Second Obligation.

SERIES SIGNATURES	SEAL	A.B.P.	GOOD	V. FINE	UNC.
☐ 1862 Crittenden-Spinner*	Red	36.00	82.00	310.00	710.00
☐ 1862 Crittenden-Spinner**	Red	55.00	105.00	310.00	1100.00
☐ 1863 Crittenden-Spinner**	Red	36.00	82.00	310.00	710.00

*FIRST OBLIGATION—**SECOND OBLIGATION

FIVE DOLLAR NOTES (1869) UNITED STATES NOTES
(ALSO KNOWN AS LEGAL TENDER NOTES)

(Large Size)

NOTE NO. 34

Face Design: Portrait of President Jackson on left. Pioneer and family in center.

Back Design: Color, green. This is a companion note to the $1.00 and $2.00 notes of 1869 Rainbow Notes.

SERIES SIGNATURES	SEAL	A.B.P.	GOOD	V. FINE	UNC.
☐ 1869 Allison-Spinner	Red	42.00	82.00	260.00	710.00

FIVE DOLLAR NOTES (1875–1907) UNITED STATES NOTES
(ALSO KNOWN AS LEGAL TENDER NOTES)

(Large Size)   **NOTE NO. 35**

Back Design: Revised.
Face Design: Similar to previous Note.

SERIES SIGNATURES	SEAL	A.B.P.	GOOD	V. FINE	UNC.
☐ 1875 Allison-New	Red	21.00	42.00	130.00	405.00
☐ 1875A Allison-New	Red	17.00	32.00	75.00	610.00
☐ 1875B Allison-New	Red	17.00	32.00	75.00	610.00
☐ 1875 Allison-Wyman	Red	16.00	32.00	75.00	610.00
☐ 1878 Allison-Gilfillan	Red	32.00	63.00	125.00	530.00
☐ 1880 Scofield-Gilfillan	Brown	17.00	32.00	62.00	255.00
☐ 1880 Bruce-Gilfillan	Brown	17.00	32.00	62.00	255.00
☐ 1880 Bruce-Wyman	Brown	22.00	45.00	110.00	360.00
☐ 1880 Bruce-Wyman	Red	19.00	40.00	85.00	480.00
☐ 1880 Rosecrans-Jordan	Red	19.00	40.00	85.00	480.00
☐ 1880 Rosecrans-Hyatt	Red	19.00	40.00	85.00	480.00
☐ 1880 Rosecrans-Huston	Red	19.00	40.00	121.00	580.00
☐ 1880 Rosecrans-Huston	Brown	24.00	45.00	105.00	360.00
☐ 1880 Rosecrans-Nebeker	Brown	19.00	42.00	80.00	380.00
☐ 1880 Rosecrans-Nebeker	Red	11.00	23.00	55.00	230.00
☐ 1880 Tillman-Morgan	Red	11.00	23.00	55.00	270.00
☐ 1880 Bruce-Roberts	Red	11.00	23.00	55.00	270.00
☐ 1880 Lyons-Roberts	Red	11.00	23.00	55.00	270.00
☐ 1907 Vernon-Treat	Red	11.00	22.00	42.00	215.00
☐ 1907 Vernon-McClung	Red	11.00	22.00	42.00	215.00
☐ 1907 Napier-McClung	Red	11.00	22.00	42.00	215.00
☐ 1907 Napier-Thompson	Red	41.00	115.00	260.00	610.00
☐ 1907 Parker-Burke	Red	9.00	22.00	42.00	225.00
☐ 1907 Teehee-Burke	Red	9.00	22.00	42.00	225.00
☐ 1907 Elliott-Burke	Red	9.00	22.00	42.00	225.00
☐ 1907 Elliott-White	Red	9.00	22.00	42.00	225.00
☐ 1907 Speelman-White	Red	9.00	22.00	42.00	225.00
☐ 1907 Woods-White	Red	9.00	22.00	42.00	225.00

FIVE DOLLAR NOTES (1928) UNITED STATES NOTES
(ALSO KNOWN AS LEGAL TENDER NOTES)

(Small Size)   **NOTE NO. 36**

Face Design: Portrait of President Lincoln center. Red seal to left, red serial numbers.

Back Design: Lincoln Memorial in Washington, D.C.

SERIES SIGNATURES	SEAL	A.B.P.	GOOD	V. FINE	UNC.
☐ 1928 Woods-Mellon	Red	5.50	7.00	11.00	26.00
☐ 1928A Woods-Mills	Red	5.50	7.00	11.00	52.00
☐ 1928B Julian-Morgenthau	Red	5.50	7.00	11.00	22.00
☐ 1928C Julian-Morgenthau	Red	5.50	7.00	12.00	24.00
☐ 1928D Julian-Vinson	Red	6.25	7.00	19.00	120.00
☐ 1928E Julian-Snyder	Red	6.25	7.00	11.00	21.00
☐ 1928F Clark-Snyder	Red	6.25	7.00	11.00	21.00

FIVE DOLLAR NOTES (1953–1963) UNITED STATES NOTES
(Small Size)   **NOTE NO. 37**

Face Design: Similar to previous note. Portrait of President Lincoln center.
Red seal is moved to the right, red numbers.
Back Design: Similar to previous note.

SERIES SIGNATURES	SEAL	A.B.P.	GOOD	V. FINE	UNC.
☐ 1953 Priest-Humphrey	Red	5.25	7.00	11.00	21.00
☐ 1953A Priest-Anderson	Red	5.25	7.00	11.00	16.50
☐ 1953B Smith-Dillon	Red	5.25	7.00	11.00	16.50
☐ 1953C Granahan-Dillon	Red	5.25	7.00	11.00	16.50

FIVE DOLLAR NOTES (1953–1963) UNITED STATES NOTES
(ALSO KNOWN AS LEGAL TENDER NOTES)
(Small Size)   **NOTE NO. 37A**

SERIES OF 1963
Back Design: The following notes have "IN GOD WE TRUST" on the
back.
Face Design: Similar to previous note.

SERIES SIGNATURES	SEAL	A.B.P.	GOOD	V. FINE	UNC.
☐ 1963 Granahan-Dillon	Red	5.25	7.00	11.00	14.00

Production of Five Dollar United States Notes ended in 1967.

FIVE DOLLAR NOTES (1863–1875)
NATIONAL BANK NOTES
FIRST CHARTER PERIOD (Large Size)   **NOTE NO. 38**

Face Design: The Columbus Note. The face shows Columbus in sight of land and Columbus with an Indian Princess.

Back Design: Christopher Columbus landing at San Salvador, 1492. Also the State seal left, and American Eagle right.

SERIES SIGNATURES	SEAL	A.B.P.	GOOD	V. FINE	UNC.
☐ Original Chittenden-Spinner	Red	31.00	55.00	280.00	1450.00
☐ Original Colby-Spinner	Red	31.00	55.00	280.00	1450.00
☐ Original Jeffries-Spinner	Red	200.00	460.00	1250.00	4100.00
☐ Original Allison-Spinner	Red	31.00	60.00	280.00	1450.00
☐ 1875 Allison-New	Red	31.00	60.00	280.00	1210.00
☐ 1875 Allison-Wyman	Red	31.00	60.00	280.00	1210.00
☐ 1875 Allison-Gilfillan	Red	31.00	60.00	280.00	1210.00
☐ 1875 Scofield-Gilfillan	Red	31.00	60.00	280.00	1210.00
☐ 1875 Bruce-Gilfillan	Red	31.00	60.00	280.00	1210.00
☐ 1875 Bruce-Wyman	Red	31.00	60.00	280.00	1210.00
☐ 1875 Bruce-Jordan	Red	EXTREMELY RARE			
☐ 1875 Rosecrans-Huston	Red	31.00	66.00	280.00	1175.00
☐ 1875 Rosecrans-Jordan	Red	31.00	66.00	280.00	1175.00

FIVE DOLLAR NOTES (1882) NATIONAL BANK NOTES
SECOND CHARTER PERIOD (Large Size)   **NOTE NO. 39**

First Issue—Brown seal and brown backs.
Face Design: Portrait of President Garfield left. Name of bank and city center, brown seal to right. Brown charter number.

Back Design: Brown border design similar to previous note. Center oval now has the bank's charter number in green. The top signatures are those of the treasury officials. Bottom signatures, usually hand written or probably rubber stamped, are bank officials.

SERIES	SIGNATURES	SEAL	A.B.P.	GOOD	V. FINE	UNC.
☐ 1882	Bruce-Gilfillan	Brown ...	33.00	62.00	155.00	410.00
☐ 1882	Bruce-Wyman	Brown ...	33.00	62.00	155.00	410.00
☐ 1882	Bruce-Jordan	Brown ...	33.00	62.00	155.00	410.00
☐ 1882	Rosecrans-Jordan	Brown ...	33.00	62.00	155.00	410.00
☐ 1882	Rosecrans-Hyatt	Brown ...	33.00	62.00	155.00	410.00
☐ 1882	Rosecrans-Huston	Brown ...	33.00	62.00	155.00	410.00
☐ 1882	Rosecrans-Nebeker	Brown ...	33.00	62.00	155.00	410.00
☐ 1882	Rosecrans-Morgan	Brown ...	78.00	150.00	500.00	1225.00
☐ 1882	Tillman-Morgan	Brown ...	33.00	62.00	155.00	410.00
☐ 1882	Tillman-Roberts	Brown ...	33.00	62.00	155.00	410.00
☐ 1882	Bruce-Roberts	Brown ...	33.00	62.00	155.00	410.00
☐ 1882	Lyons-Roberts	Brown ...	33.00	62.00	155.00	410.00

SERIES SIGNATURES	SEAL	A.B.P.	GOOD	V. FINE	UNC.
☐ 1882 Lyons-Treat	(Unknown in any collection)				
☐ 1882 Vernon-Treat	Brown ...	33.00	62.00	140.00	380.00

FIVE DOLLAR NOTES (1882) NATIONAL BANK NOTES
SECOND CHARTER PERIOD (Large Size)   **NOTE NO. 40**

Face Design: Similar to preceding portrait of President Garfield.

Back Design: Back is now green with date 1882–1908 in center.

SERIES SIGNATURES	SEAL	A.B.P.	GOOD	V. FINE	UNC.
☐ 1882 Rosecrans-Huston	Blue	21.00	40.00	105.00	560.00
☐ 1882 Rosecrans-Nebeker	Blue	21.00	40.00	105.00	560.00
☐ 1882 Rosecrans-Morgan	Blue	105.00	200.00	825.00	2050.00
☐ 1882 Tillman-Morgan	Blue	21.00	40.00	105.00	560.00
☐ 1882 Tillman-Roberts	Blue	21.00	40.00	105.00	560.00
☐ 1882 Bruce-Roberts	Blue	21.00	40.00	105.00	560.00
☐ 1882 Lyons-Roberts	Blue	21.00	40.00	105.00	560.00
☐ 1882 Vernon-Treat	Blue	21.00	40.00	105.00	560.00
☐ 1882 Vernon-McClung	RARE				
☐ 1882 Napier-McClung	RARE				

FIVE DOLLAR NOTES (1882) NATIONAL BANK NOTES
SECOND CHARTER PERIOD, Third Issue (Large Size)   **NOTE NO. 41**

Face Design: Same as Note No. 39. Blue Seal.

Back Design: Similar to Note No. 40, "FIVE DOLLARS" replaces
1882–1908.

SERIES	SIGNATURES	SEAL	A.B.P.	GOOD	V. FINE	UNC.
☐ 1882	Tillman-Morgan	Blue	36.00	76.00	245.00	780.00
☐ 1882	Tillman-Roberts	Blue	36.00	76.00	245.00	780.00
☐ 1882	Bruce-Roberts	Blue	36.00	76.00	245.00	780.00
☐ 1882	Lyons-Roberts	Blue	36.00	76.00	245.00	780.00
☐ 1882	Vernon-Treat	Blue	36.00	76.00	245.00	780.00
☐ 1882	Napier-McClung	Blue	36.00	76.00	245.00	780.00
☐ 1882	Teehee-Burke	Blue	EXTREMELY RARE			

FIVE DOLLAR NOTES (1902) NATIONAL BANK NOTES
THIRD CHARTER PERIOD (Large Size)   **NOTE NO. 42**

First Issue—Red seal and charter numbers.
Face Design: Portrait of President Harrison left, name of bank and city center, Treasury Seal to right, red seal and charter number.

Back Design: Landing of Pilgrims.

SERIES SIGNATURES	SEAL	A.B.P.	GOOD	V. FINE	UNC.
☐ 1902 Lyons-Roberts	Red	26.00	52.00	155.00	510.00
☐ 1902 Lyons-Treat	Red	26.00	52.00	155.00	510.00
☐ 1902 Vernon-Treat	Red	26.00	52.00	155.00	510.00

FIVE DOLLAR NOTES (1902) NATIONAL BANK NOTES

THIRD CHARTER PERIOD (Large Size)   **NOTE NO. 42A**

SERIES SIGNATURES	SEAL	A.B.P.	GOOD	V. FINE	UNC.
☐ 1902 Lyons-Roberts	Blue	8.50	19.00	46.00	360.00
☐ 1902 Lyons-Treat	Blue	8.50	19.00	46.00	360.00
☐ 1902 Vernon-Treat	Blue	8.50	19.00	46.00	360.00
☐ 1902 Vernon-McClung	Blue	8.50	19.00	46.00	180.00
☐ 1902 Napier-McClung	Blue	8.50	19.00	46.00	180.00
☐ 1902 Napier-Thompson	Blue	16.00	30.00	62.00	510.00
☐ 1902 Napier-Burke	Blue	8.50	19.00	46.00	180.00
☐ 1902 Parker-Burke	Blue	8.50	19.00	46.00	180.00
☐ 1902 Teehee-Burke	Blue	8.50	19.00	62.00	315.00

FIVE DOLLAR NOTES (1902) NATIONAL BANK NOTES

THIRD CHARTER PERIOD (Large Size)   **NOTE NO. 42B**

Third Issue—Blue seal and numbers. The following notes do not have date of 1902–1908 on the back.

SERIES SIGNATURES	SEAL	A.B.P.	GOOD	V. FINE	UNC.
☐ 1902 Lyons-Roberts	Blue	8.50	19.00	46.00	142.00
☐ 1902 Lyons-Treat	Blue	8.50	19.00	46.00	142.00
☐ 1902 Vernon-Treat	Blue	8.50	19.00	46.00	142.00
☐ 1902 Vernon-McClung	Blue	8.50	19.00	46.00	142.00
☐ 1902 Napier-McClung	Blue	8.50	19.00	46.00	142.00
☐ 1902 Napier-Thompson	Blue	8.50	19.00	46.00	142.00
☐ 1902 Napier-Burke	Blue	8.50	19.00	46.00	142.00
☐ 1902 Parker-Burke	Blue	8.50	19.00	46.00	142.00
☐ 1902 Teehee-Burke	Blue	8.50	19.00	46.00	142.00
☐ 1902 Elliott-Burke	Blue	8.50	19.00	46.00	142.00
☐ 1902 Elliott-White	Blue	8.50	19.00	46.00	142.00
☐ 1902 Speelman-White	Blue	8.50	19.00	46.00	142.00
☐ 1902 Woods-White	Blue	8.50	19.00	46.00	142.00
☐ 1902 Woods-Tate	Blue	8.50	19.00	46.00	142.00
☐ 1902 Jones-Woods	Blue	41.00	82.00	182.00	415.00

FIVE DOLLAR NOTES (1929) NATIONAL BANK NOTES
(Small Size)   NOTE NO. 43

TYPE I

TYPE II

Face Design: Portrait of President Lincoln in center, name of bank to left, brown seal to the right. TYPE I—Charter number in black. TYPE II—Similar, charter number added in brown.

Back Design: Lincoln Memorial.

SERIES SIGNATURES	SEAL	A.B.P.	GOOD	V. FINE	UNC.
☐ 1929 TYPE I Jones-Woods	Brown ...	6.50	9.00	23.00	65.00
☐ 1929 TYPE II Jones-Woods	Brown ...	7.50	11.00	23.00	65.00

FIVE DOLLAR NOTES (1870)
NATIONAL GOLD BANK NOTES

(Large Size)

NOTE NO. 44

Face Design: Vignettes of Columbus sighting land. Presentation of an Indian Princess. Red seal. Signatures, Allison-Spinner.

Back Design: California State Seal left, gold coins center, American Eagle right.

DATE	BANK	CITY	A.B.P.	GOOD	V. GOOD
☐ 1870	First National Gold Bank	San Francisco ...	265.00	510.00	780.00
☐ 1872	National Gold Bank and Trust Company	San Francisco ...	265.00	510.00	780.00
☐ 1872	National Gold Bank of D.O. Mills and Company	Sacramento	355.00	680.00	1050.00
☐ 1873	First National Gold Bank	Santa Barbara ...	355.00	680.00	1050.00
☐ 1873	First National Gold Bank	Stockton	355.00	680.00	1050.00
☐ 1874	Farmers Nat'l Gold Bank	San Jose	355.00	680.00	1050.00

FIVE DOLLAR NOTES (1886–1891) SILVER CERTIFICATES
(Large Size)   **NOTE NO. 45**

Face Design: Portrait of President Grant.

Back Design: Five silver dollars.

SERIES SIGNATURES	SEAL	A.B.P.	GOOD	V. FINE	UNC.
☐ 1886 Rosecrans-Jordan	Red	82.00	180.00	610.00	2210.00
☐ 1886 Rosecrans-Hyatt	Red Sm	82.00	180.00	610.00	2210.00
☐ 1886 Rosecrans-Hyatt	Red Lg	82.00	180.00	610.00	2210.00
☐ 1886 Rosecrans-Huston	Red Lg	82.00	180.00	700.00	2500.00
☐ 1886 Rosecrans-Huston	Brown	82.00	180.00	610.00	2210.00
☐ 1886 Rosecrans-Nebeker	Brown	82.00	180.00	700.00	2550.00
☐ 1886 Rosecrans-Nebeker	Red Sm	82.00	180.00	610.00	2325.00

FIVE DOLLAR NOTES (1891) SILVER CERTIFICATES

(Large Size)

NOTE NO. 46

Face Design: Similar to previous note.

Back Design: Revised.

SERIES	SIGNATURES	SEAL	A.B.P.	GOOD	V. FINE	UNC.
☐ 1891	Rosecrans-Nebeker	Red	56.00	105.00	365.00	1675.00
☐ 1891	Tillman-Morgan	Red	56.00	115.00	650.00	1910.00

FIVE DOLLAR NOTES (1896) SILVER CERTIFICATES
(Large Size)   **NOTE NO. 47**

Face Design: Portrait of General Grant and General Sheridan.

LAST NOTE OF THE POPULAR EDUCATIONAL SERIES

Back Design: Five females representing electricity as the dominant force in the world.

SERIES SIGNATURES	SEAL	A.B.P.	GOOD	V. FINE	UNC.
☐ 1896 Tillman-Morgan	Red	140.00	255.00	605.00	2675.00
☐ 1896 Bruce-Roberts	Red	140.00	255.00	605.00	2675.00
☐ 1896 Lyons-Roberts	Red	140.00	255.00	605.00	2675.00

FIVE DOLLAR NOTES (1899) SILVER CERTIFICATES

(Large Size)

Face Design: Portrait of Indian Chief.

Back Design: Green "V" and "5."

SERIES	SIGNATURES	SEAL	A.B.P.	GOOD	V. FINE	UNC.
☐ 1899	Lyons-Roberts	Blue	27.00	62.00	212.00	705.00
☐ 1899	Lyons-Treat	Blue	27.00	62.00	212.00	705.00
☐ 1899	Vernon-Treat	Blue	27.00	62.00	212.00	705.00
☐ 1899	Vernon-McClung	Blue	27.00	62.00	212.00	705.00
☐ 1899	Napier-McClung	Blue	27.00	62.00	212.00	705.00
☐ 1899	Napier-Thompson	Blue	42.00	80.00	400.00	2675.00
☐ 1899	Parker-Burke	Blue	27.00	62.00	212.00	705.00
☐ 1899	Teehee-Burke	Blue	27.00	62.00	212.00	705.00
☐ 1899	Elliott-Burke	Blue	27.00	62.00	212.00	705.00
☐ 1899	Elliott-White	Blue	27.00	62.00	212.00	705.00
☐ 1899	Speelman-White	Blue	27.00	62.00	212.00	705.00

FIVE DOLLAR NOTES (1923) SILVER CERTIFICATES
(Large Size)

Face Design: Portrait of President Lincoln in oval, nickname "Porthole Note," blue seal left, blue "5" right.

Back Design: Obverse of Great Seal of the United States.

SERIES SIGNATURES	SEAL	A.B.P.	GOOD	V. FINE	UNC.
☐ 1923 Speelman-White	Blue	40.00	82.00	215.00	1180.00

FIVE DOLLAR NOTES (1934) SILVER CERTIFICATES

(Small Size)   **NOTE NO. 50**

First Issue—Small size of $5.00 Silver Certificates 1934.
Face Design: Portrait of President Lincoln, blue "5" to left, blue seal to right.

Back Design: All small-size $5.00 notes have the same back design.

SERIES SIGNATURES	SEAL	A.B.P.	GOOD	V. FINE	UNC.
☐ 1934 Julian-Morgenthau	Blue	5.50	6.00	11.00	26.00
☐ 1934A Julian-Morgenthau	Blue	5.50	6.00	11.00	26.00
☐ 1934A Julian-Morgenthau	Yellow	6.25	13.00	30.00	180.00

This note, with Yellow Treasury Seal, was a Special Issue during World War II for military use in combat areas of North Africa and Europe.

SERIES SIGNATURES	SEAL	A.B.P.	GOOD	V. FINE	UNC.
☐ 1934B Julian-Vinson	Blue	5.50	6.50	10.00	29.00
☐ 1934C Julian-Snyder	Blue	5.50	6.50	8.50	15.50
☐ 1934D Clark-Snyder	Blue	5.50	6.50	8.50	15.50

FIVE DOLLAR NOTES (1953) SILVER CERTIFICATES
(Small Size)   **NOTE NO. 51**

Face Design: The following notes are similar to the previous note. The face design has been revised. Gray ''5'' replaces blue ''5'' to left of Lincoln. Blue seal is slightly smaller.

Back Design: Same as previous note.

SERIES SIGNATURES	SEAL	A.B.P.	GOOD	V. FINE	UNC.
☐ 1953 Priest-Humphrey	Blue	5.50	6.10	8.50	15.00
☐ 1953A Priest-Anderson	Blue	5.50	6.10	8.50	15.00
☐ 1953B Smith-Dillon	Blue	5.50	6.10	8.50	15.00

Production of Five Dollar Silver Certificates ended in 1962.

FIVE DOLLAR NOTES (1890) TREASURY NOTES
(Large Size)

Face Design: Portrait of General George Henry Thomas (1816–1870), the "Rock of Chickamaugua."

Back Design: Note No. 52.

SERIES	SIGNATURES	SEAL	A.B.P.	GOOD	V. FINE	UNC.
☐ 1890	Rosecrans-Huston	Brown ...	55.00	100.00	450.00	1825.00
☐ 1890	Rosecrans-Nebeker	Brown ...	55.00	100.00	450.00	1825.00
☐ 1890	Rosecrans-Nebeker	Red	55.00	100.00	450.00	1825.00

Back Design: Note No. 53.
Face Design: Same as previous note.

SERIES	SIGNATURES	SEAL	A.B.P.	GOOD	V. FINE	UNC.
☐ 1891	Rosecrans-Nebeker	Red	40.00	81.00	165.00	710.00
☐ 1891	Tillman-Morgan	Red	40.00	81.00	195.00	960.00
☐ 1891	Bruce-Roberts	Red	40.00	81.00	195.00	960.00
☐ 1891	Lyons-Roberts	Red	40.00	80.00	195.00	860.00

FIVE DOLLAR NOTES (1914) FEDERAL RESERVE NOTES
(Large Size)   **NOTE NO. 54**

Face Design: Portrait of President Lincoln center, Federal Reserve Seal left, Treasury Seal right.

Back Design: Scene of Columbus in sight of land left, Landing of Pilgrims right.

SERIES OF 1914—RED TREASURY SEAL AND RED NUMBERS

SERIES	CITY	SIGNATURES	SEAL	A.B.P.	GOOD	V. FINE	UNC.
☐ 1914	Boston	Burke-McAdoo	Red	16.50	42.00	92.00	360.00
☐ 1914	New York	Burke-McAdoo	Red	16.50	42.00	92.00	360.00
☐ 1914	Philadelphia	Burke-McAdoo	Red	16.50	42.00	92.00	360.00
☐ 1914	Cleveland	Burke-McAdoo	Red	16.50	42.00	92.00	360.00
☐ 1914	Richmond	Burke-McAdoo	Red	16.50	42.00	92.00	360.00
☐ 1914	Atlanta	Burke-McAdoo	Red	16.50	42.00	92.00	360.00
☐ 1914	Chicago	Burke-McAdoo	Red	16.50	42.00	92.00	360.00
☐ 1914	St. Louis	Burke-McAdoo	Red	16.50	42.00	92.00	360.00
☐ 1914	Minneapolis	Burke-McAdoo	Red	16.50	42.00	92.00	360.00
☐ 1914	Kansas City	Burke-McAdoo	Red	16.50	42.00	92.00	360.00
☐ 1914	Dallas	Burke-McAdoo	Red	16.50	42.00	92.00	360.00
☐ 1914	San Francisco	Burke-McAdoo	Red	16.50	42.00	92.00	360.00

FIVE DOLLAR NOTES (1914) FEDERAL RESERVE NOTES

NOTE NO. 54A

SERIES OF 1914—BLUE TREASURY SEAL AND BLUE NUMBERS

	SERIES CITY	SIGNATURES	SEAL	A.B.P.	GOOD	V. FINE	UNC.
☐	1914 Boston	Burke-McAdoo	Blue	7.50	13.00	27.00	125.00
☐	1914 Boston	Burke-Glass	Blue	7.50	13.00	27.00	125.00
☐	1914 Boston	Burke-Huston	Blue	7.50	13.00	27.00	125.00
☐	1914 Boston	White-Mellon	Blue	7.50	13.00	27.00	125.00
☐	1914 New York	Burke-McAdoo	Blue	7.50	13.00	27.00	125.00
☐	1914 New York	Burke-Glass	Blue	7.50	13.00	27.00	125.00
☐	1914 New York	Burke-Huston	Blue	7.50	13.00	27.00	125.00
☐	1914 New York	White-Mellon	Blue	7.50	13.00	27.00	125.00
☐	1914 Philadelphia	Burke-McAdoo	Blue	7.50	13.00	27.00	125.00
☐	1914 Philadelphia	Burke-Glass	Blue	7.50	13.00	27.00	125.00
☐	1914 Philadelphia	Burke-Huston	Blue	7.50	13.00	27.00	125.00
☐	1914 Philadelphia	White-Mellon	Blue	7.50	13.00	27.00	125.00
☐	1914 Cleveland	Burke-McAdoo	Blue	7.50	13.00	27.00	125.00
☐	1914 Cleveland	Burke-Glass	Blue	7.50	13.00	27.00	125.00
☐	1914 Cleveland	Burke-Huston	Blue	7.50	13.00	27.00	125.00
☐	1914 Cleveland	White-Mellon	Blue	7.50	13.00	27.00	125.00
☐	1914 Richmond	Burke-McAdoo	Blue	7.50	13.00	27.00	125.00
☐	1914 Richmond	Burke-Glass	Blue	7.50	13.00	27.00	125.00
☐	1914 Richmond	Burke-Huston	Blue	7.50	13.00	27.00	125.00
☐	1914 Richmond	White-Mellon	Blue	7.50	13.00	27.00	125.00
☐	1914 Atlanta	Burke-McAdoo	Blue	7.50	13.00	27.00	125.00
☐	1914 Atlanta	Burke-Glass	Blue	7.50	13.00	27.00	125.00
☐	1914 Atlanta	Burke-Huston	Blue	7.50	13.00	27.00	125.00
☐	1914 Atlanta	White-Mellon	Blue	7.50	13.00	27.00	125.00
☐	1914 Chicago	Burke-McAdoo	Blue	7.50	13.00	27.00	125.00
☐	1914 Chicago	Burke-Glass	Blue	7.50	13.00	27.00	125.00
☐	1914 Chicago	Burke-Huston	Blue	7.50	13.00	27.00	125.00
☐	1914 Chicago	White-Mellon	Blue	7.50	13.00	27.00	125.00
☐	1914 St. Louis	Burke-McAdoo	Blue	7.50	13.00	27.00	125.00
☐	1914 St. Louis	Burke-Glass	Blue	7.50	13.00	27.00	125.00
☐	1914 St. Louis	Burke-Huston	Blue	7.50	13.00	27.00	125.00
☐	1914 St. Louis	White-Mellon	Blue	7.50	13.00	27.00	125.00
☐	1914 Minneapolis	Burke-McAdoo	Blue	7.50	13.00	27.00	125.00
☐	1914 Minneapolis	Burke-Glass	Blue	7.50	13.00	27.00	125.00
☐	1914 Minneapolis	Burke-Huston	Blue	7.50	13.00	27.00	125.00
☐	1914 Minneapolis	White-Mellon	Blue	7.50	13.00	27.00	125.00
☐	1914 Kansas City	Burke-McAdoo	Blue	7.50	13.00	27.00	125.00
☐	1914 Kansas City	Burke-Glass	Blue	7.50	13.00	27.00	125.00
☐	1914 Kansas City	Burke-Huston	Blue	7.50	13.00	27.00	125.00
☐	1914 Kansas City	White-Mellon	Blue	7.50	13.00	27.00	125.00
☐	1914 Dallas	Burke-McAdoo	Blue	7.50	13.00	27.00	125.00
☐	1914 Dallas	Burke-Glass	Blue	7.50	13.00	27.00	125.00
☐	1914 Dallas	Burke-Huston	Blue	7.50	13.00	27.00	125.00
☐	1914 Dallas	White-Mellon	Blue	7.50	13.00	27.00	125.00

SERIES CITY	SIGNATURES	SEAL	A.B.P.	GOOD	V. FINE	UNC.
☐ 1914 San Francisco	Burke-McAdoo	Blue	7.50	13.00	27.00	125.00
☐ 1914 San Francisco	Burke-Glass	Blue	7.50	13.00	27.00	125.00
☐ 1914 San Francisco	Burke-Huston	Blue	7.50	13.00	27.00	125.00
☐ 1914 San Francisco	White-Mellon	Blue	7.50	13.00	27.00	125.00

FIVE DOLLAR NOTES (1928) FEDERAL RESERVE NOTES
(Small Size)   **NOTE NO. 55**

Face Design: Portrait of President Lincoln center, black Federal Reserve Seal with numeral for district in center. City of issuing bank in seal circle. Green Treasury Seal to right.
Design: Similar to Note No. 50, Lincoln Memorial in Washington, D.C.

SERIES OF 1928—SIGNATURES OF TATE AND MELLON, GREEN SEAL

BANK	A.B.P.	GOOD	V. FINE	UNC.	BANK	A.B.P.	GOOD	V. FINE	UNC.
☐ Boston	6.00	7.50	13.00	39.00	☐ Chicago	6.00	7.50	13.00	39.00
☐ New York	6.00	7.50	13.00	39.00	☐ St. Louis	6.00	7.50	13.00	39.00
☐ Philadelphia	6.00	7.50	13.00	39.00	☐ Minneapolis	6.00	7.50	13.00	39.00
☐ Cleveland	6.00	7.50	13.00	39.00	☐ Kansas City	6.00	7.50	13.00	39.00
☐ Richmond	6.00	7.50	13.00	39.00	☐ Dallas	6.00	7.50	13.00	39.00
☐ Atlanta	6.00	7.50	13.00	39.00	☐ San Francisco	6.00	7.50	13.00	39.00

SERIES OF 1928A—SIGNATURES OF WOODS-MELLON, GREEN SEAL

BANK	A.B.P.	GOOD	V. FINE	UNC.	BANK	A.B.P.	GOOD	V. FINE	UNC.
☐ Boston	6.00	7.50	13.00	39.00	☐ Chicago	6.00	7.50	13.00	39.00
☐ New York	6.00	7.50	13.00	39.00	☐ St. Louis	6.00	7.50	13.00	39.00
☐ Philadelphia	6.00	7.50	13.00	39.00	☐ Minneapolis	6.00	7.50	13.00	39.00
☐ Cleveland	6.00	7.50	13.00	39.00	☐ Kansas City	6.00	7.50	13.00	39.00
☐ Richmond	6.00	7.50	13.00	39.00	☐ Dallas	6.00	7.50	13.00	39.00
☐ Atlanta	6.00	7.50	13.00	39.00	☐ San Francisco	6.00	7.50	13.00	39.00

SERIES OF 1928B—SIGNATURES OF WOODS-MELLON, GREEN SEAL
Black Federal Reserve Seal now has a Letter for District
in place of the Numeral.

(Small Size)

BANK	A.B.P.	GOOD	V. FINE	UNC.	BANK	A.B.P.	GOOD	V. FINE	UNC.
☐ Boston	5.50	7.50	13.00	40.00	☐ Chicago	5.50	7.50	13.00	40.00
☐ New York	5.50	7.50	13.00	40.00	☐ St. Louis	5.50	7.50	13.00	40.00
☐ Philadelphia	5.50	7.50	13.00	40.00	☐ Minneapolis	5.50	7.50	13.00	40.00
☐ Cleveland	5.50	7.50	13.00	40.00	☐ Kansas City	5.50	7.50	13.00	40.00
☐ Richmond	5.50	7.50	13.00	40.00	☐ Dallas	5.50	7.50	13.00	40.00
☐ Atlanta	5.50	7.50	13.00	40.00	☐ San Francisco	5.50	7.50	13.00	40.00

FIVE DOLLAR NOTES (1928) FEDERAL RESERVE NOTES
SERIES OF 1928C—SIGNATURES OF WOODS-MILLS, GREEN SEAL

BANK	A.B.P.	GOOD	V. FINE	UNC.	BANK	A.B.P.	GOOD	V. FINE	UNC.
☐ Cleveland	42.00	80.00	180.00	400.00	☐ San				
☐ Atlanta	42.00	80.00	180.00	400.00	Francisco	42.00	80.00	180.00	400.00

This series not issued by other banks.

SERIES OF 1928D—SIGNATURES OF WOODS-WOODIN, GREEN SEAL

BANK	A.B.P.	GOOD	V. FINE	UNC.	BANK	A.B.P.	GOOD	V. FINE	UNC.
☐ Atlanta	50.00	100.00	250.00	800.00	This series not issued by other banks.				

SERIES OF 1934—JULIAN-MORGENTHAU, GREEN SEAL
"Redeemable in Gold" removed from obligation
over Federal Reserve Seal.

Note: The Green Treasury Seal on this note is known in a light and dark color. The light seal is worth about 10% to 20% more in most cases.

BANK	A.B.P.	V. FINE	UNC.	BANK	A.B.P.	V. FINE	UNC.
☐ Boston	5.50	8.50	26.00	☐ St. Louis	5.50	8.50	26.00
☐ New York	5.50	8.50	26.00	☐ Minneapolis	5.50	8.50	26.00
☐ Philadelphia	5.50	8.50	26.00	☐ Kansas City	5.50	8.50	26.00
☐ Cleveland	5.50	8.50	26.00	☐ Dallas	5.50	8.50	26.00
☐ Richmond	5.50	8.50	26.00	☐ San Francisco	5.50	8.50	26.00
☐ Atlanta	5.50	8.50	26.00	☐ San Francisco*	16.00	29.00	145.00
☐ Chicago	5.50	8.50	26.00				

*This note with BROWN Treasury Seal and surcharged HAWAII. For use in Pacific area of Operations during World War II.

(Small Size)   **NOTE NO. 56**

SERIES OF 1934–1934A—1934A—JULIAN-MORGENTHAU, Surprinted HAWAII, used in Pacific area during World War II. Used with Brown Treasury Seal.

SERIES OF 1934A—JULIAN-MORGENTHAU, GREEN SEAL

BANK	A.B.P.	V. FINE	UNC.	BANK	A.B.P.	V. FINE	UNC.
☐ Boston	5.50	8.50	26.00	☐ Atlanta	5.50	8.50	26.00
☐ New York	5.50	8.50	26.00	☐ Chicago	5.50	8.50	26.00
☐ Philadelphia	5.50	8.50	26.00	☐ St. Louis	5.50	8.50	26.00
☐ Cleveland	5.50	8.50	26.00	☐ San Francisco	5.50	8.50	26.00
☐ Richmond	5.50	8.50	26.00	☐ San Francisco*	15.50	29.00	122.00

*This note with BROWN Treasury Seal and surcharged HAWAII. For use in Pacific area of operations during World War II.

FIVE DOLLAR NOTES (1934) FEDERAL RESERVE NOTES

(Small Size)   **NOTE NO. 56**

Face Design: Same as Note No. 55.
Back Design: Same as Note No. 50.

SERIES OF 1934B—SIGNATURES OF JULIAN-VINSON, GREEN SEAL

BANK & CITY	A.B.P.	V. FINE	UNC.	BANK & CITY	A.B.P.	V. FINE	UNC.
☐ Boston	5.50	10.00	26.00	☐ Chicago	5.50	10.00	26.00
☐ New York	5.50	10.00	26.00	☐ St. Louis	5.50	10.00	26.00
☐ Philadelphia	5.50	10.00	26.00	☐ Minneapolis	5.50	10.00	26.00
☐ Cleveland	5.50	10.00	26.00	☐ Kansas City	5.50	10.00	26.00
☐ Richmond	5.50	10.00	26.00	☐ Dallas	Not Issued		
☐ Atlanta	5.50	10.00	26.00	☐ San Francisco	5.50	10.00	26.00

SERIES OF 1934C—SIGNATURES OF JULIAN-SNYDER, GREEN SEAL

BANK & CITY	A.B.P.	V. FINE	UNC.	BANK & CITY	A.B.P.	V. FINE	UNC.
☐ Boston	5.50	9.00	24.00	☐ Chicago	5.50	9.00	24.00
☐ New York	5.50	9.00	24.00	☐ St. Louis	5.50	9.00	24.00
☐ Philadelphia	5.50	9.00	24.00	☐ Minneapolis	5.50	9.00	24.00
☐ Cleveland	5.50	9.00	24.00	☐ Kansas City	5.50	9.00	24.00
☐ Richmond	5.50	9.00	24.00	☐ Dallas	5.50	9.00	24.00
☐ Atlanta	5.50	9.00	24.00	☐ San Francisco	5.50	9.00	24.00

SERIES OF 1934D—SIGNATURES OF CLARK-SNYDER, GREEN SEAL

BANK & CITY	A.B.P.	V. FINE	UNC.	BANK & CITY	A.B.P.	V. FINE	UNC.
☐ Boston	5.25	6.50	21.00	☐ Chicago	5.25	6.50	21.00
☐ New York	5.25	6.50	21.00	☐ St. Louis	5.25	6.50	21.00
☐ Philadelphia	5.25	6.50	21.00	☐ Minneapolis	5.25	6.50	21.00
☐ Cleveland	5.25	6.50	21.00	☐ Kansas City	5.25	6.50	21.00
☐ Richmond	5.25	6.50	21.00	☐ Dallas	5.25	6.50	21.00
☐ Atlanta	5.25	6.50	21.00	☐ San Francisco	5.25	6.50	21.00

FIVE DOLLAR NOTES (1950) FEDERAL RESERVE NOTES
BLACK FEDERAL RESERVE SEAL AND GREEN TREASURY SEALS ARE NOW SMALLER

(Small Size)   NOTE NO. 57

Face Design: Similar to Note No. 55.
Back Design: Similar to Note No. 50.

FIVE DOLLAR NOTES (1950–1963)
FEDERAL RESERVE NOTES

(Small Size)   NOTE NO. 57
SERIES OF 1950—SIGNATURES OF CLARK-SNYDER, GREEN SEAL

BANK & CITY	A.B.P.	V. FINE	UNC.	BANK & CITY	A.B.P.	V. FINE	UNC.
☐ Boston	5.50	8.50	23.00	☐ Chicago	5.50	8.50	23.00
☐ New York	5.50	8.50	23.00	☐ St. Louis	5.50	8.50	23.00
☐ Philadelphia	5.50	8.50	23.00	☐ Minneapolis	5.50	8.50	23.00
☐ Cleveland	5.50	8.50	23.00	☐ Kansas City	5.50	8.50	23.00
☐ Richmond	5.50	8.50	23.00	☐ Dallas	5.50	8.50	23.00
☐ Atlanta	5.50	8.50	23.00	☐ San-Francisco	5.50	8.50	23.00

SERIES OF 1950A—PRIEST-HUMPHREY, GREEN SEAL

	UNC.		UNC.		UNC.		UNC.
Boston	16.00	Cleveland	21.00	Chicago	21.00	Kansas City	21.00
New York	16.00	Richmond	21.00	St. Louis	21.00	Dallas	21.00
Philadelphia	16.00	Atlanta	21.00	Minneapolis	21.00	San Francisco	21.00

SERIES OF 1950B—PRIEST-ANDERSON, GREEN SEAL

Boston	19.00	Cleveland	19.00	Chicago	19.00	Kansas City	19.00
New York	19.00	Richmond	19.00	St. Louis	19.00	Dallas	19.00
Philadelphia	19.00	Atlanta	19.00	Minneapolis	19.00	San Francisco	19.00

SERIES OF 1950C—SMITH-DILLON, GREEN SEAL

Boston	19.00	Cleveland	19.00	Chicago	19.00	Kansas City	19.00
New York	19.00	Richmond	19.00	St. Louis	19.00	Dallas	19.00
Philadelphia	19.00	Atlanta	19.00	Minneapolis	19.00	San Francisco	19.00

SERIES OF 1950D—GRANAHAN-DILLON, GREEN SEAL

Boston . . . . 19.00 Cleveland . . . . . 19.00 Chicago . . . . . . 19.00 Kansas City . . . 19.00
New York . . . . . 19.00 Richmond . . . . . 19.00 St. Louis . . . . . . 19.00 Dallas 19.00
Philadelphia . . . 19.00 Atlanta . . . . 19.00 Minneapolis . . . 19.00 San Francisco 19.00

SERIES OF 1950E—GRANAHAN-FOWLER, GREEN SEAL

New York . . . . . 26.00 Chicago . . . . . . 26.00 San Francisco 26.00

This note was issued by only three banks.

FIVE DOLLAR NOTES (1963) FEDERAL RESERVE NOTES
("IN GOD WE TRUST" IS ADDED ON THE BACK)

(Small Size)   **NOTE NO. 57A**

SERIES OF 1963—GRANAHAN-DILLON, GREEN SEAL

	UNC.		UNC.		UNC.		UNC.
Boston 16.00		Cleveland 16.00		Chicago 16.00		Kansas City . . . 16.00	
New York 16.00		Richmond . . . . NONE		St. Louis 16.00		Dallas 16.00	
Philadelphia . . . 16.00		Atlanta 16.00		Minneapolis . . NONE		San Francisco 16.00	

SERIES OF 1963A—GRANAHAN-FOWLER, GREEN SEAL

Boston . . . . 15.00 Cleveland . . . . . 15.00 Chicago . . . . . . 15.00 Kansas City . . . 15.00
New York . . . . . 15.00 Richmond . . . . NONE St. Louis . . . . . . 15.00 Dallas 15.00
Philadelphia . . . 15.00 Atlanta . . . . 15.00 Minneapolis . . . 15.00 San Francisco 15.00

FIVE DOLLAR NOTES (1969) FEDERAL RESERVE NOTES
(WORDING IN GREEN TREASURY SEAL CHANGED
FROM LATIN TO ENGLISH)

(Small Size)   **NOTE NO. 57B**

SERIES OF 1969—ELSTON-KENNEDY, GREEN SEAL

Boston . . . . 12.50 Cleveland . . . . 12.50 Chicago . . . . . . 12.50 Kansas City . . 12.50
New York . . . 12.50 Richmond . . . . 12.50 St. Louis . . . . . 12.50 Dallas 12.50
Philadelphia . . 12.50 Atlanta . . . . 12.50 Minneapolis . . 12.50 San Francisco 12.50

SERIES OF 1969A—KABIS-CONNALLY, GREEN SEAL

Boston . . . . 12.50 Cleveland . . . . 12.50 Chicago . . . . . . 12.50 Kansas City . . 12.50
New York . . . . 12.50 Richmond . . . . 12.50 St. Louis . . . . . 12.50 Dallas 12.50
Philadelphia . . 12.50 Atlanta . . . . 12.50 Minneapolis . . . 12.50 San Francisco 12.50

FIVE DOLLAR NOTES (1969) FEDERAL RESERVE NOTES
(WORDING IN GREEN TREASURY SEAL CHANGED
FROM LATIN TO ENGLISH)

(Small Size)   **NOTE NO. 57B**

SERIES OF 1969B—BANUELOS-CONNALLY, GREEN SEAL

	UNC.		UNC.		UNC.		UNC.
Boston	8.50	Cleveland	8.50	Chicago	8.50	Kansas City	8.50
New York	8.50	Richmond	8.50	St. Louis	8.50	Dallas	8.50
Philadelphia	8.50	Atlanta	8.50	Minneapolis	8.50	San Francisco	8.50

SERIES OF 1969C—BANUELOS-SHULTZ, GREEN SEAL

Boston	8.50	Cleveland	8.50	Chicago	8.50	Kansas City	8.50
New York	8.50	Richmond	8.50	St. Louis	8.50	Dallas	8.50
Philadelphia	8.50	Atlanta	8.50	Minneapolis	8.50	San Francisco	8.50

SERIES OF 1974—NEFF-SIMON, GREEN SEAL

Boston	8.50	Cleveland	8.50	Chicago	8.50	Kansas City	8.50
New York	8.50	Richmond	8.50	St. Louis	8.50	Dallas	8.50
Philadelphia	8.50	Atlanta	8.50	Minneapolis	8.50	San Francisco	8.50

SERIES OF 1977—MORTON-BLUMENTHAL, GREEN SEAL

Boston	8.50	Cleveland	8.50	Chicago	8.50	Kansas City	8.50
New York	8.50	Richmond	8.50	St. Louis	8.50	Dallas	8.50
Philadelphia	8.50	Atlanta	8.50	Minneapolis	8.50	San Francisco	8.50

SERIES OF 1977A—MORTON-MILLER, GREEN SEAL

Boston	8.50	Cleveland	8.50	Chicago	8.50	Kansas City	8.50
New York	8.50	Richmond	8.50	St. Louis	8.50	Dallas	8.50
Philadelphia	8.50	Atlanta	8.50	Minneapolis	8.50	San Francisco	8.50

SERIES OF 1981—BUCHANAN-REGAN, GREEN SEAL

Boston	8.50	Cleveland	8.50	Chicago	8.50	Kansas City	8.50
New York	8.50	Richmond	8.50	St. Louis	8.50	Dallas	8.50
Philadelphia	8.50	Atlanta	8.50	Minneapolis	8.50	San Francisco	8.50

SERIES OF 1981A—ORTEGA-REGAN, GREEN SEAL

Boston	8.50	Cleveland	8.50	Chicago	8.50	Kansas City	8.50
New York	8.50	Richmond	8.50	St. Louis	8.50	Dallas	8.50
Philadelphia	8.50	Atlanta	8.50	Minneapolis	8.50	San Francisco	8.50

SERIES OF 1985—ORTEGA-BAKER, GREEN SEAL

Boston	6.50	Cleveland	6.50	Chicago	6.50	Kansas City	6.50
New York	6.50	Richmond	6.50	St. Louis	6.50	Dallas	6.50
Philadelphia	6.50	Atlanta	6.50	Minneapolis	6.50	San Francisco	6.50

FIVE DOLLAR NOTES (1918)
FEDERAL RESERVE BANK NOTES
(ALL WITH BLUE SEAL AND BLUE SERIAL NUMBERS)
(Large Size)   **NOTE NO. 58**

Face Design: Portrait of President Lincoln with Reserve City in center.
Back Design: Same as Note No. 54.

BANK & CITY	SERIES	GOV'T SIGNATURES	BANK SIGNATURES	A.B.P.	GOOD	V. FINE	UNC.
☐ Boston	1918	Teehee-Burke	Bullen-Morse ..	260.00	610.00	1550.00	2550.00
☐ New York	1918	Teehee-Burke	Hendricks-Strong	16.50	39.00	81.00	480.00
☐ Phila.	1918	Teehee-Burke	Hardt-Passmore	16.50	39.00	81.00	480.00
☐ Phila.	1918	Teehee-Burke	Dyer-Passmore	16.50	39.00	81.00	480.00
☐ Cleveland	1918	Teehee-Burke	Baxter-Fancher	16.50	39.00	81.00	480.00
☐ Cleveland	1918	Teehee-Burke	Davis-Fancher	16.50	39.00	81.00	480.00
☐ Cleveland	1918	Elliott-Burke	Davis-Fancher	16.50	39.00	81.00	480.00
☐ Atlanta	1915	Teehee-Burke	Bell-Wellborn	16.50	39.00	120.00	610.00
☐ Atlanta	1915	Teehee-Burke	Pike-McCord ..	16.50	39.00	120.00	610.00
☐ Atlanta	1918	Teehee-Burke	Pike-McCord ..	16.50	39.00	81.00	480.00
☐ Atlanta	1918	Teehee-Burke	Bell-Wellborn	16.50	39.00	81.00	480.00
☐ Atlanta	1918	Elliott-Burke	Bell-Wellborn	16.50	39.00	81.00	480.00
☐ Chicago	1915	Teehee-Burke	McLallen-McDougal	16.50	39.00	120.00	610.00
☐ Chicago	1918	Teehee-Burke	McCloud-McDougal	16.50	39.00	81.00	480.00
☐ Chicago	1918	Teehee-Burke	Cramer-McDougal	16.50	39.00	81.00	480.00
☐ St. Louis	1918	Teehee-Burke	Attebery-Wells	16.50	39.00	81.00	480.00
☐ St. Louis	1918	Teehee-Burke	Attebery-Biggs	16.50	39.00	81.00	480.00
☐ St. Louis	1918	Elliott-Burke	White-Biggs ...	16.50	39.00	81.00	480.00
☐ Minn.	1918	Teehee-Burke	Cook-Wold ...	16.50	39.00	81.00	480.00
☐ Kan. City	1915	Teehee-Burke	Anderson-Miller	16.50	39.00	120.00	610.00
☐ Kan. City	1915	Teehee-Burke	Cross-Miller ...	16.50	39.00	120.00	610.00
☐ Kan. City	1915	Teehee-Burke	Helm-Miller ...	16.50	39.00	120.00	610.00
☐ Kan. City	1918	Teehee-Burke	Anderson-Miller	16.50	39.00	81.00	480.00
☐ Kan. City	1918	Elliott-Burke	Helm-Miller ...	16.50	39.00	81.00	480.00
☐ Dallas	1915	Teehee-Burke	Hoopes-Van Zandt	16.50	39.00	120.00	610.00
☐ Dallas	1915	Teehee-Burke	Talley-VanZandt	16.50	39.00	120.00	610.00
☐ Dallas	1918	Teehee-Burke	Talley-VanZandt	16.50	39.00	81.00	480.00
☐ San Fran.	1915	Teehee-Burke	Clerk-Lynch ...	16.50	39.00	120.00	610.00
☐ San Fran.	1918	Teehee-Burke	Clerk-Lynch ...	16.50	39.00	81.00	480.00

FIVE DOLLAR NOTES (1929)
FEDERAL RESERVE BANK NOTES

(Small Size)   **NOTE No. 59**

Face Design: Portrait of President Lincoln.
SERIES 1929—Brown seal.

BANK & CITY	SIGNATURES	A.B.P.	GOOD	V. FINE	UNC.
☐ Boston	Jones-Woods	5.50	8.50	19.00	62.00
☐ New York	Jones-Woods	5.50	8.50	17.00	46.00
☐ Philadelphia	Jones-Woods	5.50	8.50	19.00	62.00
☐ Cleveland	Jones-Woods	5.50	8.50	19.00	55.00
☐ Richmond	Jones-Woods	5.50	8.50	25.00	82.00
☐ Atlanta	Jones-Woods	5.50	8.50	20.00	82.00
☐ Chicago	Jones-Woods	5.50	8.50	19.00	62.00
☐ St. Louis	Jones-Woods	5.50	8.50	17.00	53.00
☐ Minneapolis	Jones-Woods	5.50	8.50	22.00	53.00
☐ Kansas City	Jones-Woods	5.50	8.50	19.00	78.00
☐ Dallas	Jones-Woods	82.00	160.00	390.00	1850.00
☐ San Francisco	Jones-Woods	6.50	11.00	24.00	92.00

TEN DOLLAR NOTES

ORDER OF ISSUE

TEN DOLLAR NOTES (1861) DEMAND NOTES
NO TREASURY SEAL

(Large Size)

NOTE NO. 60

Face Design: Portrait of President Lincoln left, female figure with sword and shield.

Back Design: Ornate designs of "TEN."

CITY	A.B.P.	GOOD	V. GOOD
☐ Boston (I)	310.00	810.00	1425.00
☐ New York (I)	310.00	810.00	1425.00
☐ Philadelphia (I)	310.00	810.00	1425.00
☐ Cincinnati (I)	750.00	1600.00	RARE
☐ St. Louis (I)	750.00	1600.00	RARE
☐ Boston (II)	210.00	410.00	880.00
☐ New York (II)	210.00	410.00	880.00
☐ Philadelphia (II)	210.00	410.00	880.00
☐ Cincinnati (II)	210.00	410.00	880.00
☐ St. Louis (II)	210.00	410.00	880.00

TEN DOLLAR NOTES (1862–1863) UNITED STATES NOTES
(ALSO KNOWN AS LEGAL TENDER NOTES)

(Large Size) **NOTE NO. 61**

Back Design
Face Design: Similar to previous note.

SERIES	SIGNATURES	SEAL	A.B.P.	GOOD	V. FINE	UNC.
☐ 1862	Chittenden-Spinner*	Red	80.00	160.00	510.00	1425.00
☐ 1862	Chittenden-Spinner**	Red	80.00	160.00	510.00	1425.00
☐ 1863	Chittenden-Spinner**	Red	65.00	130.00	510.00	1500.00

*First Obligation: Similar to Note No. 33.
**Second Obligation: Shown above.

TEN DOLLAR NOTES (1869) UNITED STATES NOTES

(Large) **NOTE NO. 62**

Face Design: Portrait of Daniel Webster left, presentation of Indian Princess right. (This note is nicknamed "Jackass Note," because the EAGLE between the signatures resembles a donkey when it is held upside down.)

SERIES	SIGNATURES	SEAL	A.B.P.	GOOD	V. FINE	UNC.
☐ 1869	Allison-Spinner	Red	80.00	170.00	510.00	1480.00

TEN DOLLAR NOTES (1875–1880) UNITED STATES NOTES
(Large Size)

Face Design: Similar to previous note.

Back Design: Revised.

SERIES SIGNATURES	SEAL	A.B.P.	GOOD	V. FINE	UNC.
☐ 1875 Allison-New	Red	46.00	97.00	160.00	1150.00
☐ Same as above—SERIES A	Red	46.00	97.00	260.00	1150.00
☐ 1878 Allison-Gilfillan	Red	46.00	97.00	220.00	1400.00
☐ 1880 Scofield-Gilfillan	Brown	46.00	97.00	150.00	1025.00
☐ 1880 Bruce-Gilfillan	Brown	32.00	70.00	160.00	1025.00
☐ 1880 Bruce-Wyman	Brown	32.00	70.00	160.00	1025.00
☐ 1880 Bruce-Wyman	Red Plain	32.00	70.00	160.00	1025.00
☐ 1880 Rosecrans-Jordan	Red Plain	32.00	70.00	160.00	1100.00
☐ 1880 Rosecrans-Hyatt	Red Plain	32.00	70.00	160.00	1025.00
☐ 1880 Rosecrans-Hyatt	Red Spikes	32.00	70.00	160.00	1025.00
☐ 1880 Rosecrans-Huston	Red Spikes	32.00	70.00	160.00	1025.00
☐ 1880 Rosecrans-Huston	Brown	32.00	70.00	160.00	1025.00
☐ 1880 Rosecrans-Nebeker	Brown	32.00	70.00	160.00	750.00

SERIES SIGNATURES	SEAL	A.B.P.	GOOD	V. FINE	UNC.
☐ 1880 Rosecrans-Nebeker	Red	32.00	67.00	150.00	710.00
☐ 1880 Tillman-Morgan	Red	32.00	67.00	150.00	710.00
☐ 1880 Bruce-Roberts	Red	32.00	67.00	150.00	710.00
☐ 1880 Lyons-Roberts	Red	32.00	67.00	150.00	710.00

TEN DOLLAR NOTES (1901) UNITED STATES NOTES
LEGAL TENDER (Large Size) **NOTE NO. 64**

Face Design: American Bison (buffalo) center, portrait of Lewis left, portrait of Clark right.

Back Design: Female allegorical figure in arch.

SERIES SIGNATURES	SEAL	A.B.P.	GOOD	V. FINE	UNC.
☐ 1901 Lyons-Roberts	Red	46.00	87.00	275.00	1240.00
☐ 1901 Lyons-Treat	Red	46.00	87.00	275.00	1240.00
☐ 1901 Vernon-Treat	Red	46.00	87.00	275.00	1240.00
☐ 1901 Vernon-McClung	Red	46.00	87.00	275.00	1240.00
☐ 1901 Napier-McClung	Red	46.00	87.00	275.00	1240.00
☐ 1901 Parker-Burke	Red	46.00	87.00	275.00	1240.00
☐ 1901 Teehee-Burke	Red	46.00	87.00	275.00	1240.00
☐ 1901 Elliott-White	Red	46.00	87.00	275.00	1240.00
☐ 1901 Speelman-White	Red	46.00	87.00	275.00	1240.00

TEN DOLLAR NOTES (1923) UNITED STATES NOTES
(Large Size)   **NOTE NO. 65**

Face Design: Portrait of President Jackson center, red seal left, red "X" to right.

Back Design

SERIES SIGNATURES	SEAL	A.B.P.	GOOD	V. FINE	UNC.
☐ 1923 Speelman-White	Red	65.00	125.00	610.00	2350.00

TEN DOLLAR NOTES (1863–1875) NATIONAL BANK NOTES

FIRST CHARTER PERIOD (Large Size)　　　　　　　**NOTE NO. 66**

Face Design: Benjamin Franklin and kite left, name of bank and city center. Effigy of Liberty and Eagle right.

Back Design: Border green, center black. DeSoto on horseback at Mississippi River.

SERIES	SIGNATURES	SEAL	A.B.P.	GOOD	V. FINE	UNC.
☐ Original	Chittenden-Spinner	Red	38.00	105.00	310.00	2050.00
☐ Original	Colby-Spinner	Red	38.00	105.00	310.00	2050.00
☐ Original	Jeffries-Spinner	Red	182.00	450.00	1900.00	RARE
☐ Original	Allison-Spinner	Red	38.00	105.00	250.00	2050.00
☐ 1875	Allison-New	Red	35.00	105.00	250.00	1465.00
☐ 1875	Allison-Wyman	Red	35.00	105.00	250.00	1465.00
☐ 1875	Allison-Gilfillan	Red	35.00	105.00	250.00	1465.00
☐ 1875	Scofield-Gilfillan	Red	35.00	105.00	250.00	1465.00
☐ 1875	Bruce-Gilfillan	Red	35.00	105.00	250.00	1465.00
☐ 1875	Bruce-Wyman	Red	35.00	105.00	250.00	1465.00
☐ 1875	Rosecrans-Huston	Red	35.00	105.00	250.00	1465.00
☐ 1875	Rosecrans-Nebeker	Red	35.00	105.00	250.00	1465.00

TEN DOLLAR NOTES (1882) NATIONAL BANK NOTES

SECOND CHARTER PERIOD (Large Size)

NOTE NO. 68

First Issue—Brown seal and brown backs.
Face Design: Similar to previous Notes Nos. 66–67.
Back Design: Similar to Note No. 39, but border in brown with green Charter Number.

SERIES	SIGNATURES	SEAL	A.B.P.	GOOD	V. FINE	UNC.
☐ 1882	Bruce-Gilfillan	Brown ...	36.00	75.00	170.00	525.00
☐ 1882	Bruce-Wyman	Brown ...	36.00	75.00	170.00	525.00
☐ 1882	Bruce-Jordan	Brown ...	36.00	75.00	170.00	525.00
☐ 1882	Rosecrans-Jordan	Brown ...	36.00	75.00	170.00	525.00
☐ 1882	Rosecrans-Hyatt	Brown ...	36.00	75.00	170.00	525.00
☐ 1882	Rosecrans-Huston	Brown ...	36.00	75.00	170.00	525.00
☐ 1882	Rosecrans-Nebeker	Brown ...	35.00	75.00	170.00	525.00
☐ 1882	Rosecrans-Morgan	Brown ...	160.00	280.00	775.00	1200.00
☐ 1882	Tillman-Morgan	Brown ...	36.00	75.00	170.00	525.00
☐ 1882	Tillman-Roberts	Brown ...	36.00	75.00	170.00	525.00
☐ 1882	Bruce-Roberts	Brown ...	36.00	75.00	170.00	525.00
☐ 1882	Lyons-Roberts	Brown ...	36.00	75.00	170.00	525.00
☐ 1882	Lyons-Treat	Brown ...	36.00	75.00	170.00	525.00
☐ 1882	Vernon-Treat	Brown ...	36.00	75.00	170.00	525.00

Second Issue—Blue seal, green back with date 1882–1908.
Face Design: Similar to Note No. 66.
Back Design: Similar to Note No. 40.

(Large Size)

NOTE NO. 69

SERIES	SIGNATURES	SEAL	A.B.P.	GOOD	V. FINE	UNC.
☐ 1882	Rosecrans-Huston	Blue	22.00	42.00	145.00	575.00
☐ 1882	Rosecrans-Nebeker	Blue	22.00	42.00	145.00	575.00
☐ 1882	Rosecrans-Morgan	Blue	85.00	180.00	700.00	1250.00
☐ 1882	Tillman-Morgan	Blue	22.00	42.00	145.00	575.00
☐ 1882	Tillman-Roberts	Blue	22.00	42.00	145.00	575.00
☐ 1882	Bruce-Roberts	Blue	22.00	42.00	145.00	575.00
☐ 1882	Lyons-Roberts	Blue	22.00	42.00	145.00	575.00
☐ 1882	Vernon-Treat	Blue	22.00	42.00	145.00	575.00
☐ 1882	Vernon-McClung	Blue	22.00	42.00	145.00	575.00
☐ 1882	Napier-McClung	Blue	22.00	42.00	145.00	575.00

TEN DOLLAR NOTES (1882) NATIONAL BANK NOTES
NOTE NO. 70

Third Issue—Blue seal, green back with value in block letters.
Face Design: Similar to previous notes (see Note No. 66).
Back Design: Similar to Note No. 41.

SERIES	SIGNATURES	SEAL	A.B.P.	GOOD	V. FINE	UNC.
☐ 1882	Tillman-Roberts	Blue	36.00	76.00	280.00	2550.00
☐ 1882	Lyons-Roberts	Blue	36.00	76.00	280.00	2550.00
☐ 1882	Vernon-Treat	Blue	36.00	76.00	280.00	2550.00
☐ 1882	Napier-McClung	Blue	32.00	62.00	265.00	1850.00

These notes may exist with other signatures, but are very rare.

TEN DOLLAR NOTES (1902) NATIONAL BANK NOTES
THIRD CHARTER PERIOD (Large Size)　　　　　**NOTE NO. 71**

First Issue—Red seal and red Charter numbers.
Face Design: Portrait of President McKinley left, name of bank and city
in center.

SERIES	SIGNATURES	SEAL	A.B.P.	GOOD	V. FINE	UNC.
☐ 1902	Lyons-Roberts	Red	32.00	62.00	170.00	425.00
☐ 1902	Lyons-Treat	Red	32.00	62.00	170.00	425.00
☐ 1902	Vernon-Treat	Red	32.00	62.00	170.00	875.00

TEN DOLLAR NOTES (1902) NATIONAL BANK NOTES

THIRD CHARTER PERIOD (Large Size)

NOTE NO. 71A

Second Issue— Blue seal and numbers, 1902–1908 on the back.
Back Design: Same as Note No. 70, date 1902–1908.
Face Design: Same as Note No. 71.

SERIES	SIGNATURES	SEAL	A.B.P.	GOOD	V. FINE	UNC.
☐ 1902	Lyons-Roberts	Blue	12.50	22.00	52.00	225.00
☐ 1902	Lyons-Treat	Blue	12.50	22.00	52.00	225.00
☐ 1902	Vernon-Treat	Blue	12.50	22.00	52.00	225.00
☐ 1902	Vernon-McClung	Blue	12.50	22.00	52.00	225.00
☐ 1902	Napier-McClung	Blue	12.50	22.00	52.00	225.00
☐ 1902	Napier-Thompson	Blue	12.50	26.00	82.00	750.00
☐ 1902	Napier-Burke	Blue	12.50	22.00	52.00	225.00
☐ 1902	Parker-Burke	Blue	12.50	22.00	52.00	225.00
☐ 1902	Teehee-Burke	Blue	16.00	31.00	92.00	225.00

Third Issue—Blue seal and numbers, without date on back.

SERIES	SIGNATURES	SEAL	A.B.P.	GOOD	V. FINE	UNC.
☐ 1902	Lyons-Roberts	Blue	12.50	19.00	37.00	125.00
☐ 1902	Lyons-Treat	Blue	12.50	19.00	37.00	125.00
☐ 1902	Vernon-Treat	Blue	12.50	19.00	37.00	125.00
☐ 1902	Vernon-McClung	Blue	12.50	19.00	37.00	125.00
☐ 1902	Napier-McClung	Blue	12.50	19.00	37.00	125.00
☐ 1902	Napier-Thompson	Blue	16.00	25.00	73.00	510.00
☐ 1902	Napier-Burke	Blue	12.50	19.00	38.00	125.00
☐ 1902	Parker-Burke	Blue	12.50	19.00	38.00	125.00
☐ 1902	Teehee-Burke	Blue	12.50	19.00	38.00	125.00
☐ 1902	Elliott-Burke	Blue	12.50	19.00	38.00	125.00
☐ 1902	Elliott-White	Blue	12.50	19.00	38.00	125.00
☐ 1902	Speelman-White	Blue	12.50	19.00	38.00	125.00
☐ 1902	Woods-White	Blue	12.50	19.00	39.00	125.00
☐ 1902	Woods-Tate	Blue	12.50	19.50	39.00	125.00
☐ 1902	Jones-Woods	Blue	42.00	80.00	310.00	1325.00

TEN DOLLAR NOTES (1929) NATIONAL BANK NOTES

(Small Size)

NOTE NO. 72

Face Design—TYPE I: Portrait of Hamilton center, name of bank left, brown seal right, Charter number black.

Face Design—TYPE II: Charter number added in brown.

Back Design: United States Treasury Building.

SERIES SIGNATURES	SEAL	A.B.P.	GOOD	V. FINE	UNC.
☐ 1929—TYPE I Jones-Woods	Brown ...	11.00	13.00	22.00	62.00
☐ 1929—TYPE II Jones-Woods	Brown ...	11.00	13.00	24.00	67.00

TEN DOLLAR NOTES (1870–1875)
NATIONAL GOLD BANK NOTES

(Large Size)

NOTE NO. 67

Face Design: Similar to Note No. 66.

Back Design: State Seal left, gold coins center, American Eagle right.
SIGNATURES OF ALLISON-SPINNER, RED TREASURY SEAL

DATE BANK	CITY	A.B.P.	GOOD	V. GOOD
☐ 1870 First National Gold Bank	San Francisco	260.00	580.00	1625.00
☐ 1872 National Gold Bank and Trust Company	San Francisco	260.00	580.00	1625.00
☐ 1872 National Gold Bank of D.O. Mills and Company	Sacramento	365.00	810.00	1910.00
☐ 1873 First National Gold Bank	Santa Barbara	365.00	810.00	1910.00
☐ 1873 First National Gold Bank	Stockton	365.00	810.00	1910.00
☐ 1874 Farmers Nat'l Gold Bank	San Jose	365.00	810.00	1910.00
☐ 1874 First National Gold Bank	Petaluma	365.00	810.00	1910.00
☐ 1875 First National Gold Bank	Oakland	365.00	810.00	1910.00

TEN DOLLAR NOTES (1880) SILVER CERTIFICATES

(Large Size)   **NOTE NO. 73**

Face Design: Portrait of Robert Morris left.

Back Design: Printed in black ink, large letters "SILVER."

SERIES SIGNATURES	SEAL	A.B.P.	GOOD	V. FINE	UNC.
☐ 1880 Scofield-Gilfillan	Brown	70.00	130.00	710.00	3550.00
☐ 1880 Bruce-Gilfillan	Brown	70.00	130.00	710.00	3550.00
☐ 1880 Bruce-Wyman	Brown	70.00	130.00	710.00	3550.00
☐ 1880 Bruce-Wyman	Red	72.00	142.00	810.00	3050.00

TEN DOLLAR NOTES (1886) SILVER CERTIFICATES
(Large Size)   **NOTE NO. 74**

Face Design:
Portrait of
Thomas A.
Hendricks in
center.

SERIES SIGNATURES	SEAL	A.B.P.	GOOD	V. FINE	UNC.
☐ 1886 Rosecrans-Jordan	Small Red	82.00	145.00	510.00	2450.00
☐ 1886 Rosecrans-Hyatt	Small Red	82.00	145.00	510.00	2450.00
☐ 1886 Rosecrans-Hyatt	Large Red	82.00	145.00	510.00	2450.00
☐ 1886 Rosecrans-Huston	Large Red	82.00	145.00	510.00	2450.00
☐ 1886 Rosecrans-Huston	Large Brown	82.00	145.00	510.00	2450.00
☐ 1886 Rosecrans-Nebeker	Large Brown	82.00	145.00	510.00	2450.00
☐ 1886 Rosecrans-Nebeker	Small Red	82.00	145.00	510.00	2450.00

TEN DOLLAR NOTES (1891–1908) SILVER CERTIFICATES
(Large Size)   **NOTE NO. 75**

Face Design:
Same as
Note No. 74.
Back Design

SERIES	SIGNATURES	SEAL	A.B.P.	GOOD	V. FINE	UNC.
☐ 1891	Rosecrans-Nebeker	Red	39.00	77.00	210.00	1350.00
☐ 1891	Tillman-Morgan	Red	39.00	77.00	210.00	1410.00
☐ 1891	Bruce-Roberts	Red	39.00	77.00	210.00	1410.00
☐ 1891	Lyons-Roberts	Red	39.00	77.00	210.00	1410.00
☐ 1891	Vernon-Treat	Blue	39.00	77.00	210.00	1410.00
☐ 1891	Vernon-McClung	Blue	39.00	77.00	210.00	1410.00
☐ 1891	Parker-Burke	Blue	39.00	77.00	210.00	1410.00

TEN DOLLAR NOTES (1933) SILVER CERTIFICATES

(Small Size) **NOTE NO. 76**

Face Design: Portrait of Alexander Hamilton, center. Blue seal to left, blue numbers.

Back Design: Green United States Treasury Building.

SERIES	SIGNATURES	SEAL	A.B.P.	GOOD	V. FINE	UNC.
☐ 1933	Julian-Woodin	Blue	210.00	510.00	1650.00	5100.00

TEN DOLLAR NOTES (1934) SILVER CERTIFICATES
(Small Size)   **NOTE NO. 77**

Face Design: Blue "10" to left of portrait. Treasury Seal is now to right.
Back Design: Similar to previous issue.

TEN DOLLAR NOTES (1934) SILVER CERTIFICATES
(Small Size)   **NOTE NO. 77**

SERIES SIGNATURES	SEAL	A.B.P.	GOOD	V. FINE	UNC.
☐ 1934 Julian-Morgenthau	Blue	11.00	13.00	26.00	55.00
☐ 1934 Julian-Morgenthau*	Yellow	175.00	360.00	1100.00	7200.00
☐ 1934A Julian-Morgenthau	Blue	11.00	13.00	18.00	35.00
☐ 1934A Julian-Morgenthau*	Yellow	12.00	16.00	23.00	145.00
☐ 1934B Julian-Vinson	Blue	12.00	22.00	75.00	675.00
☐ 1934C Julian-Snyder	Blue	12.00	13.00	22.00	55.00
☐ 1934D Clark-Snyder	Blue	12.00	13.00	22.00	55.00

*Silver Certificates with a yellow seal were a special issue for use in combat areas of North Africa and Europe during World War II.

TEN DOLLAR NOTES (1953) SILVER CERTIFICATES

(Small Size) **NOTE NO. 78**

Face Design: Gray "10" to left of portrait, Treasury Seal is smaller.
Back Design: Back similar to previous note.

SERIES	SIGNATURES	SEAL	A.B.P.	GOOD	V. FINE	UNC.
☐ 1953	Priest-Humphrey	Blue	11.00	12.50	20.00	45.00
☐ 1953A	Priest-Anderson	Blue	40.00	12.50	40.00	120.00
☐ 1953B	Smith-Dillon	Blue	11.00	12.50	20.00	45.00

ABOVE NOTE ONLY—720,000 ISSUED.
NOTE: Last issue of $10.00 Silver Certificates. These were not issued with "In God We Trust" on the back. Production ended in 1962.

TEN DOLLAR (1879) REFUNDING CERTIFICATES

NOTE NO. 78A

Face Design: Portrait of Benjamin Franklin.

Back Design: Large "TEN," ornate cornucopia border.

SERIES SIGNATURES	SEAL	A.B.P.	GOOD	V. FINE	UNC.
☐ 1879 Scofield-Gilfillan, PAY TO ORDER ...	Red				VERY RARE
☐ 1879 Scofield-Gilfillan, PAY TO BEARER ..	Red	180.00	380.00	1250.00	

TEN DOLLAR NOTES (1907) GOLD CERTIFICATES

(Large Size)

Face Design: Portrait of Hillegas center, yellow "X" left, yellow seal right, yellow numbers.

Back Design: The backs are a bright yellow color.

SERIES SIGNATURES	SEAL	A.B.P.	GOOD	V. FINE	UNC.
☐ 1907 Vernon-Treat	Gold	12.50	22.00	110.00	510.00
☐ 1907 Vernon-McClung	Gold	12.50	22.00	110.00	510.00
☐ 1907 Napier-McClung	Gold	12.50	22.00	110.00	420.00
☐ 1907 Napier-Thompson	Gold	21.00	40.00	140.00	1000.00
☐ 1907 Parker-Burke	Gold	12.50	22.00	110.00	420.00
☐ 1907 Teehee-Burke	Gold	12.50	22.00	110.00	420.00
☐ 1922 Speelman-White	Gold	12.50	22.00	110.00	420.00

TEN DOLLAR NOTES (1928) GOLD CERTIFICATES

(Small Size)   **NOTE NO. 80**

Face Design: Portrait of Alexander Hamilton center, yellow seal to left, yellow numbers.

Back Design: Printed in green ink.

SERIES SIGNATURES	SEAL	A.B.P.	GOOD	V. FINE	UNC.
☐ 1928 Woods-Mellon	Gold	15.00	20.00	60.00	280.00

TEN DOLLAR NOTES (1890) TREASURY NOTES

(Large Size)   **NOTE NO. 81**

Face Design: Portrait of General Philip Sheridan.

Back Design:
Very ornate
large "TEN."

SERIES SIGNATURES	SEAL	A.B.P.	GOOD	V. FINE	UNC.
☐ 1890 Rosecrans-Huston	Lg. Brown	65.00	160.00	500.00	2850.00
☐ 1890 Rosecrans-Nebeker	Lg. Brown	65.00	160.00	500.00	3450.00
☐ 1890 Rosecrans-Nebeker	Sm. Red	50.00	95.00	500.00	2850.00

TEN DOLLAR NOTES (1891) TREASURY NOTES

(Large Size)   **NOTE NO. 81A**

Face Design:
Same as No. 81.
Back Design:
Ornate small
"TEN."

SERIES SIGNATURES	SEAL	A.B.P.	GOOD	V. FINE	UNC.
☐ 1891 Rosecrans-Nebeker	Sm. Red	40.00	85.00	260.00	925.00

SERIES SIGNATURES	SEAL		A.B.P.	GOOD	V. FINE	UNC.
☐ 1891 Tillman-Morgan	Sm.	Red	38.00	80.00	250.00	900.00
☐ 1891 Bruce-Roberts	Sm.	Red	38.00	80.00	250.00	900.00

TEN DOLLAR NOTES (1914) FEDERAL RESERVE NOTES
(Large Size)   NOTE NO. 82

Face Design: Portrait of President Jackson center, Federal Reserve Seal left, Treasury Seal right.

Back Design: Scenes of farming and industry.

SIGNATURES OF BURKE-McADOO, RED SEALS AND RED SERIAL NUMBERS

SERIES CITY	SEAL	A.B.P.	GOOD	V. FINE	UNC.
☐ 1914 Boston	Red	16.50	32.00	85.00	410.00
☐ 1914 New York	Red	16.50	32.00	85.00	410.00
☐ 1914 Philadelphia	Red	16.50	32.00	85.00	410.00
☐ 1914 Cleveland	Red	16.50	32.00	85.00	410.00
☐ 1914 Richmond	Red	16.50	32.00	85.00	410.00
☐ 1914 Atlanta	Red	16.50	32.00	85.00	410.00
☐ 1914 Chicago	Red	16.50	32.00	85.00	410.00
☐ 1914 St. Louis	Red	16.50	32.00	85.00	410.00

SERIES CITY		SEAL	A.B.P.	GOOD	V. FINE	UNC.
☐ 1914 Minneapolis		Red	16.50	31.00	85.00	410.00
☐ 1914 Kansas City		Red	16.50	31.00	85.00	410.00
☐ 1914 Dallas		Red	16.50	31.00	85.00	410.00
☐ 1914 San Francisco		Red	16.50	31.00	85.00	410.00

TEN DOLLAR NOTES (1914) FEDERAL RESERVE NOTES

(Large Size)   NOTE NO. 82A

BANK & CITY	SIGNATURES	SEAL	A.B.P.	V. FINE	UNC.
☐ Boston	Burke-McAdoo	Blue	17.50	54.00	155.00
☐ Boston	Burke-Glass	Blue	17.50	54.00	155.00
☐ Boston	Burke-Huston	Blue	17.50	54.00	155.00
☐ Boston	White-Mellon	Blue	17.50	54.00	155.00
☐ New York	Burke-McAdoo	Blue	17.50	54.00	155.00
☐ New York	Burke-Glass	Blue	17.50	54.00	155.00
☐ New York	Burke-Huston	Blue	17.50	54.00	155.00
☐ New York	White-Mellon	Blue	17.50	54.00	155.00
☐ Philadelphia	Burke-McAdoo	Blue	17.50	54.00	155.00
☐ Philadelphia	Burke-Glass	Blue	17.50	54.00	155.00
☐ Philadelphia	Burke-Huston	Blue	17.50	54.00	155.00
☐ Philadelphia	White-Mellon	Blue	17.50	54.00	155.00
☐ Cleveland	Burke-McAdoo	Blue	17.50	54.00	155.00
☐ Cleveland	Burke-Glass	Blue	17.50	54.00	155.00
☐ Cleveland	Burke-Huston	Blue	17.50	54.00	155.00
☐ Cleveland	White-Mellon	Blue	17.50	54.00	155.00
☐ Richmond	Burke-McAdoo	Blue	17.50	54.00	155.00
☐ Richmond	Burke-Glass	Blue	17.50	54.00	155.00
☐ Richmond	Burke-Huston	Blue	17.50	54.00	155.00
☐ Richmond	White-Mellon	Blue	17.50	54.00	155.00
☐ Atlanta	Burke-McAdoo	Blue	17.50	54.00	155.00
☐ Atlanta	Burke-Glass	Blue	17.50	54.00	155.00
☐ Atlanta	Burke-Huston	Blue	17.50	54.00	155.00
☐ Atlanta	White-Mellon	Blue	17.50	54.00	155.00
☐ Chicago	Burke-McAdoo	Blue	17.50	54.00	155.00
☐ Chicago	Burke-Glass	Blue	17.50	54.00	155.00
☐ Chicago	Burke-Huston	Blue	17.50	54.00	155.00
☐ Chicago	White-Mellon	Blue	17.50	54.00	155.00
☐ St. Louis	Burke-McAdoo	Blue	17.50	54.00	155.00
☐ St. Louis	Burke-Glass	Blue	17.50	54.00	150.00
☐ St. Louis	Burke-Huston	Blue	31.00	54.00	155.00
☐ St. Louis	White-Mellon	Blue	17.50	54.00	155.00
☐ Minneapolis	Burke-McAdoo	Blue	17.50	54.00	155.00
☐ Minneapolis	Burke-Glass	Blue	17.50	54.00	155.00
☐ Minneapolis	Burke-Huston	Blue	17.50	54.00	155.00
☐ Minneapolis	White-Mellon	Blue	17.50	54.00	155.00
☐ Kansas City	Burke-McAdoo	Blue	17.50	54.00	155.00
☐ Kansas City	Burke-Glass	Blue	17.50	54.00	155.00
☐ Kansas City	Burke-Huston	Blue	17.50	54.00	155.00
☐ Kansas City	White-Mellon	Blue	17.50	54.00	155.00

BANK & CITY	SIGNATURES	SEAL	A.B.P.	V. FINE	UNC.
☐ Dallas	Burke-McAdoo	Blue	17.50	54.00	155.00
☐ Dallas	Burke-Glass	Blue	17.50	54.00	155.00
☐ Dallas	Burke-Huston	Blue	17.50	54.00	155.00
☐ Dallas	White-Mellon	Blue	17.50	54.00	155.00
☐ San Francisco	Burke-McAdoo	Blue	17.50	54.00	155.00
☐ San Francisco	Burke-Glass	Blue	17.50	54.00	155.00
☐ San Francisco	Burke-Huston	Blue	17.50	54.00	155.00
☐ San Francisco	White-Mellon	Blue	17.50	54.00	155.00

TEN DOLLAR NOTES (1928–1928A)
FEDERAL RESERVE NOTES

(Small Size)

NOTE NO. 83

Face Design: Portrait of Alexander Hamilton center, black Federal Reserve Seal left, with number, green Treasury Seal to the right.

Back Design: United States Treasury Building.

SERIES OF 1928—SIGNATURES OF TATE-MELLON, GREEN SEAL

BANK & CITY	A.B.P.	V. FINE	UNC.	BANK & CITY	A.B.P.	V. FINE	UNC.
☐ Boston	12.00	21.00	55.00	☐ Chicago	12.00	21.00	55.00
☐ New York	12.00	21.00	55.00	☐ St. Louis	12.00	21.00	55.00
☐ Philadelphia	12.00	21.00	55.00	☐ Minneapolis	12.00	21.00	55.00
☐ Cleveland	12.00	21.00	55.00	☐ Kansas City	12.00	21.00	55.00

BANK & CITY	A.B.P.	V. FINE	UNC.	BANK & CITY	A.B.P.	V. FINE	UNC.
☐ Richmond	12.00	21.00	55.00	☐ Dallas	12.00	21.00	55.00
☐ Atlanta	12.00	21.00	55.00	☐ San Francisco	12.00	21.00	55.00

SERIES OF 1928A—SIGNATURES OF WOODS-MELLON, GREEN SEAL

BANK & CITY	A.B.P.	V. FINE	UNC.	BANK & CITY	A.B.P.	V. FINE	UNC.
☐ Boston	12.00	17.00	50.00	☐ Chicago	12.00	17.00	50.00
☐ New York	12.00	17.00	50.00	☐ St. Louis	12.00	17.00	50.00
☐ Philadelphia	12.00	17.00	50.00	☐ Minneapolis	12.00	17.00	50.00
☐ Cleveland	12.00	17.00	50.00	☐ Kansas City	12.00	17.00	50.00
☐ Richmond	12.00	17.00	50.00	☐ Dallas	12.00	17.00	50.00
☐ Atlanta	12.00	17.00	50.00	☐ San Francisco	12.00	17.00	50.00

TEN DOLLAR NOTES (1928B–1928C)
FEDERAL RESERVE NOTES

(Small Issue)   **NOTE NO. 83A**

Face Design: Alexander Hamilton Black Federal Reserve Seal left has letter instead of number.

Back Design: Same as Note No. 83.

SERIES OF 1928B—SIGNATURES OF WOODS-MELLON, GREEN SEAL

BANK & CITY	A.B.P.	V. FINE	UNC.	BANK & CITY	A.B.P.	V. FINE	UNC.
☐ Boston	12.00	15.00	36.00	☐ Chicago	12.00	15.00	36.00
☐ New York	12.00	15.00	36.00	☐ St. Louis	12.00	15.00	36.00
☐ Philadelphia	12.00	15.00	36.00	☐ Minneapolis	12.00	15.00	36.00
☐ Cleveland	12.00	15.00	36.00	☐ Kansas City	12.00	15.00	36.00
☐ Richmond	12.00	15.00	36.00	☐ Dallas	12.00	15.00	36.00
☐ Atlanta	12.00	15.00	36.00	☐ San Francisco	12.00	15.00	36.00

SERIES OF 1928C—SIGNATURES OF WOODS-MILLS, GREEN SEAL

BANK & CITY	A.B.P.	V. FINE	UNC.	BANK & CITY	A.B.P.	V. FINE	UNC.
☐ New York	36.00	62.00	115.00	☐ Atlanta	36.00	62.00	115.00
☐ Cleveland	36.00	62.00	115.00	☐ Chicago	36.00	62.00	115.00
☐ Richmond	36.00	62.00	115.00				

TEN DOLLAR NOTES (1934) FEDERAL RESERVE NOTES

(Small Size)   **NOTE NO. 83B**

SERIES OF 1934—SIGNATURES OF JULIAN-MORGENTHAU, GREEN SEAL

BANK & CITY	A.B.P.	V. FINE	UNC.	BANK & CITY	A.B.P.	V. FINE	UNC.
☐ Boston	12.00	15.00	31.00	☐ Chicago	12.00	15.00	31.00
☐ New York	12.00	15.00	31.00	☐ St. Louis	12.00	15.00	31.00
☐ Philadelphia	12.00	15.00	31.00	☐ Minneapolis	12.00	15.00	31.00
☐ Cleveland	12.00	15.00	31.00	☐ Kansas City	12.00	15.00	31.00
☐ Richmond	12.00	15.00	31.00	☐ Dallas	12.00	15.00	31.00
☐ Atlanta	12.00	15.00	31.00	☐ San Francisco	12.00	15.00	31.00

NOTE: The green Treasury Seal on this note is known in a light and dark color. The light seal is worth about 10% to 20% more in most cases. "Redeemable in Gold" removed from obligation over Federal Reserve Seal.

TEN DOLLAR NOTES (1934) FEDERAL RESERVE NOTES

(Small Size)   **NOTE NO. 83B**

SERIES OF 1934A—SIGNATURES OF JULIAN-MORGENTHAU, GREEN SEAL

BANK & CITY	A.B.P.	V. FINE	UNC.	BANK & CITY	A.B.P.	V. FINE	UNC.
☐ Boston	12.00	15.00	26.00	☐ Chicago	12.00	15.00	26.00
☐ New York	12.00	15.00	26.00	☐ St. Louis	12.00	15.00	26.00
☐ Philadelphia	12.00	15.00	26.00	☐ Minneapolis	12.00	15.00	26.00
☐ Cleveland	12.00	15.00	26.00	☐ Kansas City	12.00	15.00	26.00
☐ Richmond	12.00	15.00	26.00	☐ Dallas	12.00	15.00	26.00
☐ Atlanta	12.00	15.00	26.00	☐ San Francisco*	12.00	15.00	26.00

*San Francisco—1934A with brown seal and overprinted HAWAII on face and back. Special issue for use in combat areas during World War II. Value in V. Fine $35.00, Value in Unc. $250.00.

SERIES OF 1934B—SIGNATURES OF JULIAN-VINSON, GREEN SEAL

BANK & CITY	A.B.P.	V. FINE	UNC.	BANK & CITY	A.B.P.	V. FINE	UNC.
☐ Boston	12.00	15.00	31.00	☐ Chicago	12.00	15.00	31.00
☐ New York	12.00	15.00	31.00	☐ St. Louis	12.00	15.00	31.00
☐ Philadelphia	12.00	15.00	31.00	☐ Minneapolis	12.00	15.00	31.00
☐ Cleveland	12.00	15.00	31.00	☐ Kansas City	12.00	15.00	31.00
☐ Richmond	12.00	15.00	31.00	☐ Dallas	12.00	15.00	31.00
☐ Atlanta	12.00	15.00	31.00	☐ San Francisco	12.00	15.00	31.00

SERIES OF 1934C—SIGNATURES OF JULIAN-SNYDER, GREEN SEAL

BANK & CITY	A.B.P.	V. FINE	UNC.	BANK & CITY	A.B.P.	V. FINE	UNC.
☐ Boston	12.00	15.00	26.00	☐ Chicago	12.00	13.00	26.00
☐ New York	12.00	15.00	26.00	☐ St. Louis	12.00	13.00	26.00
☐ Philadelphia	12.00	15.00	26.00	☐ Minneapolis	12.00	13.00	26.00
☐ Cleveland	12.00	15.00	26.00	☐ Kansas City	12.00	13.00	26.00
☐ Richmond	12.00	15.00	26.00	☐ Dallas	12.00	13.00	26.00
☐ Atlanta	12.00	15.00	26.00	☐ San Francisco	12.00	13.00	26.00

SERIES OF 1934D—SIGNATURES OF CLARK-SNYDER, GREEN SEAL

BANK & CITY	A.B.P.	V. FINE	UNC.	BANK & CITY	A.B.P.	V. FINE	UNC.
☐ Boston	12.00	13.00	26.00	☐ Chicago	12.00	13.00	26.00
☐ New York	12.00	13.00	26.00	☐ St. Louis	12.00	13.00	26.00

BANK & CITY	A.B.P.	V. FINE	UNC.	BANK & CITY	A.B.P.	V. FINE	UNC.
☐ Philadelphia	12.00	13.00	26.00	☐ Minneapolis	12.00	13.00	26.00
☐ Cleveland	12.00	13.00	26.00	☐ Kansas City	12.00	13.00	26.00
☐ Richmond	12.00	13.00	26.00	☐ Dallas	12.00	13.00	26.00
☐ Atlanta	12.00	13.00	26.00	☐ San Francisco	12.00	13.00	26.00

TEN DOLLAR NOTES (1950) FEDERAL RESERVE NOTES

(Small Size)   **NOTE NO. 83C**
SERIES OF 1950—CLARK-SNYDER SIGNATURES, GREEN SEAL

UNC.

Issued for all Federal Reserve Banks 35.00

TEN DOLLAR NOTES (1950) FEDERAL RESERVE NOTES

(Small Size)   **NOTE NO. 83C**
SERIES OF 1950A—SIGNATURES OF PRIEST-HUMPHREY, GREEN SEAL
Issued for all Federal Reserve Banks 25.00
SERIES OF 1950B—SIGNATURES OF PRIEST-ANDERSON, GREEN SEAL
Issued for all Federal Reserve Banks 25.00
SERIES OF 1950C—SIGNATURES OF SMITH-DILLON, GREEN SEAL
Issued for all Federal Reserve Banks 24.00
SERIES OF 1950D—SIGNATURES OF GRANAHAN-DILLON, GREEN SEAL
Issued for all Federal Reserve Banks 23.00
SERIES OF 1950E—SIGNATURES OF GRANAHAN-FOWLER, GREEN SEAL

BANK	UNC.	BANK	UNC.
☐ New York	24.00	☐ San Francisco	24.00
☐ Chicago	24.00	ONLY DISTRICTS USED	

TEN DOLLAR NOTES (1963) FEDERAL RESERVE NOTES
("IN GOD WE TRUST" ADDED ON BACK)

(Small Size)   **NOTE NO. 83D**
SERIES OF 1963—SIGNATURES OF GRANAHAN-DILLON, GREEN SEAL
Issued for all banks except Minneapolis 23.00
SERIES OF 1963A—SIGNATURES OF GRANAHAN-FOWLER, GREEN SEAL
Issued for all Federal Reserve Banks 23.00

TEN DOLLAR NOTES (1969) FEDERAL RESERVE NOTES
(WORDING IN GREEN TREASURY SEAL CHANGED
FROM LATIN TO ENGLISH)

(Small Size)   **NOTE NO. 83E**
SERIES OF 1969—SIGNATURES OF ELSTON-KENNEDY
Issued for all Federal Reserve Banks 23.00
SERIES OF 1969A—SIGNATURES OF KABIS-CONNALLY
Issued for all Federal Reserve Banks 21.00

SERIES OF 1969B—SIGNATURES OF BANUELOS-CONNALLY
Issued for all Federal Reserve Banks 20.00
SERIES OF 1969C—SIGNATURES OF BANUELOS-SHULTZ
Issued for all Federal Reserve Banks 20.00
SERIES OF 1974—SIGNATURES OF NEFF-SIMON
Issued for all Federal Reserve Banks 18.00
SERIES OF 1977—SIGNATURES OF MORTON-BLUMENTHAL
Issued for all Federal Reserve Banks 18.00
SERIES OF 1977A—SIGNATURES OF MORTON-MILLER
Issued for all Federal Reserve Banks 18.00
SERIES OF 1981—SIGNATURES OF BUCHANAN-REGAN, GREEN SEAL
Issued for all Federal Reserve Banks 16.00
SERIES OF 1981A—SIGNATURES OF ORTEGA-REGAN, GREEN SEAL
Issued for all Federal Reserve Banks 16.00
SERIES OF 1985—SIGNATURES OF ORTEGA-BAKER, GREEN SEAL
Issued for all Federal Reserve Banks 13.00

TEN DOLLAR NOTES (1915–1918)
FEDERAL RESERVE BANK NOTES

(Large Size)

NOTE NO. 84

Face Design: Portrait of President Jackson to left, bank and city in center, blue seal to the right.

Back Design: Similar to Note No. 82.

BANK & CITY	SERIES	GOV'T SIGNATURES	BANK SIGNATURES	A.B.P.	GOOD	V. FINE	UNC.
☐ New York	1918	Teehee-Burke	Hendricks-Strong	42.00	87.00	380.00	2250.00
☐ Atlanta	1915	Teehee-Burke	Bell-Wellborn	55.00	100.00	510.00	2100.00
☐ Atlanta	1918	Elliott-Burke	Bell-Wellborn	42.00	87.00	380.00	2250.00
☐ Chicago	1915	Teehee-Burke	McLallen-McDougal	42.00	87.00	410.00	1650.00
☐ Chicago	1918	Teehee-Burke	McCloud-McDougal	42.00	87.00	500.00	2250.00
☐ St. Louis	1918	Teehee-Burke	Attebery-Wells	42.00	87.00	380.00	2250.00
☐ Kan. City	1915	Teehee-Burke	Anderson-Miller	42.00	87.00	380.00	1650.00
☐ Kan. City	1915	Teehee-Burke	Cross-Miller ...	42.00	87.00	380.00	1650.00
☐ Kan. City	1915	Teehee-Burke	Helm-Miller ...	42.00	87.00	380.00	1650.00
☐ Dallas	1915	Teehee-Burke	Hoopes-VanZandt	42.00	87.00	510.00	1650.00
☐ Dallas	1915	Teehee-Burke	Gilbert-VanZandt	42.00	120.00	610.00	2400.00
☐ Dallas	1915	Teehee-Burke	Talley-VanZandt	42.00	87.00	510.00	1650.00

TEN DOLLAR NOTES (1929)
FEDERAL RESERVE BANK NOTES

(Small Size)

NOTE NO. 85

Face Design: Portrait of Alexander Hamilton.

Back Design: Same as all small size $10.00 notes.
SIGNATURES OF JONES-WOODS, BROWN SEAL

BANK	SEAL	A.B.P.	GOOD	V. FINE	UNC.
☐ Boston	Brown ...	12.00	12.50	32.00	73.00
☐ New York	Brown ...	12.00	12.50	32.00	52.00
☐ Philadelphia	Brown ...	12.00	12.50	32.00	73.00
☐ Cleveland	Brown ...	12.00	12.50	32.00	73.00
☐ Richmond	Brown ...	12.00	12.50	32.00	92.00
☐ Atlanta	Brown ...	12.00	12.50	32.00	73.00
☐ Chicago	Brown ...	12.00	12.50	32.00	65.00
☐ St. Louis	Brown ...	12.00	12.50	32.00	65.00
☐ Minneapolis	Brown ...	12.00	12.50	32.00	84.00
☐ Kansas City	Brown ...	12.00	12.50	32.00	72.00
☐ Dallas	Brown ...	125.00	200.00	400.00	1650.00
☐ San Francisco	Brown ...	12.00	12.50	32.00	110.00

TWENTY DOLLAR NOTES

ORDER OF ISSUE

TWENTY DOLLAR NOTES (1861) DEMAND NOTES

(Large Size)

NOTE NO. 86

Face Design: Liberty with sword and shield.

Back Design: Intricate design of numerals "20," Demand Notes have no Treasury Seal.

SERIES	PAYABLE AT	A.B.P.	GOOD	V. GOOD
☐ 1861	Boston (I)	RARE	RARE	RARE
☐ 1861	New York (I)	1650.00	4000.00	6600.00
☐ 1861	Philadelphia (I)	1650.00	4000.00	6600.00
☐ 1861	Cincinnati (I)	RARE	RARE	RARE
☐ 1861	St. Louis (I)	(Unknown in any collection)		
☐ 1861	Boston (II)	RARE	RARE	RARE
☐ 1861	New York (II)	1650.00	4000.00	6600.00
☐ 1861	Philadelphia (II)	1650.00	4000.00	6600.00
☐ 1861	Cincinnati (II)	RARE	RARE	RARE
☐ 1861	St. Louis (II)	(Unknown in any collection)		

NOTE: Counterfeits and expertly repaired specimens exist. Use caution in buying.

TWENTY DOLLAR NOTES (1862–1863)
UNITED STATES NOTES
(ALSO KNOWN AS LEGAL TENDER NOTES)

(Large Size)

NOTE NO. 86A

Face Design: Liberty with sword and shield.

Back Design: Second obligation. This note was also issued with first obligation on the back. See Notes Nos. 33 and 33A.

SERIES	SIGNATURES	SEAL	A.B.P.	GOOD	V. FINE	UNC.
☐ 1862	Chittenden-Spinner*	Red	96.00	210.00	720.00	3050.00
☐ 1862	Chittenden-Spinner**	Red	96.00	210.00	720.00	3050.00
☐ 1863	Chittenden-Spinner**	Red	96.00	210.00	720.00	2900.00

*First Obligation: Similar to Note No. 33.
**Second Obligation: Shown above.

TWENTY DOLLAR NOTES (1869) UNITED STATES NOTES
(ALSO KNOWN AS LEGAL TENDER NOTES)

(Large Size)   **NOTE NOS. 87–87A**

Face
Design

87 SERIES SIGNATURES	SEAL	A.B.P.	GOOD	V. FINE	UNC.
☐ 1869 Allison-Spinner	Red	112.00	210.00	1050.00	2100.00

87A SERIES Back Design: Revised

☐ 1875 Allison-New	Red	46.00	96.00	510.00	1150.00
☐ 1878 Allison-Gilfillan	Red	44.00	83.00	510.00	1425.00
☐ 1880 Scofield-Gilfillan	Brown Lg	44.00	83.00	320.00	1210.00
☐ 1880 Bruce-Gilfillan	Brown Lg	46.00	97.00	510.00	1550.00
☐ 1880 Bruce-Wyman	Brown Lg	44.00	82.00	510.00	1610.00
☐ 1880 Bruce-Wyman	Red Lg ..	44.00	83.00	320.00	1225.00
☐ 1880 Rosecrans-Jordan	Red Lg ..	44.00	83.00	320.00	1225.00
☐ 1880 Rosecrans-Hyatt	Red Plain	44.00	83.00	320.00	1225.00
☐ 1880 Rosecrans-Hyatt	Red Spikes	44.00	83.00	710.00	1825.00
☐ 1880 Rosecrans-Huston	Red Lg ..	44.00	83.00	710.00	1825.00
☐ 1880 Rosecrans-Huston	Brown Lg	44.00	83.00	400.00	1210.00
☐ 1880 Rosecrans-Nebeker	Brown Lg	44.00	83.00	710.00	1850.00
☐ 1800 Rosecrans-Nebeker	Red Sm..	44.00	83.00	310.00	1225.00
☐ 1880 Tillman-Morgan	Red Sm..	33.00	66.00	310.00	950.00
☐ 1880 Bruce-Roberts	Red Sm..	33.00	66.00	310.00	950.00
☐ 1880 Lyons-Roberts	Red Sm..	33.00	66.00	310.00	950.00
☐ 1880 Vernon-Treat	Red Sm..	33.00	66.00	310.00	950.00
☐ 1880 Vernon-McClung	Red Sm..	33.00	66.00	310.00	950.00
☐ 1880 Teehee-Burke	Red Sm..	33.00	66.00	310.00	950.00
☐ 1880 Elliott-White	Red Sm..	33.00	66.00	310.00	950.00

TWENTY DOLLAR NOTES (1863–1875)
NATIONAL BANK NOTES
FIRST CHARTER PERIOD (Large Size)   **NOTE NO. 88**

Face Design: Battle of Lexington left, name of bank in center. Columbia with flag right.

Back Design: Green border, black center picture of baptism of Pocahontas.

SERIES	SIGNATURES	SEAL	A.B.P.	GOOD	V. FINE	UNC.
☐ Original	Chittenden-Spinner	Red	90.00	210.00	710.00	3250.00
☐ Original	Colby-Spinner	Red	90.00	210.00	710.00	3250.00
☐ Original	Jeffries-Spinner	Red	360.00	710.00	1600.00	5100.00
☐ Original	Allison-Spinner	Red	85.00	210.00	620.00	3250.00
☐ 1875	Allison-New	Red	85.00	210.00	710.00	3250.00
☐ 1875	Allison-Wyman	Red	85.00	210.00	710.00	3250.00
☐ 1875	Allison-Gilfillan	Red	85.00	210.00	710.00	3250.00
☐ 1875	Scofield-Gilfillan	Red	85.00	210.00	710.00	3250.00
☐ 1875	Bruce-Gilfillan	Red	85.00	210.00	710.00	3250.00
☐ 1875	Bruce-Wyman	Red	85.00	210.00	710.00	3250.00
☐ 1875	Rosecrans-Huston	Red	85.00	210.00	710.00	3250.00
☐ 1875	Rosecrans-Nebeker	Red	85.00	210.00	610.00	4100.00
☐ 1875	Tillman-Morgan	Red	85.00	210.00	610.00	4100.00

TWENTY DOLLAR NOTES (1882) NATIONAL BANK NOTES

SECOND CHARTER PERIOD (Large Size) **NOTE NO. 88A**

First Issue—Brown seal and brown backs.
Face Design: Similar to Note No. 88.
Back Design: Similar to Note No. 39, border is brown, green Charter number in center.

SERIES SIGNATURES	SEAL	A.B.P.	GOOD	V. FINE	UNC.
☐ 1882 Bruce-Gilfillan	Brown ...	29.00	55.00	140.00	510.00
☐ 1882 Bruce-Wyman	Brown ...	29.00	55.00	140.00	510.00
☐ 1882 Bruce-Jordan	Brown ...	29.00	55.00	140.00	510.00
☐ 1882 Rosecrans-Jordan	Brown ...	29.00	55.00	140.00	510.00
☐ 1882 Rosecrans-Hyatt	Brown ...	29.00	55.00	140.00	510.00
☐ 1882 Rosecrans-Huston	Brown ...	29.00	55.00	140.00	510.00
☐ 1882 Rosecrans-Nebeker	Brown ...	29.00	55.00	140.00	510.00
☐ 1882 Rosecrans-Morgan	Brown ...	130.00	280.00	780.00	1850.00
☐ 1882 Tillman-Morgan	Brown ...	29.00	55.00	140.00	510.00
☐ 1882 Tillman-Roberts	Brown ...	29.00	55.00	140.00	510.00
☐ 1882 Bruce-Roberts	Brown ...	29.00	55.00	140.00	510.00
☐ 1882 Lyons-Roberts	Brown ...	29.00	55.00	140.00	510.00
☐ 1882 Lyons-Treat	Brown ...	29.00	55.00	140.00	510.00
☐ 1882 Vernon-Treat	Brown ...	29.00	55.00	140.00	510.00

SECOND CHARTER PERIOD, Second Issue **NOTE NO. 88B**

Face Design: Similar to Note No. 88.
Back Design: Similar to Note No. 40.

SERIES SIGNATURES	SEAL	A.B.P.	GOOD	V. FINE	UNC.
☐ 1882 Rosecrans-Huston	Blue	26.00	60.00	145.00	810.00
☐ 1882 Rosecrans-Nebeker	Blue	26.00	60.00	145.00	810.00
☐ 1882 Rosecrans-Morgan	Blue	125.00	300.00	760.00	1650.00
☐ 1882 Tillman-Morgan	Blue	26.00	60.00	145.00	810.00
☐ 1882 Tillman-Roberts	Blue	26.00	60.00	145.00	810.00
☐ 1882 Bruce-Roberts	Blue	26.00	60.00	145.00	810.00
☐ 1882 Lyons-Roberts	Blue	26.00	60.00	145.00	810.00
☐ 1882 Vernon-Treat	Blue	26.00	60.00	145.00	810.00
☐ 1882 Napier-McClung	Blue	26.00	60.00	145.00	810.00

SECOND CHARTER PERIOD, Third Issue (Large Size) **NOTE NO. 88C**

Face Design: Similar to Note No. 88 with blue seal.
Back Design: Similar to Note No. 41, green back, value in block letters.

SERIES SIGNATURES	SEAL	A.B.P.	GOOD	V. FINE	UNC.
☐ 1882 Tillman-Morgan	Blue	55.00	98.00	370.00	1520.00
☐ 1882 Lyons-Roberts	Blue	55.00	98.00	370.00	1520.00
☐ 1882 Lyons-Treat	Blue	55.00	98.00	370.00	1520.00
☐ 1882 Vernon-Treat	Blue	55.00	98.00	370.00	1520.00
☐ 1882 Napier-McClung	Blue	55.00	98.00	370.00	1520.00
☐ 1882 Teehee-Burke	Blue	55.00	98.00	370.00	1625.00

TWENTY DOLLAR NOTES (1902) NATIONAL BANK NOTES
THIRD CHARTER PERIOD, First Issue (Large Size) **NOTE NO. 89**

Face Design: Portrait of McCulloch left, name of bank center, Treasury
Seal right.

SERIES	SIGNATURES	SEAL	A.B.P.	GOOD	V. FINE	UNC.
☐ 1902	Lyon-Roberts	Red	32.00	62.00	165.00	610.00
☐ 1902	Lyons-Treat	Red	32.00	62.00	165.00	610.00
☐ 1902	Vernon-Treat	Red	32.00	62.00	200.00	1550.00

**Second Issue—Date 1902–1908 added on back,
Treasury seal and serial numbers blue.**

☐ 1902	Lyons-Roberts	Blue	23.00	34.00	62.00	260.00
☐ 1902	Lyons-Treat	Blue	23.00	34.00	62.00	260.00
☐ 1902	Vernon-Treat	Blue	23.00	34.00	62.00	260.00
☐ 1902	Vernon-McClung	Blue	23.00	34.00	62.00	260.00
☐ 1902	Napier-McClung	Blue	23.00	34.00	62.00	260.00
☐ 1902	Napier-Thompson	Blue	23.00	34.00	110.00	410.00
☐ 1902	Napier-Burke	Blue	23.00	34.00	62.00	260.00
☐ 1902	Parker-Burke	Blue	23.00	34.00	62.00	260.00

**Third Issue—Date 1902–1908 removed from back,
seal and serial numbers are blue.**

☐ 1902	Lyons-Roberts	Blue	23.00	33.00	55.00	225.00
☐ 1902	Lyons-Treat	Blue	23.00	33.00	55.00	225.00
☐ 1902	Vernon-Treat	Blue	23.00	33.00	55.00	225.00
☐ 1902	Vernon-McClung	Blue	23.00	33.00	55.00	225.00
☐ 1902	Napier-McClung	Blue	23.00	33.00	55.00	225.00
☐ 1902	Napier-Thompson	Blue	23.00	42.00	110.00	410.00
☐ 1902	Napier-Burke	Blue	23.00	33.00	55.00	225.00
☐ 1902	Parker-Burke	Blue	23.00	33.00	55.00	225.00
☐ 1902	Teehee-Burke	Blue	23.00	33.00	55.00	225.00
☐ 1902	Elliott-Burke	Blue	23.00	33.00	55.00	225.00
☐ 1902	Elliott-White	Blue	23.00	33.00	55.00	225.00
☐ 1902	Speelman-White	Blue	23.00	33.00	55.00	225.00
☐ 1902	Woods-White	Blue	23.00	33.00	55.00	225.00
☐ 1902	Woods-Tate	Blue	23.00	45.00	115.00	420.00
☐ 1902	Jones-Woods	Blue	210.00	435.00	910.00	4300.00

TWENTY DOLLAR NOTES (1929) NATIONAL BANK NOTES
(Small Size)   **NOTE NO. 90**

Face Design: TYPE I—Portrait of President Jackson in center, name of bank to left, brown seal right. Charter number in black.

Face Design: TYPE II.

Back Design: The White House, similar to all $20.00 small notes.

SERIES SIGNATURES	SEAL	A.B.P.	GOOD	V. FINE	UNC.
☐ 1929—Type I Jones-Woods	Brown ...	22.00	27.00	42.00	94.00
☐ 1929—TYPE II Jones-Woods	Brown ...	22.00	27.00	42.00	87.00

TWENTY DOLLAR NOTES (1880) SILVER CERTIFICATES
(Large Size)   NOTE NO. 91

Face Design: Portrait of Stephen Decatur left. "TWENTY SILVER DOL-LARS," in center.

Back Design: "SILVER" in large block letters.

SERIES SIGNATURES	SEAL	A.B.P.	GOOD	V. FINE	UNC.
☐ 1880 Scofield-Gilfillan	Brown ...	105.00	210.00	880.00	5300.00
☐ 1880 Bruce-Gilfillan	Brown ...	105.00	210.00	880.00	5300.00
☐ 1880 Bruce-Wyman	Brown ...	105.00	210.00	880.00	5300.00
☐ 1880 Bruce-Wyman	Red Sm.	460.00	1100.00	2200.00	6300.00

This note was also issued in series of 1878. They are very rare.

TWENTY DOLLAR NOTES (1886) SILVER CERTIFICATES
(Large Size)   **NOTE NO. 92**

Face Design: Portrait of Daniel Manning center, Agriculture left, Industry right.

Back Design: Double diamond design center.

SERIES SIGNATURES	SEAL	A.B.P.	GOOD	V. FINE	UNC.
☐ 1886 Rosecrans-Hyatt	Red Lg	155.00	310.00	1200.00	6550.00
☐ 1886 Rosecrans-Huston	Brown Lg	155.00	310.00	1200.00	6550.00
☐ 1886 Rosecrans-Nebeker	Brown Lg	155.00	310.00	1200.00	6550.00
☐ 1886 Rosecrans-Nebeker	Red Sm	215.00	600.00	1375.00	6850.00

TWENTY DOLLAR NOTES (1891) SILVER CERTIFICATES
(NOT ISSUED IN SMALL SIZE NOTES)

(Large Size)

NOTE NO. 93

Face Design: Same as Note No. 92.

Back Design: Revised.

SERIES	SIGNATURES	SEAL	A.B.P.	GOOD	V. FINE	UNC.
☐ 1891	Rosecrans-Nebeker	Red	43.00	86.00	280.00	2450.00
☐ 1891	Tillman-Morgan	Red	43.00	86.00	410.00	2450.00
☐ 1891	Bruce-Roberts	Red	43.00	86.00	410.00	2450.00
☐ 1891	Lyons-Roberts	Red	43.00	86.00	410.00	2450.00
☐ 1891	Parker-Burke	Blue	42.00	83.00	410.00	2450.00
☐ 1891	Teehee-Burke	Blue	42.00	83.00	410.00	2450.00

TWENTY DOLLAR NOTES (1882) GOLD CERTIFICATES
(Large Size)   **NOTE NO. 94**

Face Design: Portrait of President Garfield right, "TWENTY DOLLARS IN GOLD COIN" center.

Back Design: Large "20" left, eagle and arrows center, bright orange color.

SERIES SIGNATURES	SEAL	A.B.P.	GOOD	V. FINE	UNC.
☐ 1882 Bruce-Gilfillan	Brown ...			VERY RARE	

The above Note has a countersigned signature.

☐ 1882 Bruce-Gilfillan	Brown ...	260.00	610.00	3050.00	6850.00
☐ 1882 Bruce-Wyman	Brown ...	160.00	410.00	1800.00	3850.00
☐ 1882 Rosecrans-Huston	Brown ...	160.00	410.00	2000.00	5100.00
☐ 1882 Lyons-Roberts	Red	40.00	90.00	410.00	2025.00

TWENTY DOLLAR NOTES (1905) GOLD CERTIFICATES
(Large Size)   NOTE NO. 95

Face Design: Portrait of President Washington center, "XX" left, Treasury Seal right.

Back Design: Eagle and Shield center, printed in bright orange color.

SERIES	SIGNATURES	SEAL	A.B.P.	GOOD	V. FINE	UNC.
☐ 1905	Lyons-Roberts	Red	105.00	310.00	1050.00	8250.00
☐ 1905	Lyons-Treat	Red	105.00	310.00	1200.00	7100.00
☐ 1906	Vernon-Treat	Gold	31.00	86.00	170.00	610.00
☐ 1906	Vernon-McClung	Gold	31.00	86.00	205.00	810.00
☐ 1906	Napier-McClung	Gold	31.00	86.00	205.00	810.00
☐ 1906	Napier-Thompson	Gold	31.00	86.00	205.00	1050.00
☐ 1906	Parker-Burke	Gold	31.00	86.00	205.00	810.00
☐ 1906	Tehee-Burke	Gold	31.00	86.00	205.00	810.00
☐ 1922	Speelman-White	Gold	31.00	86.00	205.00	525.00

TWENTY DOLLAR NOTES (1928) GOLD CERTIFICATES
(Small Size)   **NOTE NO. 96**

Face Design: Portrait of President Jackson center, gold seal left, gold serial numbers.

Back Design: The White House, printed green, similar to all small size $20s.

SERIES SIGNATURES	SEAL	A.B.P.	V. FINE	UNC.
☐ 1928 Woods-Mellon	Gold	22.00	78.00	205.00

TWENTY DOLLAR NOTES (1890) TREASURY NOTES

(Large Size)   **NOTE NO. 97**

Face Design: Portrait of John Marshall, Supreme Court Chief Justice left, "20" center.

Back Design

SERIES SIGNATURES	SEAL	A.B.P.	GOOD	V. FINE	UNC.
☐ 1890 Rosecrans-Huston	Brown	150.00	310.00	1950.00	8000.00
☐ 1890 Rosecrans-Nebeker	Brown	150.00	310.00	1950.00	8000.00
☐ 1890 Rosecrans-Nebeker	Red	150.00	310.00	1950.00	8000.00

(Large Size)   **NOTE NO. 97A**

Back Design

Face Design: Same as previous note.

SERIES SIGNATURES	SEAL	A.B.P.	GOOD	V. FINE	UNC.
☐ 1891 Tillman-Morgan	Red	450.00	950.00	2700.00	10,000.00
☐ 1891 Bruce-Roberts	Red	450.00	950.00	2700.00	10,000.00

TWENTY DOLLAR NOTES (1914)
FEDERAL RESERVE NOTES

(Large Size)   **NOTE NO. 98**

Face Design: Portrait of President Cleveland center, Federal Reserve Seal left, Treasury Seal right.

Back Design: Scenes of transportation. Locomotive left, steamship right.
SERIES OF 1914—SIGNATURES OF BURKE-McADOO, RED TREASURY SEAL

BANK	A.B.P.	V. FINE	UNC.	BANK	A.B.P.	V. FINE	UNC.
☐ Boston	37.00	210.00	600.00	☐ Chicago	37.00	210.00	600.00
☐ New York	37.00	210.00	600.00	☐ St. Louis	37.00	210.00	600.00
☐ Philadelphia	37.00	210.00	600.00	☐ Minneapolis	37.00	210.00	600.00
☐ Cleveland	37.00	210.00	600.00	☐ Kansas City	37.00	210.00	600.00
☐ Richmond	37.00	210.00	600.00	☐ Dallas	37.00	210.00	600.00
☐ Atlanta	37.00	210.00	600.00	☐ San Francisco	37.00	210.00	600.00

SERIES OF 1914—WITH BLUE TREASURY SEAL AND BLUE SERIAL NUMBERS

This note was issued with signatures of BURKE-McADOO, BURKE-GLASS, BURKE-HUSTON and WHITE-MELLON.

	A.B.P.	V. FINE	UNC.
Issued to all Federal Reserve Banks	30.00	65.00	195.00

TWENTY DOLLAR NOTES (1928)
FEDERAL RESERVE NOTES

(Small Size)

Face Design: Portrait of President Jackson center, black Federal Reserve Seal with numeral for district in center. City of issuing bank in seal circle. Green Treasury Seal right.

Back Design: Picture of the White House, similar to all small size $20.00 notes.

SERIES OF 1928—SIGNATURES OF TATE-MELLON, GREEN SEAL

BANK	A.B.P.	V. FINE	UNC.	BANK	A.B.P.	V. FINE	UNC.
☐ Boston	23.00	30.00	62.00	☐ Chicago	23.00	30.00	62.00
☐ New York	23.00	30.00	62.00	☐ St. Louis	23.00	30.00	62.00
☐ Philadelphia	23.00	30.00	62.00	☐ Minneapolis	23.00	30.00	62.00
☐ Cleveland	23.00	30.00	62.00	☐ Kansas City	23.00	30.00	62.00
☐ Richmond	23.00	30.00	62.00	☐ Dallas	23.00	30.00	62.00
☐ Atlanta	23.00	30.00	62.00	☐ San Francisco	23.00	30.00	62.00

SERIES OF 1928A—SIGNATURES OF WOODS-MELLON, GREEN SEAL

CITY	A.B.P.	V. FINE	UNC.	CITY	A.B.P.	V. FINE	UNC.
☐ Boston	23.00	30.00	62.00	☐ Chicago	23.00	30.00	62.00
☐ New York	23.00	30.00	62.00	☐ St. Louis	23.00	30.00	62.00
☐ Philadelphia	23.00	30.00	62.00	☐ Minneapolis	NOT ISSUED		
☐ Cleveland	23.00	30.00	62.00	☐ Kansas City	23.00	30.00	62.00
☐ Richmond	23.00	30.00	62.00	☐ Dallas	23.00	30.00	62.00
☐ Atlanta	23.00	30.00	62.00	☐ San Francisco	NOT ISSUED		

TWENTY DOLLAR NOTES (1928)
FEDERAL RESERVE NOTES

(Small Size)   **NOTE NO. 100**

SERIES OF 1928B—SIGNATURES OF WOODS-MELLON, GREEN SEAL
Face and Back Design similar to Previous Note. Numeral in Federal Reserve Seal is now changed to a Letter.

BANK	A.B.P.	V. FINE	UNC.	BANK	A.B.P.	V. FINE	UNC.
☐ Boston	23.00	29.00	42.00	☐ Chicago	23.00	29.00	42.00
☐ New York	23.00	29.00	42.00	☐ St. Louis	23.00	29.00	42.00
☐ Philadelphia	23.00	29.00	42.00	☐ Minneapolis	23.00	29.00	42.00
☐ Cleveland	23.00	29.00	42.00	☐ Kansas City	23.00	29.00	42.00
☐ Richmond	23.00	29.00	42.00	☐ Dallas	23.00	29.00	42.00
☐ Atlanta	23.00	29.00	42.00	☐ San Francisco	23.00	29.00	42.00

SERIES OF 1928C—SIGNATURES OF WOODS-MILLS, GREEN SEAL
Only two banks issued this note.

BANK	A.B.P.	V. FINE	UNC.	BANK	A.B.P.	V. FINE	UNC.
☐ Chicago	82.00	210.00	325.00	☐ San Francisco	82.00	210.00	325.00

TWENTY DOLLAR NOTES (1934)
FEDERAL RESERVE NOTES

                                         NOTE NO. 100A

SIGNATURES OF JULIAN-MORGENTHAU, GREEN SEAL
Face and Back Design similar to Previous Note. "Redeemable in Gold" removed from obligation over Federal Reserve Seal.

BANK	GOOD	V. FINE	UNC.	BANK	GOOD	V. FINE	UNC.
☐ Boston	23.00	32.00	55.00	☐ St. Louis	23.00	32.00	55.00
☐ New York	23.00	32.00	55.00	☐ Minneapolis	23.00	32.00	55.00
☐ Philadelphia	23.00	32.00	55.00	☐ Kansas City	23.00	32.00	55.00
☐ Cleveland	23.00	32.00	55.00	☐ Dallas	23.00	32.00	55.00
☐ Richmond	23.00	32.00	55.00	☐ San Francisco	23.00	32.00	55.00
☐ Atlanta	23.00	32.00	55.00	☐ *San Francisco			
☐ Chicago	23.00	32.00	55.00	(HAWAII)	55.00	130.00	910.00

*The San Francisco Federal Reserve Note with brown seal and brown serial numbers, and overprinted "HAWAII" on face and back, was a special issue for the Armed Forces in the Pacific area during World War II.

TWENTY DOLLAR NOTES (1934A)
FEDERAL RESERVE NOTES

(Small Size) **NOTE NO. 101**

SERIES OF 1934A—SIGNATURES OF JULIAN-MORGENTHAU

BANK	A.B.P.	V. FINE	UNC.	BANK	A.B.P.	V. FINE	UNC.
☐ Boston	23.00	29.00	52.00	☐ St. Louis	23.00	29.00	52.00
☐ New York	23.00	29.00	52.00	☐ Minneapolis	23.00	29.00	52.00
☐ Philadelphia	23.00	29.00	52.00	☐ Kansas City	23.00	29.00	52.00
☐ Cleveland	23.00	29.00	52.00	☐ Dallas	23.00	29.00	52.00
☐ Richmond	23.00	29.00	52.00	☐ San Francisco	23.00	29.00	52.00
☐ Atlanta	23.00	29.00	52.00	☐ *San Francisco			
☐ Chicago	23.00	29.00	52.00	(HAWAII)	26.00	45.00	325.00

SERIES OF 1934B—SIGNATURES OF JULIAN-VINSON, GREEN SEAL

BANK	A.B.P.	V. FINE	UNC.	BANK	A.B.P.	V. FINE	UNC.
☐ Boston	23.00	26.00	46.00	☐ Chicago	23.00	26.00	46.00
☐ New York	23.00	26.00	46.00	☐ St. Louis	23.00	26.00	46.00
☐ Philadelphia	23.00	26.00	46.00	☐ Minneapolis	23.00	26.00	46.00
☐ Cleveland	23.00	26.00	46.00	☐ Kansas City	23.00	26.00	46.00
☐ Richmond	23.00	26.00	46.00	☐ Dallas	23.00	26.00	46.00
☐ Atlanta	23.00	26.00	46.00	☐ San Francisco	23.00	26.00	46.00

SERIES OF 1934C—SIGNATURES OF JULIAN-SNYDER, GREEN SEAL

Back Design: This has been modified with this series, balcony added to the White House.

BANK	A.B.P.	V. FINE	UNC.	BANK	A.B.P.	V. FINE	UNC.
☐ Boston	22.00	26.00	46.00	☐ Chicago	22.00	26.00	46.00
☐ New York	22.00	26.00	46.00	☐ St. Louis	22.00	26.00	46.00
☐ Philadelphia	22.00	26.00	46.00	☐ Minneapolis	22.00	26.00	46.00
☐ Cleveland	22.00	26.00	46.00	☐ Kansas City	22.00	26.00	46.00
☐ Richmond	22.00	26.00	46.00	☐ Dallas	22.00	26.00	46.00
☐ Atlanta	22.00	26.00	46.00	☐ San Francisco	22.00	26.00	46.00

SERIES OF 1934D—SIGNATURES OF CLARK-SNYDER, GREEN SEAL

BANK	A.B.P.	V. FINE	UNC.	BANK	A.B.P.	V. FINE	UNC.
☐ Boston	22.00	27.00	42.00	☐ Chicago	22.00	27.00	42.00
☐ New York	22.00	27.00	42.00	☐ St. Louis	22.00	27.00	42.00
☐ Philadelphia	22.00	27.00	42.00	☐ Minneapolis	22.00	27.00	42.00
☐ Cleveland	22.00	27.00	42.00	☐ Kansas City	22.00	27.00	42.00

BANK	A.B.P.	V. FINE	UNC.	BANK	A.B.P.	V. FINE	UNC.
☐ Richmond	22.00	27.00	42.00	☐ Dallas	22.00	27.00	42.00
☐ Atlanta	22.00	27.00	42.00	☐ San Francisco	22.00	27.00	42.00

TWENTY DOLLAR NOTES (1950)
FEDERAL RESERVE NOTES

(Small Size)   **NOTE NO. 102**
SERIES OF 1950—SIGNATURES OF CLARK-SNYDER, GREEN SEAL
Black Federal Reserve Seal and Green Treasury Seal are slightly smaller.

BANK	A.B.P.	UNC.	BANK	A.B.P.	UNC.
☐ Boston	22.00	45.00	☐ Chicago	22.00	45.00
☐ New York	22.00	45.00	☐ St. Louis	22.00	45.00
☐ Philadelphia	22.00	45.00	☐ Minneapolis	22.00	45.00
☐ Cleveland	22.00	45.00	☐ Kansas City	22.00	45.00
☐ Richmond	22.00	45.00	☐ Dallas	22.00	45.00
☐ Atlanta	22.00	45.00	☐ San Francisco	22.00	45.00

SERIES OF 1950A—SIGNATURES OF PRIEST-HUMPHREY, GREEN SEAL
Issued for all Federal Reserve Banks 38.00
SERIES OF 1950B—SIGNATURES OF PRIEST-ANDERSON, GREEN SEAL
Issued for all Federal Reserve Banks 38.00
SERIES OF 1950C—SIGNATURES OF SMITH-DILLON, GREEN SEAL
Issued for all Federal Reserve Banks 36.00
SERIES OF 1950D—SIGNATURES OF GRANAHAN-DILLON, GREEN SEAL
Issued for all Federal Reserve Banks 38.00
SERIES OF 1950E—SIGNATURES OF GRANAHAN-FOWLER, GREEN SEAL
Issued only for New York, Chicago and San Francisco 38.00

TWENTY DOLLAR NOTES (1963)
FEDERAL RESERVE NOTES

(Small Size)   **NOTE NO. 102A**
SERIES OF 1963—SIGNATURES OF GRANAHAN-DILLON, GREEN SEAL
Issued for all banks except Minneapolis 36.50
SERIES OF 1963A—SIGNATURES OF GRANAHAN-FOWLER, GREEN SEAL
Issued for all Federal Reserve Banks 35.00
SERIES OF 1969—SIGNATURES OF ELSTON-KENNEDY, GREEN SEAL
Issued for all Federal Reserve Banks 35.00
SERIES OF 1969A—SIGNATURES OF KABIS-CONNALLY, GREEN SEAL
Issued for all Federal Reserve Banks 35.00
SERIES OF 1969B—SIGNATURES OF BANUELOS-CONNALLY
Issued for all Federal Reserve Banks 35.00
SERIES OF 1969C—SIGNATURES OF BANUELOS-SHULTZ, GREEN SEAL
Issued for all Federal Reserve Banks 35.00
SERIES OF 1974—SIGNATURES OF NEFF-SIMON, GREEN SEAL
Issued for all Federal Reserve Banks 35.00

SERIES OF 1977—SIGNATURES OF MORTON-BLUMENTHAL, GREEN SEAL

Issued for all Federal Reserve Banks 29.00

SERIES OF 1977A—SIGNATURES OF MORTON-MILLER, GREEN SEAL

Issued for all Federal Reserve Banks 28.00

SERIES OF 1981—SIGNATURES OF BUCHANAN-REGAN, GREEN SEAL

Issued for all Federal Reserve Banks 28.00

SERIES OF 1981A—SIGNATURES OF ORTEGA-REGAN, GREEN SEAL

Issued for all Federal Reserve Banks 26.00

SERIES OF 1985—SIGNATURES OF ORTEGA-BAKER, GREEN SEAL

Issued for all Federal Reserve Banks 24.00

TWENTY DOLLAR NOTES (1915–1918)
FEDERAL RESERVE BANK NOTES
(ALL HAVE BLUE SEALS)

(Large Size)　　　　　　　　　　　　　　　　　　NOTE NO. 103

Face Design: Portrait of President Cleveland left, name of bank and city center, blue Seal right.

Back Design: Locomotive and steamship, same as Page 140, similar to Note No. 98.

BANK & CITY	SERIES	GOV'T SIGNATURES	BANK SIGNATURES	A.B.P.	GOOD	V. FINE	UNC.
☐ Atlanta	1915	Teehee-Burke	Bell-Wellborn	57.00	105.00	375.00	2550.00
☐ Atlanta	1918	Elliott-Burke	Bell-Wellborn	57.00	108.00	380.00	1850.00
☐ Chicago	1915	Teehee-Burke	McLallen-McDougal	57.00	110.00	510.00	2050.00
☐ St. Louis	1918	Teehee-Burke	Attebery-Wells	57.00	110.00	485.00	3600.00
☐ Kan. City	1915	Teehee-Burke	Anderson-Miller	57.00	105.00	510.00	2100.00
☐ Kan. City	1915	Teehee-Burke	Cross-Miller ...	57.00	105.00	510.00	2100.00
☐ Dallas	1915	Teehee-Burke	Hoopes-VanZandt.....	57.00	108.00	510.00	4050.00
☐ Dallas	1915	Teehee-Burke	Gilbert-VanZandt.....	57.00	112.00	510.00	2100.00
☐ Dallas	1915	Teehee-Burke	Talley-VanZandt.....	57.00	112.00	510.00	2100.00

TWENTY DOLLAR NOTES (1929)
FEDERAL RESERVE BANK NOTES

(Small Size)

NOTE NO. 103A

Face Design: Portrait of President Jackson center, name of Bank and city left, blue Seal right.

Back Design: The White House.

BANK	A.B.P.	V. FINE	UNC.	BANK	A.B.P.	V. FINE	UNC.
☐ Boston	22.00	27.00	84.00	☐ Chicago	22.00	27.00	84.00
☐ New York	22.00	27.00	84.00	☐ St. Louis	22.00	27.00	84.00
☐ Philadelphia	22.00	27.00	84.00	☐ Minneapolis	22.00	27.00	84.00
☐ Cleveland	22.00	27.00	84.00	☐ Kansas City	22.00	27.00	84.00
☐ Richmond	22.00	27.00	84.00	☐ Dallas	24.00	33.00	410.00
☐ Atlanta	22.00	27.00	84.00	☐ San Francisco	24.00	42.00	180.00

FIFTY DOLLAR NOTES

ORDER OF ISSUE

FIFTY DOLLAR NOTES (1862–1863)
UNITED STATES NOTES
(ALSO KNOWN AS LEGAL TENDER NOTES)

(Large Size)   **NOTE NO. 104**

Face Design: Portrait of Hamilton to left.

Back Design

SERIES SIGNATURES	SEAL	A.B.P.	GOOD	V. FINE	UNC.
☐ 1862 Chittenden-Spinner*	Red	1200.00	1800.00	6000.00	18,000.00
☐ 1862 Chittenden-Spinner**	Red	1200.00	1800.00	6000.00	18,000.00
☐ 1863 Chittenden-Spinner**	Red	1200.00	1800.00	6000.00	18,000.00

*First Obligation: Similar to Note No. 33.
**Second Obligation: Shown above.

FIFTY DOLLAR NOTES (1869) UNITED STATES NOTES
(ALSO KNOWN AS LEGAL TENDER NOTES)

(Large Size)

NOTE NO. 105

Face Design: Portrait of Henry Clay to right.

Back Design

SERIES SIGNATURES	SEAL	A.B.P.	GOOD	V. FINE	UNC.
☐ 1869 Allison-Spinner	Red	2000.00	3000.00	6500.00	19,500.00

Note: Only 24 pieces of this note remain unredeemed.

FIFTY DOLLAR NOTES (1874–1880)
UNITED STATES NOTES

(Large Size)

NOTE NO. 106

Face Design: Franklin to left.

Back Design

SERIES	SIGNATURES	SEAL		A.B.P.	GOOD	V. FINE	UNC.
☐ 1874	Allison-Spinner	Sm.	Red	280.00	600.00	1900.00	4700.00
☐ 1875	Allison-Wyman	Sm.	Red	280.00	600.00	1900.00	4700.00
☐ 1878	Allison-Gilfillan	Sm.	Red	280.00	600.00	1900.00	4700.00
☐ 1880	Bruce-Gilfillan	Lg.	Brown	125.00	225.00	850.00	3200.00
☐ 1880	Bruce-Wyman	Lg.	Brown	125.00	225.00	850.00	3200.00
☐ 1880	Rosecrans-Jordan	Lg.	Red ..	125.00	225.00	800.00	2800.00
☐ 1880	Rosecrans-Hyatt	Lg.	Red ..	125.00	225.00	800.00	2800.00
☐ 1880	Rosecrans-Hyatt	Lg.	Red ..	125.00	225.00	800.00	2800.00
☐ 1880	Rosecrans-Huston	Lg.	Red ..	125.00	225.00	800.00	2800.00
☐ 1880	Rosecrans-Huston	Lg.	Red	125.00	225.00	800.00	2800.00
☐ 1880	Tillman-Morgan	Sm.	Red	125.00	225.00	800.00	2800.00
☐ 1880	Bruce-Roberts	Sm.	Red	125.00	225.00	800.00	2800.00
☐ 1880	Lyons-Roberts	Sm.	Red	125.00	225.00	800.00	2800.00

FIFTY DOLLAR NOTES (1875) NATIONAL BANK NOTES
FIRST CHARTER PERIOD (Large Size)
NOTE NO. 107

Face Design: Washington crossing Delaware left, Washington at Valley Forge, right.

Back Design: Embarkation of the Pilgrims.

SERIES SIGNATURES	SEAL	A.B.P.	V. FINE	UNC.
☐ Original Chittenden-Spinner	Red/rays	1900.00	3375.00	9600.00
☐ Original Colby-Spinner	Red/rays	1900.00	3375.00	9600.00
☐ Original Allison-Spinner	Red/rays	1900.00	3375.00	9600.00
☐ 1875 Allison-New	Red/Scals	1675.00	3100.00	8650.00
☐ 1875 Allison-Wyman	Red/Scals	1675.00	3100.00	8650.00
☐ 1875 Allison-Gilfillan	Red/Scals	1675.00	3100.00	8650.00
☐ 1875 Scofield-Gilfillan	Red/Scals	1675.00	3100.00	8650.00
☐ 1875 Bruce-Gilfillan	Red/Scals	1675.00	3100.00	8650.00
☐ 1875 Bruce-Wyman	Red/Scals	1675.00	3100.00	8650.00
☐ 1875 Rosecrans-Huston	Red/Scals	1675.00	3100.00	8650.00
☐ 1875 Rosecrans-Nebeker	Red/Scals	1675.00	3100.00	8650.00
☐ 1875 Tillman-Morgan	Red/Scals	1675.00	3100.00	8650.00

FIFTY DOLLAR NOTES (1882) NATIONAL BANK NOTES
SECOND CHARTER PERIOD (Large Size) **NOTE NO. 108**

First Issue—Brown seal and brown back.
Back Design of Note No. 108.
Face Design: Similar to Note No. 107.

SERIES SIGNATURES	SEAL	A.B.P.	GOOD	V. FINE	UNC.
☐ 1882 Bruce-Gilfillan	Brown ...	110.00	230.00	550.00	2300.00
☐ 1882 Bruce-Wyman	Brown ...	110.00	230.00	550.00	2300.00
☐ 1882 Bruce-Jordan	Brown ...	110.00	230.00	550.00	2300.00
☐ 1882 Rosecrans-Jordan	Brown ...	110.00	230.00	550.00	2300.00
☐ 1882 Rosecrans-Hyatt	Brown ...	110.00	230.00	550.00	2300.00
☐ 1882 Rosecrans-Huston	Brown ...	110.00	230.00	550.00	2300.00
☐ 1882 Rosecrans-Nebeker	Brown ...	110.00	230.00	550.00	2300.00
☐ 1882 Rosecrans-Morgan	Brown ...	285.00	535.00	1550.00	2850.00
☐ 1882 Tillman-Morgan	Brown ...	110.00	230.00	550.00	2300.00
☐ 1882 Tillman-Roberts	Brown ...	110.00	230.00	550.00	2300.00
☐ 1882 Bruce-Roberts	Brown ...	110.00	230.00	550.00	2300.00
☐ 1882 Lyons-Roberts	Brown ...	110.00	230.00	550.00	2300.00
☐ 1882 Vernon-Treat	Brown ...	285.00	535.00	1550.00	2850.00

FIFTY DOLLAR NOTES (1882) NATIONAL BANK NOTES
SECOND CHARTER PERIOD (Large Size)
NOTE NO. 108A

Second Issue—Blue seal, green back with date 1902–1908.
Face Design: Washington crossing Delaware left, Washington at Valley Forge, right.

Back Design

SERIES SIGNATURES	SEAL	A.B.P.	GOOD	V. FINE	UNC.
☐ 1882 Rosecrans-Huston	Blue	135.00	280.00	1100.00	3100.00
☐ 1882 Rosecrans-Nebeker	Blue	135.00	280.00	1100.00	3100.00
☐ 1882 Tillman-Morgan	Blue	135.00	280.00	1100.00	3100.00
☐ 1882 Tillman-Roberts	Blue	135.00	280.00	1100.00	3100.00
☐ 1882 Bruce-Roberts	Blue	135.00	280.00	1100.00	3100.00
☐ 1882 Lyons-Roberts	Blue	135.00	280.00	1100.00	3100.00
☐ 1882 Vernon-Treat	Blue	135.00	280.00	1100.00	3100.00
☐ 1882 Napier-McClung	Blue	135.00	280.00	1100.00	3100.00

FIFTY DOLLAR NOTES (1902) NATIONAL BANK NOTES
THIRD CHARTER PERIOD (Large Size)   **NOTE NO. 109**

First Issues—Red seal and numbers.
Face Design: Portrait of Sherman left. Name of bank center. Treasury
Seal and numbers.

SERIES SIGNATURES	SEAL	A.B.P.	GOOD	V. FINE	UNC.
☐ 1902 Lyons-Roberts	Red	230.00	380.00	1850.00	5100.00
☐ 1902 Lyons-Treat	Red	230.00	380.00	1850.00	5100.00
☐ 1902 Vernon-Treat	Red	230.00	380.00	1850.00	5100.00

Second Issue—Treasury Seal
Numbers remain blue, date 1902–1908 added on back.

☐ 1902 Lyons-Roberts	Blue	60.00	70.00	165.00	710.00
☐ 1902 Lyons-Treat	Blue	60.00	70.00	165.00	710.00
☐ 1902 Vernon-Treat	Blue	60.00	70.00	165.00	710.00
☐ 1902 Vernon-McClung	Blue	60.00	70.00	165.00	710.00
☐ 1902 Napier-McClung	Blue	60.00	70.00	165.00	710.00
☐ 1902 Napier-Thompson	Blue	65.00	90.00	165.00	710.00
☐ 1902 Napier-Burke	Blue	60.00	70.00	165.00	710.00
☐ 1902 Parker-Burke	Blue	60.00	70.00	165.00	710.00
☐ 1902 Teehee-Burke	Blue	60.00	70.00	165.00	710.00

Third Issue—Treasury Seal
Numbers remain blue, date of 1902–1908 removed from back.

☐ 1902 Lyons-Roberts	Blue	60.00	70.00	135.00	520.00
☐ 1902 Lyons-Treat	Blue	60.00	70.00	135.00	520.00
☐ 1902 Vernon-Treat	Blue	60.00	70.00	135.00	520.00
☐ 1902 Vernon-McClung	Blue	60.00	70.00	135.00	520.00
☐ 1902 Napier-McClung	Blue	60.00	70.00	135.00	520.00
☐ 1902 Napier-Thompson	Blue	60.00	70.00	135.00	520.00
☐ 1902 Napier-Burke	Blue	60.00	70.00	135.00	520.00
☐ 1902 Teehee-Burke	Blue	60.00	70.00	135.00	520.00
☐ 1902 Parker-Burke	Blue	60.00	70.00	135.00	520.00
☐ 1902 Elliott-Burke	Blue	60.00	70.00	135.00	520.00
☐ 1902 Elliott-White	Blue	60.00	70.00	135.00	520.00
☐ 1902 Speelman-White	Blue	60.00	70.00	135.00	520.00
☐ 1902 Woods-White	Blue	60.00	70.00	135.00	520.00

FIFTY DOLLAR NOTES (1929) NATIONAL BANK NOTES
(Small Size)   **NOTE NO. 110**

Face Design: Portrait of President Grant center. Bank left, brown seal right. Brown serial numbers, black charter numbers.

Back Design: The Capitol.

SERIES	SIGNATURES	SEAL	A.B.P.	V. FINE	UNC.
☐ 1929 TYPE I*	Jones-Wood	Brown	60.00	90.00	170.00
☐ 1929 TYPE II*	Jones-Wood	Brown	65.00	110.00	620.00

*See Page 72. TYPE I—Charter number in black. TYPE II—Similar. Charter number added in brown.

FIFTY DOLLAR NOTES (1878–1880) SILVER CERTIFICATES
(Large Size)
NOTE NO. 111

Face Design: Portrait of Edward Everett.

Back Design

SERIES SIGNATURES	SEAL	A.B.P.	GOOD	V. FINE
☐ 1878 Varied	Red	VERY RARE		
☐ 1880 Scofield-Gilfillan	Brown	1050.00	1900.00	5600.00
☐ 1880 Bruce-Gilfillan	Brown	1050.00	1900.00	5600.00
☐ 1880 Bruce-Wyman	Brown	1050.00	1900.00	5600.00
☐ 1880 Rosecrans-Huston	Brown	1050.00	1900.00	5600.00
☐ 1880 Rosecrans-Nebeker	Red	1050.00	1900.00	5600.00

FIFTY DOLLAR NOTES (1891) SILVER CERTIFICATES

(Large Size)   **NOTE NO. 111A**

Face Design: Portrait of Edward Everett.

Back Design

SERIES SIGNATURES	SEAL	A.B.P.	GOOD	V. FINE	UNC.
☐ 1891 Rosecrans-Nebeker	Red	210.00	380.00	1100.00	6200.00
☐ 1891 Tillman-Morgan	Red	210.00	380.00	1100.00	6200.00
☐ 1891 Bruce-Roberts	Red	210.00	380.00	1100.00	6200.00
☐ 1891 Lyons-Roberts	Red	210.00	380.00	1100.00	6200.00
☐ 1891 Vernon-Treat	Red	210.00	380.00	1100.00	6200.00
☐ 1891 Parker-Burke	Blue	210.00	380.00	1100.00	6200.00

FIFTY DOLLAR NOTES (1882) GOLD CERTIFICATES
(Large Size)   **NOTE NO. 112**

Face Design: Portrait of Silas Wright to left.

Back Design: Bright yellow color.

SERIES SIGNATURES	SEAL	A.B.P.	GOOD	V. FINE	UNC.
☐ 1882 Bruce-Gilfillan	Brown ...	210.00	775.00	3300.00	13,000.00
☐ 1882 Bruce-Wyman	Brown ...	210.00	775.00	3300.00	13,000.00
☐ 1882 Rosecrans-Hyatt	Red	210.00	380.00	1100.00	4600.00
☐ 1882 Rosecrans-Huston	Brown ...	210.00	775.00	2800.00	13,000.00
☐ 1882 Lyons-Roberts	Red	210.00	380.00	1100.00	4600.00
☐ 1882 Lyons-Treat	Red	210.00	380.00	1100.00	4600.00
☐ 1882 Vernon-Treat	Red	210.00	380.00	1100.00	4600.00
☐ 1882 Vernon-McClung	Red	210.00	380.00	1100.00	4600.00
☐ 1882 Napier-McClung	Red	210.00	380.00	1100.00	4600.00

FIFTY DOLLAR NOTES (1913) GOLD CERTIFICATES
(Large Size)   **NOTE NO. 113**

Face Design: Portrait of President Grant.

Back Design: Bright yellow color.

SERIES SIGNATURES	SEAL	A.B.P.	GOOD	V. FINE	UNC.
☐ 1913 Parker-Burke	Gold	105.00	210.00	430.00	3600.00
☐ 1913 Teehee-Burke	Gold	105.00	210.00	510.00	4100.00
☐ 1922 Speelman-White	Gold	65.00	150.00	320.00	1325.00

FIFTY DOLLAR NOTES (1928) GOLD CERTIFICATES

(Small Size) **NOTE NO. 114**

Back Design: Same as Note No. 110.

SERIES SIGNATURES	SEAL	A.B.P.	GOOD	V. FINE	UNC.
☐ 1928 Woods-Mellon	Gold	60.00	69.00	130.00	825.00

FIFTY DOLLAR NOTES (1891) TREASURY NOTES

(Large Size) **NOTE NO. 114A**

Face Design: Portrait of William H. Seward. Only 25 pieces remain unredeemed.
Back Design: Green.

SERIES SIGNATURES	SEAL	A.B.P.	GOOD	V. FINE	UNC.
☐ 1891 Rosecrans-Nebeker	Red	2600.00	4100.00	9600.00	RARE

FIFTY DOLLAR NOTES (1914) FEDERAL RESERVE NOTES

(Large Size)   NOTE NO. 115

SERIES OF 1914—SIGNATURES OF BURKE-McADOO, RED SEAL AND RED SERIAL NUMBERS*

CITY	A.B.P.	GOOD	V. FINE	UNC.	CITY	A.B.P.	GOOD	V. FINE	UNC.
☐ Boston	65.00	105.00	230.00	1100.00	☐ Chicago ...	65.00	105.00	230.00	1100.00
☐ New York ..	65.00	105.00	230.00	1100.00	☐ St. Louis ...	65.00	105.00	230.00	1100.00
☐ Philadelphia	65.00	105.00	230.00	1100.00	☐ Minneapolis	65.00	105.00	230.00	1100.00
☐ Cleveland...	65.00	105.00	230.00	1100.00	☐ Kansas City	65.00	105.00	230.00	1100.00
☐ Richmond ..	65.00	105.00	230.00	1100.00	☐ Dallas	65.00	105.00	230.00	1100.00
☐ Atlanta	65.00	105.00	230.00	1100.00	☐ San Fran...	65.00	105.00	230.00	1100.00

SERIES OF 1914—DESIGN CONTINUES AS PREVIOUS NOTE. THE SEAL AND SERIAL NUMBERS ARE NOW BLUE.

(This note was issued with various signatures for each bank.)

BANK	A.B.P.	GOOD	V. FINE	UNC.	BANK	A.B.P.	GOOD	V. FINE	UNC.
☐ Boston.......	45.00	80.00	135.00	610.00	☐ Chicago	45.00	80.00	135.00	610.00
☐ New York ...	45.00	80.00	135.00	610.00	☐ St. Louis	45.00	80.00	135.00	610.00
☐ Philadelphia ..	45.00	80.00	135.00	610.00	☐ Minneapolis ..	45.00	80.00	135.00	610.00
☐ Cleveland	45.00	80.00	135.00	610.00	☐ Kansas City ..	45.00	80.00	135.00	610.00
☐ Richmond	45.00	80.00	135.00	610.00	☐ Dallas	45.00	80.00	135.00	610.00
☐ Atlanta.......	45.00	80.00	135.00	610.00	☐ San Fran.	45.00	80.00	135.00	610.00

*Signatures: Burke-McAdoo, Burke-Glass, Burke-Huston, White-Mellon.

FIFTY DOLLAR NOTES (1928)
FEDERAL RESERVE NOTES

(Small Size)   **NOTE NO. 116**

Face Design: Portrait of President Grant center. Black Federal Reserve
Seal with number to left. Green Treasury Seal to right.
Back Design: Same as Note No. 110.
SERIES OF 1928—SIGNATURES OF WOODS-MELLON, GREEN SEAL

	A.B.P.	UNC.
Issued for all Federal Reserve Banks	70.00	160.00

(Small Size)   **NOTE NO. 116A**
SERIES OF 1928A—SIGNATURES OF WOODS-MELLON, GREEN SEAL
LETTER REPLACES NUMERAL IN FEDERAL RESERVE SEAL

Issued for all Federal Reserve Banks	70.00	130.00

(Small Size)   **NOTE NO. 116B**
SERIES OF 1934—SIGNATURES OF JULIAN-MORGENTHAU, GREEN SEAL

Issued for all Federal Reserve Banks	60.00	110.00

SERIES OF 1934A—SIGNATURES OF JULIAN-MORGENTHAU, GREEN SEAL

Issued for all Federal Reserve Banks except Philadelphia	60.00	100.00

SERIES OF 1934B—SIGNATURES OF JULIAN-VINSON, GREEN SEAL

Issued for all Federal Reserve Banks except Boston and New York	60.00	110.00

SERIES OF 1934C—SIGNATURES OF JULIAN-SNYDER, GREEN SEAL

Issued for all Federal Reserve Banks except San Francisco	60.00	96.00

SERIES OF 1934D—SIGNATURES OF CLARK-SNYDER, GREEN SEAL

Issued for Cleveland, St. Louis, Minneapolis, Kansas City, San Francisco	60.00	92.00

FIFTY DOLLAR NOTES (1950) FEDERAL RESERVE NOTES

(Small Size)   **NOTE NO. 116C**

**SERIES OF 1950—SIGNATURES OF CLARK-SNYDER, FEDERAL RESERVE
AND TREASURY SEALS ARE NOW SMALLER**

	UNC.
Issued for all Federal Reserve Banks	80.00

SERIES OF 1950A—SIGNATURES OF PRIEST-HUMPHREY

Issued for all Federal Reserve Banks except Minneapolis	78.00

SERIES OF 1950B—SIGNATURES OF PRIEST-ANDERSON

Issued for all Federal Reserve Banks except Atlanta and Minneapolis	73.00

SERIES OF 1950C—SIGNATURES OF SMITH-DILLON

Issued for all Federal Reserve Banks except Atlanta	75.00

SERIES OF 1950D—SIGNATURES OF GRANAHAN-DILLON

Issued for all Federal Reserve Banks	70.00

SERIES OF 1950E—SIGNATURES OF GRANAHAN-FOWLER

Issued only for New York, Chicago, San Francisco	70.00

FIFTY DOLLAR NOTES (1963) FEDERAL RESERVE NOTES

("IN GOD WE TRUST" ADDED ON BACK)

(Small Size)   **NOTE NO. 116D**

**SERIES OF 1963, NO NOTES WERE PRINTED; SERIES OF
1963A—SIGNATURES OF GRANAHAN-FOWLER**

Issued for all Federal Reserve Banks	70.00

FIFTY DOLLAR NOTES (1969) FEDERAL RESERVE NOTES

(WORDING IN GREEN SEAL CHANGED FROM LATIN TO ENGLISH)

                                                         NOTE NO. 116E

SERIES OF 1969—SIGNATURES OF ELSTON-KENNEDY

Issued for all Federal Reserve Banks	62.00

SERIES OF 1969A—SIGNATURES OF KABIS-CONNALLY

Issued for all Federal Reserve Banks	62.00

SERIES OF 1969B—SIGNATURES OF BANUELOS-CONNALLY

Issued for Boston, New York, Philadelphia, Richmond, Atlanta, Chicago, Dallas	62.00

SERIES OF 1969C—SIGNATURES OF BANUELOS-SHULTZ

Issued for all Federal Reserve Banks	62.00

SERIES OF 1974—SIGNATURES OF NEFF-SIMON

Issued for all Federal Reserve Banks	65.00

SERIES OF 1977—SIGNATURES OF MORTON-BLUMENTHAL

Issued for all Federal Reserve Banks	62.00

SERIES OF 1977A—SIGNATURES OF MORTON-MILLER

Issued for all Federal Reserve Banks	65.00

SERIES OF 1981—BUCHANAN-REGAN, GREEN SEAL
Issued for all Federal Reserve Banks 60.00
SERIES OF 1981A—SIGNATURES OF ORTEGA-REGAN, GREEN SEAL
Issued for all Federal Reserve Banks 60.00
SERIES OF 1985—SIGNATURES OF ORTEGA-BAKER, GREEN SEAL
Issued for all Federal Reserve Banks 55.00

FIFTY DOLLAR NOTES (1918)
FEDERAL RESERVE BANK NOTES

(Large Size)   **NOTE NO. 117**

Face Design: Portrait of President Grant to left, Federal Reserve Bank in center, blue seal right.
Back Design: Female figure of Panama between merchant ship and battleship. Plates were made for all 12 Federal Reserve Districts. Only St. Louis bank issued. Less than 30 notes are known today.

CITY	SERIES	GOV'T SIGNATURES	BANK SIGNATURES	A.B.P.	FINE	UNC.
☐ St. Louis	1918	Teehee-Burke	Attebery-Wells	2400.00	3700.00	10,800.00

FIFTY DOLLAR NOTES (1929) FEDERAL RESERVE BANK

(Small Size)
NOTE NO. 117A

Face Design:
Portrait of Grant
center, name of
bank left, brown
serial numbers,
black letter for
Federal Reserve
District.

Back Design:
Same as Note
No. 110.

BANK	SERIES	SIGNATURES	SEAL	A.B.P.	V. FINE	UNC.
☐ New York	1929	Jones-Woods	Brown	50.00	110.00	260.00
☐ Cleveland	1929	Jones-Woods	Brown	50.00	110.00	260.00
☐ Chicago	1929	Jones-Woods	Brown	50.00	110.00	270.00
☐ Minneapolis	1929	Jones-Woods	Brown	50.00	110.00	265.00
☐ Kansas City	1929	Jones-Woods	Brown	50.00	110.00	265.00
☐ Dallas	1929	Jones-Woods	Brown	50.00	110.00	320.00
☐ San Francisco	1929	Jones-Woods	Brown	50.00	110.00	525.00

ONE HUNDRED DOLLAR NOTES

ORDER OF ISSUE

ONE HUNDRED DOLLAR NOTES (1862–1863) U.S. NOTES
(ALSO KNOWN AS LEGAL TENDER NOTES)

(Large Size)

NOTE NO. 118

Face Design: Eagle with spread wings left, three discs with "100," red seal numbers.

Back Design: Green, two variations of the wording in obligation.

SERIES SIGNATURES	SEAL	A.B.P.	GOOD	V. FINE	UNC.
☐ 1862 Chittenden-Spinner*	Red	1250.00	2100.00	7650.00	16,700.00
☐ 1862 Chittenden-Spinner**	Red	1250.00	2100.00	7650.00	16,700.00
☐ 1863 Chittenden-Spinner**	Red	1250.00	2100.00	7650.00	16,700.00

*First Obligation: Similar to Note No. 33.
**Second Obligation: Shown above.

ONE HUNDRED DOLLAR NOTES (1869–1880) U.S. NOTES
(Large Size)   **NOTE NO. 119**

Face Design: Portrait of President Lincoln.

Back Design: No. 119.

Back Design: No. 119A.

SERIES SIGNATURES	SEAL		A.B.P.	GOOD	V. FINE	UNC.
☐ 1869 Allison-Spinner	Red		1300.00	2700.00	8600.00	16,000.00

THE FOLLOWING NOTES HAVE A MODIFIED BACK DESIGN

(Small Size)   **NOTE NO. 119A**

SERIES SIGNATURES	SEAL		A.B.P.	GOOD	V. FINE	UNC.
☐ 1875 Allison-New	Sm.	Red	1300.00	2700.00	8700.00	11,500.00
☐ 1875 Allison-Wyman	Sm.	Red	1300.00	2700.00	8700.00	11,500.00
☐ 1878 Allison-Gilfillan	Sm.	Red.	1300.00	2700.00	8700.00	11,500.00
☐ 1880 Bruce-Gilfillan	Lg.	Brown	400.00	650.00	1800.00	6500.00
☐ 1880 Bruce-Wyman	Lg.	Brown	400.00	650.00	1800.00	6500.00
☐ 1880 Rosecrans-Jordan	Lg.	Red ..	400.00	650.00	1800.00	6500.00
☐ 1880 Rosecrans-Hyatt	Lg.	Red ..	400.00	650.00	1800.00	6500.00
☐ 1880 Rosecrans-Hyatt	Lg.	Red ..	400.00	650.00	1800.00	6500.00
☐ 1880 Rosecrans-Huston	Lg.	Red ..	400.00	650.00	1800.00	6500.00
☐ 1880 Rosecrans-Huston	Lg.	Brown	400.00	650.00	1800.00	6500.00
☐ 1880 Tillman-Morgan	Sm.	Red	400.00	650.00	1800.00	6500.00
☐ 1880 Bruce-Roberts	Sm.	Red	400.00	650.00	1800.00	6500.00
☐ 1880 Lyons-Roberts	Sm.	Red	400.00	650.00	1800.00	6500.00

ONE HUNDRED DOLLAR NOTES (1966) U.S. NOTES
(ALSO KNOWN AS LEGAL TENDER NOTES)

(Small Size)   **NOTE NO. 119B**

Face Design: Portrait of Franklin, red seal, red serial numbers.

Back Design: Independence Hall.

SERIES SIGNATURES	SEAL	V. FINE	UNC.
☐ 1966* Granahan-Fowler	Red	130.00	230.00
☐ 1966A Elston-Kennedy	Red	140.00	350.00

*This is the first note to be issued with the new Treasury Seal with wording in English instead of Latin.

ONE HUNDRED DOLLAR NOTES (1875)
NATIONAL BANK NOTES
(ALL HAVE RED SEAL)

FIRST CHARTER PERIOD (Large Size)   **NOTE NO. 120**

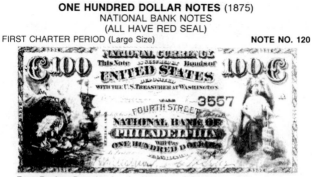

Face Design: Perry leaving the Lawrence, left.

Face Design: Border green, center black, Signing of the Declaration of Independence.

SERIES SIGNATURES	SEAL	A.B.P.	GOOD	V. FINE
☐ Original Chittenden-Spinner	Red	675.00	1400.00	3850.00
☐ Original Colby-Spinner	Red	675.00	1400.00	3850.00
☐ Original Allison-Spinner	Red	675.00	1400.00	3850.00
☐ 1875 Allison-New	Red	675.00	1400.00	3850.00
☐ 1875 Allison-Wyman	Red	675.00	1400.00	3850.00
☐ 1875 Allison-Gilfillan	Red	675.00	1400.00	3850.00
☐ 1875 Scofield-Gilfillan	Red	675.00	1400.00	3850.00
☐ 1875 Bruce-Gilfillan	Red	675.00	1400.00	3850.00
☐ 1875 Bruce-Wyman	Red	675.00	1400.00	3850.00
☐ 1875 Rosecrans-Huston	Red	675.00	1400.00	3850.00
☐ 1875 Tillman-Morgan	Red	675.00	1400.00	3850.00

ONE HUNDRED DOLLAR NOTES (1882)
NATIONAL BANK NOTES

SECOND CHARTER PERIOD (Large Size)　　　　　　　**NOTE NO. 120A**
    First Issue—Brown seal and brown backs.
    Face Design: Similar to Note No. 120.
    Back Design: Similar to Note No. 39.

SERIES	SIGNATURES	SEAL	A.B.P.	GOOD	V. FINE	UNC.
☐ 1882	Bruce-Gilfillan	Brown ...	130.00	320.00	650.00	3600.00
☐ 1882	Bruce-Wyman	Brown ...	130.00	320.00	650.00	3600.00
☐ 1882	Bruce-Jordan	Brown ...	130.00	320.00	650.00	3600.00
☐ 1882	Rosecrans-Jordan	Brown ...	130.00	320.00	650.00	3600.00
☐ 1882	Rosecrans-Hyatt	Brown ...	130.00	320.00	650.00	3600.00
☐ 1882	Rosecrans-Huston	Brown ...	130.00	320.00	650.00	3600.00
☐ 1882	Rosecrans-Nebeker	Brown ...	130.00	320.00	650.00	3600.00
☐ 1882	Rosecrans-Morgan	Brown ...	130.00	320.00	650.00	3600.00
☐ 1882	Tillman-Morgan	Brown ...	130.00	320.00	650.00	3600.00
☐ 1882	Tillman-Roberts	Brown ...	130.00	320.00	650.00	3600.00
☐ 1882	Bruce-Roberts	Brown ...	130.00	320.00	650.00	3600.00
☐ 1882	Lyons-Roberts	Brown ...	130.00	320.00	650.00	3600.00

SECOND CHARTER PERIOD (Large Size)　　　　　　　**NOTE NO. 121**
    Second Issue—Blue seal, green back with date 1902–1908.
    Face Design: Similar to note No. 120.
    Back Design: Green with date 1882–1908, center.

SERIES	SIGNATURES	SEAL	A.B.P.	V. FINE	UNC.
☐ 1882	Rosecrans-Huston	Blue	340.00	650.00	4150.00
☐ 1882	Rosecrans-Nebeker	Blue	340.00	650.00	4150.00
☐ 1882	Tillman-Morgan	Blue	340.00	650.00	4150.00
☐ 1882	Tillman-Roberts	Blue	340.00	650.00	4150.00
☐ 1882	Bruce-Roberts	Blue	340.00	650.00	4150.00
☐ 1882	Lyons-Roberts	Blue	340.00	650.00	4150.00
☐ 1882	Vernon-Treat	Blue	340.00	650.00	4150.00
☐ 1882	Napier-McClung	Blue	340.00	650.00	4150.00

This note was also issued with (value) "ONE HUNDRED DOLLARS" on the back. Very rare.

ONE HUNDRED DOLLAR NOTES (1902)
NATIONAL BANK NOTES
THIRD CHARTER PERIOD (Large Size)   **NOTE NO. 122**

Face Design: Portrait of John J. Knox, left.

First Issue—Red seal.
Back Design: Male figures with shield and flags.

SERIES	SIGNATURES	SEAL	A.B.P.	GOOD	V. FINE	UNC.
☐ 1902	Lyons-Roberts	Red	240.00	450.00	1400.00	7200.00
☐ 1902	Lyons-Treat	Red	240.00	450.00	1400.00	7200.00
☐ 1902	Vernon-Treat	Red	240.00	450.00	1400.00	7200.00

Second Issue—Design is similar to previous note. Seal and serial numbers are now blue, back of note has date 1902–1908 added.

☐		Blue	115.00	130.00	260.00	750.00

Third Issue—Design continues as previous notes. Seal and serial numbers remain blue, date 1902–1908 removed from back.

The notes of the **Second and Third Issue** appeared with various signatures: Lyons-Roberts, Lyons-Treat, Vernon-Treat, Vernon-McClung, Napier-McClung, Parker-Burke, Teehee-Burke, Elliott-Burke, Elliott-White, Speelman-White, Woods-White.

☐		Blue	120.00	135.00	240.00	650.00

ONE HUNDRED DOLLAR NOTES (1929)
NATIONAL BANK NOTES

(Small Size)

NOTE NO. 123

Face Design: Portrait of Franklin, center. Name of bank and city, left. Brown seal, right.

SERIES SIGNATURES	SEAL	A.B.P.	V. FINE	UNC.
☐ 1929 TYPE I Jones-Woods	Brown	130.00	160.00	260.00
☐ 1929 TYPE II Jones-Woods	Brown	130.00	160.00	625.00

ONE HUNDRED DOLLAR NOTES (1878)
SILVER CERTIFICATES

SERIES SIGNATURES	SEAL	A.B.P.	GOOD	V. FINE	UNC.
☐ 1878 Scofield-Gilfillan-White	Red			UNIQUE	
☐ 1878 Scofield-Gilfillan-Hopper	Red		NO SPECIMENS KNOWN		
☐ 1878 Scofield-Gilfillan-Hillhouse	Red		NO SPECIMENS KNOWN		
☐ 1878 Scofield-Gilfillan-Anthony	Red			UNIQUE	
☐ 1878 Scofield-Gilfillan-Wyman	Red		NO SPECIMENS KNOWN		
☐ 1878 Scofield-Gilfillan-Wyman (printed signature of Wyman)	Red			VERY RARE	
☐ 1880 Scofield-Gilfillan	Brown		EXTREMELY RARE		
☐ 1880 Bruce-Gilfillan	Brown	1400.00	2400.00	7000.00	15,000.00
☐ 1880 Bruce-Wyman	Brown	1400.00	2400.00	7000.00	15,000.00
☐ 1880 Rosecrans-Huston	Brown	1400.00	2400.00	7000.00	15,000.00
☐ 1880 Rosecrans-Nebeker	Red	1400.00	2400.00	7000.00	15,000.00

ONE HUNDRED DOLLAR NOTES (1891)
SILVER CERTIFICATES

(Large Size)   **NOTE NO. 124**

Face Design: Portrait of President Monroe.

SERIES SIGNATURES		SEAL	A.B.P.	GOOD	V. FINE	UNC.
☐ 1891 Rosecrans-Nebeker		Red	500.00	700.00	2400.00	11,000.00
☐ 1891 Tillman-Morgan		Red	500.00	700.00	2400.00	11,000.00

This note was also issued in the Series of 1878 and 1880. They are very rare.

ONE HUNDRED DOLLAR NOTES (1882–1922)
GOLD CERTIFICATES

(Large Size)   **NOTE NO. 125**

Face Design: Portrait of Thomas H. Benton.

SERIES SIGNATURES	SEAL	A.B.P.	GOOD	V. FINE	UNC.
☐ 1882 Bruce-Gilfillan	Lg. Brown	375.00	750.00	3500.00	RARE
☐ 1882 Bruce-Wyman	Lg. Brown	375.00	750.00	3500.00	RARE
☐ 1882 Rosecrans-Hyatt	Lg. Red ..	375.00	750.00	3500.00	RARE
☐ 1882 Rosecrans-Huston	Lg. Brown	375.00	750.00	3500.00	RARE
☐ 1882 Lyons-Roberts	Sm. Red .	125.00	275.00	650.00	4000.00
☐ 1882 Lyons-Treat	Sm. Red .	125.00	275.00	650.00	4000.00
☐ 1882 Vernon-Treat	Sm. Red .	125.00	275.00	650.00	4000.00
☐ 1882 Vernon-McClung	Sm. Red .	125.00	275.00	650.00	4000.00
☐ 1882 Napier-McClung	Sm. Red .	125.00	275.00	650.00	4000.00
☐ 1882 Napier-Thompson	Sm. Red .	125.00	275.00	650.00	4000.00
☐ 1882 Napier-Burke	Sm. Red .	125.00	275.00	650.00	4000.00
☐ 1882 Parker-Burke	Sm. Red .	125.00	275.00	650.00	4000.00
☐ 1882 Teehee-Burke	Sm. Red .	125.00	275.00	650.00	4000.00
☐ 1922 Speelman-White	Sm. Red .	125.00	275.00	650.00	4000.00

ONE HUNDRED DOLLAR NOTES (1928)
GOLD CERTIFICATES

(Small Size)   **NOTE NO. 126**

Face Design: Portrait of Franklin, center. Yellow seal to left. Yellow numbers.

SERIES SIGNATURES	SEAL	A.B.P.	GOOD	V. FINE	UNC.
☐ 1928 Woods-Mellon	Gold	110.00	135.00	200.00	777.00

ONE HUNDRED DOLLAR NOTES (1890–1891)
TREASURY NOTES

(Large Size)

NOTE NO. 127

Face Design: Portrait of Commodore Farragut to right.

Back Design: Large "100," called "Watermelon Note."

Back Design: "One Hundred" in scalloped medallion.

SERIES SIGNATURES	SEAL	A.B.P.	GOOD	V. FINE	UNC.
☐ 1890 Rosecrans-Huston	Brown	3500.00	6000.00	13,000.00	RARE
☐ 1891 Rosecrans-Nebeker	Red	3500.00	6000.00	13,000.00	RARE

ONE HUNDRED DOLLAR NOTES (1914)
FEDERAL RESERVE NOTES

(Large Size)

NOTE NO. 128

Face Design: Portrait of Franklin in center.
Back Design: Group of five allegorical figures.
SERIES OF 1914—SIGNATURES OF BURKE-McADOO, RED SEAL AND RED SERIAL NUMBERS

CITY	A.B.P.	GOOD	V. FINE	UNC.	CITY	A.B.P.	GOOD	V. FINE	UNC.
☐ Boston	110.00	150.00	350.00	1550.00	☐ Chicago	110.00	150.00	350.00	1550.00
☐ New York	110.00	150.00	350.00	1550.00	☐ St. Louis	110.00	150.00	350.00	1550.00
☐ Philadelphia	110.00	150.00	350.00	1550.00	☐ Minneapolis	110.00	150.00	350.00	1550.00
☐ Cleveland	110.00	150.00	350.00	1550.00	☐ Kansas City	110.00	150.00	350.00	1550.00
☐ Richmond	110.00	150.00	350.00	1550.00	☐ Dallas	110.00	150.00	350.00	1550.00
☐ Atlanta	110.00	150.00	350.00	1550.00	☐ San Fran.	110.00	150.00	350.00	1550.00

SERIES OF 1914—DESIGN CONTINUES AS PREVIOUS NOTE. THE SEAL AND SERIAL NUMBERS ARE NOW BLUE.

*(This note was issued with various signatures for each bank.)

BANK	A.B.P.	V. FINE	UNC.	BANK	A.B.P.	V. FINE	UNC.
☐ Boston	110.00	170.00	500.00	☐ Chicago	110.00	170.00	500.00
☐ New York	110.00	170.00	500.00	☐ St. Louis	110.00	170.00	500.00
☐ Philadelphia	110.00	170.00	500.00	☐ Minneapolis	110.00	170.00	500.00
☐ Cleveland	110.00	170.00	500.00	☐ Kansas City	110.00	170.00	500.00
☐ Richmond	110.00	170.00	500.00	☐ Dallas	110.00	170.00	500.00
☐ Atlanta	110.00	170.00	500.00	☐ San Francisco	110.00	170.00	500.00

*Signatures: Burke-McAdoo, Burke-Glass, Burke-Huston, White-Mellon.

ONE HUNDRED DOLLAR NOTES (1928)
FEDERAL RESERVE NOTES

(Small Size)

NOTE NO. 129

Face Design: Portrait of Franklin, Black Federal Reserve Seal left with number, green Treasury Seal right.

SERIES OF 1928—SIGNATURES OF WOODS-MELLON, GREEN SEAL

CITY	A.B.P.	V. FINE	UNC.	CITY	A.B.P.	V. FINE	UNC.
☐ Boston	115.00	140.00	200.00	☐ Chicago	115.00	140.00	200.00
☐ New York	115.00	140.00	200.00	☐ St. Louis	115.00	140.00	200.00
☐ Philadelphia	115.00	140.00	200.00	☐ Minneapolis	115.00	140.00	200.00
☐ Cleveland	115.00	140.00	200.00	☐ Kansas City	115.00	140.00	200.00
☐ Richmond	115.00	140.00	200.00	☐ Dallas	115.00	140.00	200.00
☐ Atlanta	115.00	140.00	200.00	☐ San Francisco	115.00	140.00	200.00

SERIES OF 1928A—SIGNATURES OF WOODS-MELLON, GREEN SEAL
NUMBER IN BLACK, FEDERAL RESERVE SEAL
IS CHANGED TO A LETTER

(Small Size)

NOTE NO. 129A

CITY	A.B.P.	V. FINE	UNC.	CITY	A.B.P.	V. FINE	UNC.
☐ Boston	115.00	145.00	210.00	☐ Chicago	115.00	145.00	210.00
☐ New York	115.00	145.00	210.00	☐ St. Louis	115.00	145.00	210.00
☐ Philadelphia	115.00	145.00	210.00	☐ Minneapolis	115.00	145.00	210.00
☐ Cleveland	115.00	145.00	210.00	☐ Kansas City	115.00	145.00	210.00
☐ Richmond	115.00	145.00	210.00	☐ Dallas	115.00	145.00	210.00
☐ Atlanta	115.00	145.00	210.00	☐ San Francisco	115.00	145.00	210.00

SERIES OF 1934—SIGNATURES OF JULIAN-MORGENTHAU, GREEN SEAL

SERIES OF 1934A—SIGNATURES OF JULIAN-MORGENTHAU, GREEN SEAL

(The above two notes were issued on all Federal Reserve Districts.)
SERIES OF 1934B*—SIGNATURES OF JULIAN-VINSON, GREEN SEAL

SERIES OF 1934C*—SIGNATURES OF JULIAN-SNYDER, GREEN SEAL

SERIES OF 1934D*—SIGNATURES OF CLARK-SNYDER, GREEN SEAL

*(Not all Districts issued these series.)

	A.B.P.	V. FINE	UNC.
AVERAGE PRICES ARE FOR ABOVE FIVE ISSUES	120.00	140.00	225.00

ONE HUNDRED DOLLAR NOTES (1950)
FEDERAL RESERVE NOTES, GREEN SEAL

(Small Size)   **NOTE NO. 129C**

SERIES OF 1950—SIGNATURES OF CLARK-SNYDER
Issued for all Federal Reserve Banks 170.00

SERIES OF 1950A—SIGNATURES OF PRIEST-HUMPHREY
Issued for all Federal Reserve Banks 160.00

SERIES OF 1950B—SIGNATURES OF PRIEST-ANDERSON
Issued for all Federal Reserve Banks 155.00

SERIES OF 1950C—SIGNATURES OF SMITH-DILLON
Issued for all Federal Reserve Banks 155.00

SERIES OF 1950D—SIGNATURES OF GRANAHAN-DILLON
Issued for all Federal Reserve Banks 155.00

SERIES OF 1950E—SIGNATURES OF GRANAHAN-FOWLER
Issued for New York, Chicago, San Francisco only 155.00

ONE HUNDRED DOLLAR NOTES (1963)
FEDERAL RESERVE NOTES

NOTE NO. 129D

SERIES OF 1963—NO NOTES WERE PRINTED FOR THIS SERIES

SERIES OF 1963A—"IN GOD WE TRUST" ADDED ON BACK

SERIES OF 1963B—SIGNATURES OF GRANAHAN-FOWLER
Issued for all Federal Reserve Banks 150.00

ONE HUNDRED DOLLAR NOTES (1969)
FEDERAL RESERVE NOTES

NOTE NO. 129E

SERIES OF 1969—ENGLISH WORDING IN TREASURY SEAL

SERIES OF 1969—SIGNATURES OF ELSTON-KENNEDY
Issued for all Federal Reserve Banks 140.00

SERIES OF 1969A—SIGNATURES OF KABIS-CONNALLY
Issued for all Federal Reserve Banks 140.00

SERIES OF 1969B—NO NOTES WERE PRINTED

SERIES OF 1969C—SIGNATURES OF BANUELOS-SHULTZ
Issued for all Federal Reserve Banks 135.00

SERIES OF 1974—SIGNATURES OF NEFF-SIMON
Issued for all Federal Reserve Banks 134.00

SERIES OF 1977—SIGNATURES OF MORTON-BLUMENTHAL
Issued for all Federal Reserve Banks 128.00

SERIES OF 1977A—SIGNATURES OF MORTON-MILLER
Issued for all Federal Reserve Banks 128.00

SERIES OF 1981—SIGNATURES OF BUCHANAN-REGAN, GREEN SEAL
Issued for all Federal Reserve Banks 125.00

SERIES OF 1981A—SIGNATURES OF ORTEGA-REGAN, GREEN SEAL
Issued for all Federal Reserve Banks 120.00
SERIES OF 1985—SIGNATURES OF ORTEGA-BAKER, GREEN SEAL
Issued for all Federal Reserve Banks 120.00

ONE HUNDRED DOLLAR NOTES (1929)
FEDERAL RESERVE BANK NOTES
(ISSUED ONLY IN SERIES OF 1929)

(Small Size)   **NOTE NO. 129F**

Face Design: Portrait of Franklin, brown seal and numbers.

Back Design

BANK & CITY	SIGNATURES	SEAL	A.B.P.	V. FINE	UNC.
☐ New York	Jones-Woods	Brown	120.00	135.00	260.00
☐ Cleveland	Jones-Woods	Brown	120.00	135.00	260.00
☐ Richmond	Jones-Woods	Brown	120.00	135.00	260.00
☐ Chicago	Jones-Woods	Brown	120.00	135.00	260.00
☐ Minneapolis	Jones-Woods	Brown	120.00	135.00	260.00
☐ Kansas City	Jones-Woods	Brown	120.00	135.00	260.00
☐ Dallas	Jones-Woods	Brown	120.00	135.00	400.00

FIVE HUNDRED, ONE THOUSAND, FIVE HUNDRED AND TEN THOUSAND DOLLAR NOTES
*(Production of notes in denominations above one hundred dollars was discontinued in 1969.)

SPECIAL REPORT: UNCUT SHEETS

As very few notes exist in the form of full uncut sheets, this is a limited area for the collector. Also, the prices are high, well out of range for most hobbyists.

Uncut sheets available on the market are of small-size notes exclusively. In most instances it is not known precisely how they reached public hands. Some were undoubtedly presented as souvenir gifts to Treasury Department officials. In any event, uncut sheets have never been illegal to own, since the notes they comprise are precisely the same as those released into general circulation.

The sheets differ in the number of notes, from a low of six in National Currency sheets to a high of eighteen for some sheets of United States (Legal Tender) Notes and Silver Certificates. Others have twelve notes. These differences are due entirely to the printing method being used at their time of manufacture. Any given note was always printed in sheets of the same size, with the same number of specimens per sheet. If you have an uncut sheet with twelve notes, it means that all notes from the series were printed twelve to a sheet.

The condition standards for uncut sheets are the same as those for single notes. Obviously, an uncut sheet did not circulate as money, but some specimens became worn or damaged as a result of careless storage, accident, or other causes. These impaired sheets do turn up in the market, but there is not much demand for them. Almost every buyer of uncut sheets wants uncirculated condition. Quite often an uncut sheet will be framed when you buy it. This should be considered a plus, as the frame has probably kept the sheet in immaculate condition. Just to be entirely safe, however, it is wise to examine the reverse side of the sheet for possible staining or other problems.

The following prices were current for uncut sheets in uncirculated grade at publication time. Gem uncirculated sheets in absolutely pristine condition command higher prices than those shown.

SILVER CERTIFICATES

DENOMINATION	SERIES	NUMBER OF NOTES PER SHEET	CURRENT PRICE RANGE IN UNCIRCULATED CONDITION
$1	1928	12	3500.00–4000.00
$1	1934	12	4300.00–5000.00
$5	1934	12	3000.00–4000.00
$10	1934	12	5000.00–6500.00
$1	1935	12	1800.00–2500.00
$5	1953	18	4000.00–5000.00
$10	1953	18	6000.00–7500.00

DENOMINATION	SERIES	NUMBER OF NOTES PER SHEET	CURRENT PRICE RANGE IN UNCIRCULATED CONDITION

UNITED STATES NOTES (LEGAL TENDER NOTES)

$1	1928	12	30,000.00 & UP
$2	1928	12	2500.00–3000.00
$5	1928	12	2800.00–3200.00
$2	1953	18	2500.00–3000.00
$5	1953	18	4000.00–5000.00

NATIONAL CURRENCY

$5	1929	6	1000.00–1500.00
$10	1929	6	1000.00–1500.00
$20	1929	6	1200.00–1500.00
$50	1929	6	4000.00–6000.00

MULES
(MIXED PLATE NUMBERS)

All United States currency have plate numbers on the face and back. These plate numbers are in the lower right corner somewhat close to the fine scroll design. They refer to the number of the engraved plate used to print the sheet of notes. Each plate can be used for about 100,000 impressions. It is then destroyed and a new plate with the next number in sequence is put into use.

During the term of Treasury officials Julian and Morgenthau, the plate numbers were changed from almost a microscopic to a larger size, far easier to read. Due to this improvement the series designation then in use was an advance on United States Notes, Silver Certificates and Federal Reserve Notes. The signatures remained Julian-Morgenthau. National currency and gold certificates were not affected, as these were discontinued earlier.

During the changeover period in printing, plates were sometimes mixed up, producing a note with a large number on one side and a small number on the other side. Notes of this variety are called mules, or mule notes. This is from a term applied to coins struck with the obverse or reverse die of one year and the opposite side from a die of another year.

Many collectors are eager to add one or more of these mule notes to their collection. Some of the most common mule notes are:

$2.00 UNITED STATES NOTES	**$1.00 SILVER CERTIFICATES**
1928-C 1928-D	1935 1935-A

$5.00 UNITED STATES NOTES	**$5.00 SILVER CERTIFICATES**
1928-B 1928-C 1928-D 1928-E	1934 1934-A 1934-B 1934-C

$10.00 SILVER CERTIFICATES
1934   1934-A

Mules were also issued in the Federal Reserve Note series. However, these are not as popular with collectors as the United States Notes and Silver Certificates because of the higher denominations and the 12 districts involved.

The schedule below shows some of the most common mule notes and their values in new condition. The combination of the prefix and suffix letters of the serial numbers on notes is known as "Blocks." For instance: A—A Block, B—A Block, etc.

			UNC.
$2.00 UNITED STATES NOTE	1928-D ...	B—A	400.00
		C—A	40.00
		*—A	50.00
$5.00 UNITED STATES NOTE	1928-B ...	E—A	90.00
		*—A	450.00
	1928-C ...	E—A	60.00
		*—A	125.00
$1.00 SILVER CERTIFICATE	1935	N—A	
		Thru	150.00
		P—A	
	1935-A ...	M—A	
		Thru	50.00
		V—A	
		C—B	70.00
$5.00 SILVER CERTIFICATE	1934-A ...	D—A	
		Thru	60.00
		G—A	
		*—A	160.00
$10.00 SILVER CERTIFICATE	1934	A—A	70.00
		*—A	120.00
	1934-A ...	A—A	180.00

Front   **SIZES DIFFERENT**   **Back**

INTRODUCTION TO UNITED STATES
FRACTIONAL CURRENCY

Events following the outbreak of the Civil War resulted in a shortage of circulating coinage. Trade was hampered as many merchants, especially in large cities, were unable to make change and only customers presenting the exact amount for a purchase could buy—but they were generally as short on coins as the shop proprietors. Various attempts were made to solve this problem by issuing credit slips (which most customers didn't care for), tokens (which they also didn't care for), and using postage stamps as money. Finally in 1862 the government stepped in, recognizing that the economy was being seriously hurt, and issued a series of small paper notes as equivalents of coinage denominations. They carried designs adapted from the current postage stamps of the day and were known as Postage Currency or Postal Currency. The more popular title is now Fractional Currency. There were five separate issues of fractional currency, three of which occurred during the Civil War and two thereafter, the final one as late as 1874. That a need existed for coin substitutes as late as the 1870's demonstrates the drain placed upon coinage during the war and the long period of recovery. A total of six denominations were issued, from 3¢ to 50¢, comprising 23 designs and more than 100 varieties. Because of its small size and lack of visual impact, fractional currency was long shunned by collectors. In recent years it has enjoyed an unprecedented surge of popularity, which, if continued, promises to drive prices beyond present levels. All told, more than $360,000,000 worth of fractional currency was circulated. It would be extremely plentiful today but for the fact that most notes were redeemed, leaving only about $2,000,000 outstanding. This is what collectors have to work with, and a good deal of these are badly preserved.

> **FIRST ISSUE**—Postage Currency August 21st, 1862
> 5–10–25–50
> **SECOND ISSUE**—Fractional Currency October 10th, 1863
> 5–10–25–50
> **THIRD ISSUE**—Fractional Currency December 5th, 1864
> 3–5–10–15–25–50
> **FOURTH ISSUE**—Fractional Currency July 14th, 1869
> 10–15–25–50
> **FIFTH ISSUE**—Fractional Currency February 26th, 1874
> 10–25–50

THE FRACTIONAL CURRENCY SHIELD

Fractional currency shields were sold by the Treasury Department in 1866. Specimen notes printed only on one side were used. Very good condition shields are valued at $2500 to $3000. Choice condition shields in contemporary frames can sell for $4500. Shields with pink, green or other backgrounds are more valuable.

UNITED STATES FRACTIONAL CURRENCY
These notes may be collected by issue or by denomination.
We list them here by denomination for convenience.

NOTE: Since most of these notes were hastily cut from large sheets, the margin size can vary. Specimens with larger than normal margins command premium prices.

THREE-CENT NOTES

THIRD ISSUE

NOTE NO. 142

Face Design:
Portrait of
President Washington.

Back Design:
Large "3"
green.

	A.B.P.	GOOD	V. FINE	UNC.
☐ With Light Portrait	5.00	9.00	20.00	75.00
☐ With Dark Portrait	6.00	11.00	25.00	175.00

FIVE-CENT NOTES

FIRST ISSUE

NOTE NO. 143

Face Design:
Portrait of
President Jefferson,
brown.

Back Design:
"S" black.

	A.B.P.	GOOD	V. FINE	UNC.
☐ Perforated edges. Monogram ABNCO on back	5.00	8.00	20.00	155.00
☐ Perforated edges. Without monogram on back	6.00	10.00	22.00	180.00
☐ Straight edges. Monogram ABNCO on back	3.00	6.00	12.00	110.00
☐ Straight edges. Without monogram on back	6.00	11.00	24.00	110.00

FIVE-CENT NOTES

SECOND ISSUE

NOTE NO. 144

Face Design:
Portrait of
President
Washington.

Back Design:
Shield and
brown, "5s".

	A.B.P.	GOOD	V. FINE	UNC.
☐ Value only in bronze on back	4.00	7.00	15.00	90.00
☐ Surcharges 18–63 on back	4.00	7.00	15.00	90.00
☐ Surcharges S-18-63 on back	6.00	11.00	35.00	120.00
☐ Surcharges R-1-18-63 on back—fiber paper	8.50	18.00	60.00	320.00

FIVE-CENT NOTES

THIRD ISSUE

NOTE NO. 145

Face Design:
Portrait of
Spencer M. Clark.

Back Design:
Green or red.

	A.B.P.	GOOD	V. FINE	UNC.
☐ Without letter "A" on face. Green back	5.00	9.00	13.00	155.00
☐ With letter "A" on face. Green back	6.00	10.00	16.00	155.00
☐ Without letter "A" on face. Red back	6.00	12.00	21.00	110.00
☐ With letter "A" on face. Red back	7.00	14.00	30.00	110.00

NOTE: This note was authorized to have the portraits of the explorers Lewis and Clark on the face. Mr. Spencer M. Clark, who was then head of the Bureau of Currency, flagrantly placed his own portrait on this note. This caused Congress to pass legislation forbidding the likeness of any living person on U.S. currency.

TEN-CENT NOTES

FIRST ISSUE

NOTE NO. 146

Face Design:
Portrait of
President Washington.

Back Design:
"10," black.

	A.B.P.	GOOD	V. FINE	UNC.
☐ Perforated edges. Monogram ABNCO on back	5.00	8.00	20.00	160.00
☐ Perforated edges. Without monogram on back	5.00	8.00	20.00	160.00
☐ Plain edges. Monogram ABNCO on back	4.00	5.00	12.00	80.00
☐ Plain edges. Without monogram on back	7.00	12.00	28.00	220.00

TEN-CENT NOTES

SECOND ISSUE

NOTE NO. 147

Face Design:
Portrait of
President Washington.

Back Design:
"10," green.

	A.B.P.	GOOD	V. FINE	UNC.
☐ Value only surcharge on back	5.00	9.00	15.00	90.00
☐ Surcharge 18-63 on back	5.00	10.00	20.00	105.00
☐ Surcharge S-18-63 on back	5.00	10.00	21.00	105.00
☐ Surcharge I-18-63 on back	8.00	15.00	45.00	310.00
☐ Surcharge O-63 on back	150.00	310.00	610.00	1900.00
☐ Surcharge T-1-18-63 on back—fiber paper	7.00	15.00	40.00	260.00

TEN-CENT NOTES

THIRD ISSUE

NOTE NO. 148

Face Design:
Portrait of
President
Washington.

Back Design:
"10," green or
red.

	A.B.P.	GOOD	V. FINE	UNC.
☐ Printed signatures Colby-Spinner. Green back	4.50	9.00	14.00	51.00
☐ As above. Figure "1" near left margin on face	4.50	9.00	13.00	160.00
☐ Printed signatures Colby-Spinner. Red back	5.00	10.00	18.00	2250.00
☐ As above. Figure "1" near left margin. Red back	5.50	12.00	19.00	260.00
☐ Autographed signatures Colby-Spinner. Red back	7.50	16.00	34.00	85.00
☐ Autographed signatures Jeffries-Spinner. Red back	7.00	14.00	24.00	85.00

TEN-CENT NOTES

FOURTH ISSUE

NOTE NO. 149

Face Design:
Bust of
Liberty.

Back Design:
Green with
"Ten" & "10."

	A.B.P.	GOOD	V. FINE	UNC.
☐ Large red seal. Watermarked paper	3.00	5.00	14.00	65.00
☐ Large red seal. Pink fibers in paper	3.00	5.00	15.00	65.00
☐ Large seal. Pink fibers in paper. Right end blue	4.00	7.00	20.00	70.00
☐ Large brown seal	16.00	32.00	110.00	410.00
☐ Small red seal. Pink fibers. Right end blue	4.00	6.00	18.00	70.00

TEN-CENT NOTES

FIFTH ISSUE

NOTE NO. 150

Face Design:
William
Meredith.

Back Design:
Green.

	A.B.P.	GOOD	V. FINE	UNC.
☐ Green seal. Long narrow key	4.00	7.00	16.00	75.00
☐ Red seal. Long narrow key	3.00	5.00	9.00	60.00
☐ Red seal. Short stubby key	3.00	6.00	10.00	60.00

FIFTEEN-CENT NOTES
FACES AND BACKS PRINTED SEPARATELY

THIRD ISSUE

NOTE NO. 151

Face Design:
Sherman and
President Grant.

Back Design:
Green
or red.

	NARROW MARGIN	WIDE MARGIN
☐ With printed signatures Colby-Spinner*	220.00	360.00
☐ With autographed signatures Colby-Spinner**	1250.00	RARE
☐ With autographed signatures Jeffries-Spinner**	275.00	380.00
☐ With autographed signatures Allison-Spinner**	300.00	465.00
☐ *Green back	180.00	210.00
☐ *Red back	175.00	225.00

FIFTEEN-CENT NOTES

FOURTH ISSUE

NOTE NO. 152

Face Design:
Bust
of Columbia.

Back Design:
Green
with "15s."

	A.B.P.	GOOD	V. FINE	UNC.
☐ Large seal. Watermarked paper	6.00	11.00	22.00	170.00
☐ Large seal. Pink fibers in paper	7.00	14.00	35.00	170.00
☐ Large seal. Pink fibers in paper. Right end blue	6.00	12.00	26.00	170.00
☐ Large brown seal	25.00	45.00	170.00	RARE
☐ Smaller red seal. Pink fibers. Right end blue	6.00	12.00	25.00	170.00

TWENTY-FIVE CENT NOTES

FIRST ISSUE

NOTE NO. 153

Face Design:
Five 5¢
Jefferson Stamps.

Back Design:
Black,
large "25."

	A.B.P.	GOOD	V. FINE	UNC.
☐ Perforated edges. Monogram ABNCO on back	7.00	12.00	32.00	210.00
☐ Perforated edges. Without monogram on back	7.00	13.00	42.00	315.00
☐ Straight edges. Monogram ABNCO on back	6.00	10.00	26.00	110.00
☐ Straight edges. Without monogram on back	9.00	16.00	73.00	320.00

A.B.P.—*Average Buying Price in better than good condition.*

TWENTY-FIVE-CENT NOTES

SECOND ISSUE

NOTE NO. 154

(Time and climatic condition have changed the purple color on the back of this note into many variations.)

Face Design:
Portrait of
President Washington.

Back Design:
Purple with "25."

	A.B.P.	GOOD	V. FINE	UNC.
☐ Value only surcharge on back	4.00	8.00	17.00	125.00
☐ Surcharge 18-63 on back	7.00	14.00	20.00	135.00
☐ Surcharge A-18-63 on back	5.00	11.00	18.00	130.00
☐ Surcharge 1-18-63 on back	24.00	50.00	90.00	385.00
☐ Surcharge 2-18-63 on back	7.00	13.00	21.00	135.00
☐ Surcharge S-18-63 on back	8.00	16.00	24.00	130.00
☐ Surcharge T-1-18-63 on back, fiber paper	10.00	17.00	30.00	285.00
☐ Surcharge T-2-18-63 on back, fiber paper	8.00	16.00	27.00	285.00
☐ Surcharge S-2-18-63, fiber paper		RARE		

TWENTY-FIVE-CENT NOTES

THIRD ISSUE

NOTE NO. 155

(All notes have printed signatures of Colby-Spinner.)

Face Design:
Portrait of
Fessenden.

Back Design:
Green or red
with "25 CENTS."

	A.B.P.	GOOD	V. FINE	UNC.
☐ Face—Bust of Fessenden between solid bronze surcharges. Fiber paper. Back—Green. Surcharge M-2-6-5 in corners	110.00	215.00	320.00	1550.00
☐ As above. With letter "A" in lower left corner of face	130.00	260.00	460.00	2400.00
☐ Face—Fessenden. Open scroll bronze surcharges. Fiber paper. Back—Green. Surcharges M-2-6-5 in corners	10.00	18.00	40.00	310.00
☐ As above with letter "A" in lower left corner of face	9.00	17.00	36.00	210.00
☐ Face—Fessenden. Open scroll surcharges. Plain paper. Back—Green. Value surcharges only	6.00	11.00	20.00	115.00

	A.B.P.	GOOD	V. FINE	UNC.
☐ As before. Letter "A" in lower left corner of face.				
Back—Green. Plain paper	10.00	21.00	50.00	115.00
☐ Face—Fessenden. Red back. Value surcharge only ...	7.00	12.00	22.00	160.00
☐ As above. Letter "A" in lower left corner of face	8.00	13.00	28.00	165.00

TWENTY-FIVE-CENT NOTES

FOURTH ISSUE

NOTE NO. 156

Face Design:
Portrait of
President Washington
and Treasury Seal.

Back Design:
Green.

	A.B.P.	GOOD	V. FINE	UNC.
☐ Large seal. Plain watermarked paper	4.00	9.00	18.00	82.00
☐ Large seal. Pink silk fiber in paper	4.00	8.00	17.00	82.00
☐ Large seal. Pink fibers in paper. Right end blue	4.00	8.00	21.00	92.00
☐ Large brown seal. Right end blue	36.00	72.00	300.00	1100.00
☐ Smaller red seal. Right end blue	4.00	9.00	16.00	83.00

TWENTY-FIVE-CENT NOTES

FIFTH ISSUE

NOTE NO. 157

Face Design:
Portrait of
Walker and red seal.

Back Design:
Black.

	A.B.P.	GOOD	V. FINE	UNC.
☐ With long narrow key in Treasury Seal	3.00	4.50	11.00	42.00
☐ With short stubby key in Treasury Seal	3.00	4.50	11.00	36.00

A.B.P.—*Average Buying Price in better than good condition.*

FIFTY-CENT NOTES

FIRST ISSUE

NOTE NO. 158

Face Design:
Five 10¢
Washington Stamps.

Back Design:
Green.

	A.B.P.	GOOD	V. FINE	UNC.
☐ Perforated edges. Monogram ABNCO on back	9.00	17.00	55.00	260.00
☐ Perforated edges. Without monogram on back	10.00	19.00	70.00	360.00
☐ Straight edges. Monogram ABNCO on back	8.00	15.00	42.00	115.00
☐ Straight edges. Without monogram	11.00	22.00	100.00	380.00

FIFTY-CENT NOTES

SECOND ISSUE

NOTE NO. 159

Face Design:
Portrait of
President Washington.

Back Design:
Red.

	A.B.P.	GOOD	V. FINE	UNC.
☐ Value surcharge only in back	70.00	130.00	520.00	1400.00
☐ Surcharge 18-63 on back	8.00	15.00	32.00	215.00
☐ Surcharge A-18-63 on back	6.00	12.00	25.00	210.00
☐ Surcharge I-18-63	6.00	12.00	24.00	210.00
☐ Surcharge O-1-18-63. Fiber paper	7.00	15.00	28.00	215.00
☐ Surcharge R-2-18-63. Fiber paper	14.00	26.00	45.00	230.00
☐ Surcharge T-1-18-63. Fiber paper	6.00	11.00	26.00	215.00
☐ Surcharge T-18-63. Fiber paper	52.00	105.00	210.00	775.00

FIFTY-CENT NOTES

THIRD ISSUE

NOTE NO. 160

(Notes with Printed Signatures of Colby-Spinner, Green Backs.)

Face Design:
Justice with
Sword,
Shield,
Scales.

Back Design:
Green
or red.

	A.B.P.	GOOD	V. FINE	UNC.
☐ Value surcharge and S-2-6-4 on back. Fiber paper	VERY RARE			
☐ Value surcharge and A-2-6-5 on back. Fiber paper	16.00	32.00	72.00	310.00
☐ As above with "1" and letter "A" on face A-2-6-5 on back	33.00	67.00	320.00	1300.00
☐ As above with "1" only on face. A-2-6-5 on back	16.00	34.00	80.00	320.00
☐ As above with letter "A" only on face. A-2-6-5 on back	18.00	38.00	92.00	325.00
☐ A-2-6-5 on back, narrowly spaced. Plain paper	6.00	10.00	34.00	310.00
☐ As above. Numeral "1" and letter "A" on face	16.00	28.00	80.00	425.00
☐ As above. Numeral "1" only on face	5.00	11.00	34.00	260.00
☐ As above. Letter "A" only on face	12.00	19.00	40.00	310.00
☐ A-2-6-5 on back, widely spaced. Plain paper	10.00	18.00	44.00	310.00
☐ As above. Numeral "1" and letter "A" on face	16.00	30.00	130.00	600.00
☐ As above. Numeral "1" only on face	7.00	14.00	50.00	415.00
☐ As above. Letter "A" only on face	9.00	16.00	52.00	460.00
☐ Without position letters or back surcharges	6.00	12.00	36.00	320.00
☐ As above with numeral "1" and letter "A" on face	17.00	35.00	65.00	485.00
☐ As above with numeral "1" only on face	5.00	11.00	30.00	310.00
☐ As above with letter "A" only on face	8.00	14.00	42.00	280.00
(Notes with Printed Signatures of Colby-Spinner, Red Backs.)				
☐ Value surcharge and S-2-6-4 on back. Fiber	90.00	190.00	410.00	1275.00
☐ As above. Numeral "1" and letter "A"	210.00	410.00	780.00	RARE
☐ As above. Numeral "1" only on face	110.00	220.00	510.00	1800.00
☐ As above. Letter "A" only on face	130.00	260.00	600.00	1650.00
☐ Value surcharge and A-2-6-5 on back. Plain	7.00	14.00	40.00	310.00
☐ As above. Numeral "1" and letter "A"	17.00	34.00	76.00	420.00
☐ As above. Numeral "1" only on face	9.00	18.00	40.00	350.00
☐ As above. Letter "A" only on face	10.00	19.00	45.00	250.00
☐ Value surcharge only on back. Plain paper	10.00	17.00	40.00	350.00
☐ As above. Numeral "1" and letter "A" on face	15.00	25.00	66.00	510.00
☐ As above. Numeral "1" only on face	11.00	22.00	45.00	320.00
☐ As above. Letter "A" only on face	12.00	24.00	62.00	420.00
(Notes with Autographed Signatures of Colby-Spinner, Red Backs.)				
☐ Value surcharge and S-2-6-4 on back. Fiber	41.00	81.00	225.00	1120.00
☐ Value surcharge and A-2-6-5 on back. Fiber	15.00	26.00	90.00	610.00
☐ Value surcharge only on back. Plain paper	10.00	20.00	60.00	400.00

FIFTY-CENT NOTES

THIRD ISSUE

NOTE NO. 161

Face Design: Bust of Spinner with surcharges.
Back Design: Green or red.

(Notes with Printed Signatures of Colby-Spinner, Green Backs.)

	A.B.P.	GOOD	V. FINE	UNC.
☐ Value surcharge and A-2-6-5 on back	9.00	17.00	70.00	320.00
☐ As above. Numeral "1" and letter "A" on face	21.00	41.00	125.00	500.00
☐ As above. Numeral "1" only on face	7.00	15.00	40.00	320.00
☐ As above. Letter "A" only on face	8.00	16.00	60.00	420.00
☐ Value surcharge only on back	6.00	12.00	30.00	380.00
☐ As above. Numeral "1" and Letter "A" on face	12.00	26.00	46.00	390.00
☐ As above. Numeral "1" only on face	6.00	12.00	32.00	420.00
☐ As above. Letter "A" only on face	7.00	15.00	32.00	410.00
(TYPE II BACK DESIGN)				
☐ Value surcharge only on back	8.00	15.00	27.00	310.00
☐ Numeral "1" and letter "A" on face	19.00	37.00	90.00	520.00
☐ Numeral "1" only on face	9.00	17.00	34.00	310.00
☐ Letter "A" only on face	9.00	18.00	34.00	390.00
(Notes with Portrait of Spinner, Printed Signatures of Colby-Spinner, Red Backs, Type I.)				
☐ Value surcharge and A-2-6-5 on back	10.00	16.00	44.00	410.00
☐ As above with numeral "1" and letter "A"	19.00	39.00	170.00	620.00
☐ As above with numeral "1" only on face	9.00	17.00	50.00	280.00
☐ As above with letter "A" only on face	11.00	22.00	60.00	320.00
(Notes with Autographed Signatures, Red Backs, Type I.)				
☐ Autographed signatures COLBY-SPINNER. Back surcharged Value and A-2-6-5	12.00	25.00	50.00	410.00
☐ Autographed signatures ALLISON-SPINNER. Back surcharged Value and A-2-6-5	14.00	28.00	72.00	660.00
☐ Autographed signatures ALLISON-NEW. Back surcharged Value and A-2-6-5	430.00	760.00	1850.00	3650.00

A.B.P.—*Average Buying Price in better than good condition.*

FIFTY-CENT NOTES

FOURTH ISSUE

NOTE NO. 162

Face Design:
Bust
of Lincoln.

Back Design:
Green.

	A.B.P.	GOOD	V. FINE	UNC.
☐ Plain paper	8.00	16.00	42.00	230.00
☐ Paper with pink fibers	9.00	17.00	49.00	240.00

FIFTY-CENT NOTES

FOURTH ISSUE

NOTE NO. 163

Face Design:
Bust
of Stanton.

Back Design:
Green
with "50."

	A.B.P.	GOOD	V. FINE	UNC.
☐ Red Seal and signatures ALLISON-SPINNER. Paper with pink fibers. Blue ends	7.00	14.00	28.00	140.00

FIFTY-CENT NOTES

FOURTH ISSUE

NOTE NO. 164

Face Design:
Bust of
Samuel Dexter.

Back Design:
Green with "50."

	A.B.P.	GOOD	V. FINE	UNC.
☐ Green seal. Pink fibers. Blue ends	6.00	11.00	26.50	115.00

FIFTY-CENT NOTES

FIFTH ISSUE

NOTE NO. 165

Face Design:
Bust
of Crawford.

Back Design:
Green with "50."

	A.B.P.	GOOD	V. FINE	UNC.
☐ Signatures ALLISON-NEW. Paper with pink fibers. Blue ends	3.50	7.00	13.00	65.00

A.B.P.—*Average Buying Price in better than good condition.*

ERROR OR FREAK NOTES

Notes have been misprinted from time to time since the earliest days of currency. The frequency of misprintings and other abnormalities has increased in recent years, due to heavier production and high-speed machinery. This has provided a major sub-hobby for note collectors. Freaks and errors have become very popular, their appeal and prices showing upward movement each year.

On the following pages we have pictured and described most of the more familiar and collectible error notes. Pricing is approximate only because many notes bearing the same general type of error differ in severity of error from one specimen to another. As a general rule, the less glaring or obvious errors carry a smaller premium value. Very valuable error notes include double denominations, or bills having the face of one denomination and reverse side of another.

Error and freak notes do turn up in everyday change. Specimens are located either in that fashion or from bank packs. As far as circulated specimens are concerned, some error notes have passed through so many hands before being noticed that the condition is not up to collector standards. This, of course, results in a very low premium valuation.

Values given below are for the specimens pictured and described. Different premiums may be attached to other specimens with similar errors, or notes showing the same errors but of different denominations.

1. MISMATCHED SERIAL NUMBERS

On ordinary notes, the serial number in the lower left of the obverse matches that in the upper right. When it fails to, even by the difference of a single digit, this is known as a MISMATCHED SERIAL NUMBER. It occurs as the result of a cylinder or cylinders in the high-speed numbering machine becoming jammed. If more than one digit is mismatched, the value will be greater.

	V. FINE	UNC.
☐ $1 Federal Reserve Note, Series 1969, Signatures Elston-Kennedy	45.00	110.00

	V. FINE	UNC.
☐ $1 Silver Certificate, Series 1957B, Signatures Granahan-Dillon	45.00	110.00

	V. FINE	UNC.
☐ $1 Federal Reserve Note, Series 1977A, Signatures Morton-Miller	90.00	215.00

2. INVERTED THIRD PRINT

The inverted third print is also known as Inverted Overprint. The Treasury Seal, District Seal, Serial Numbers and District Number are inverted on the obverse side of the note, or printed upside-down. Caused by the sheet of notes (having already received the primary design on front and back) being fed upside-down into the press for this so-called "third print." (The back design is the "first print," the front is the "second print," and these various additions comprise the "third print." It is not possible to print these "third print" items at the same time as the obverse design, since they are not standard on every bill. At one time the signatures were included in the "third print" but these are now engraved directly into the plate and are part of the "second print.")

Though very spectacular, inverted third print errors are not particularly scarce and are especially plentiful in 1974 and 1976 series notes.

	V. FINE	UNC.
☐ $5 Federal Reserve Note, Series 1974, Signatures Neff-Simon	90.00	160.00

	V. FINE	UNC.
☐ $2 Federal Reserve Note, Series 1976, Signatures Neff-Simon	140.00	450.00

	V. FINE	UNC.
☐ $1 Federal Reserve Note, Series 1974, Signatures Neff-Simon	90.00	215.00

	V. FINE	UNC.
☐ $50 Federal Reserve Note, Series 1977, Signatures Morton-Blumenthal ...	300.00	475.00

	V. FINE	UNC.
☐ $20 Federal Reserve Note, Series 1974, Signatures Neff-Simon	150.00	280.00

	V. FINE	UNC.
☐ $10 Federal Reserve Note, Series 1974, Signatures Neff-Simon	125.00	250.00

3. COMPLETE OFFSET TRANSFER

Offset transfers are not, as is often believed, caused by still-wet printed sheets coming into contact under pressure. Though very slight offsetting can occur in that manner, it would not create notes as spectacular as those pictured here, in which the offset impression is almost as strong as the primary printing. These happen as a result of the printing press being started up an instant or so before the paper is fed in. Instead of contacting the paper, the inked plate makes its impression upon the machine bed. When the paper is then fed through, it picks up this "ghost" impression from the bed, in addition to the primary impression it is supposed to receive. Each successive sheet going through the press will acquire the impression until all ink is totally removed from the machine bed. But, naturally, the first sheet will show the transfer strongest, and the others will be weaker and weaker. Obviously, the market value of such notes depends largely on the strength of the offset impression. The heavier and more noticeable it is, the more valuable the note will be—all other things being equal.

	V. FINE	UNC.
☐ $5 Federal Reserve note, Series 1977, Signatures Morton-Blumenthal. Offset of reverse side of face.		
☐ Dark	60.00	125.00
☐ Light	30.00	70.00

	V. FINE	UNC.
☐ $1 Federal Reserve note, Series 1974, Signatures Neff-Simon. Offset of reverse side of face.		
☐ Dark	80.00	190.00
☐ Light	45.00	90.00

4. PARTIAL OFFSET TRANSFER

The most logical explanation for this error is that a sheet of paper fed into the press incorrectly, became mangled or torn, and part of the inked plate contacted the printing press bed. Therefore wet ink was left on those portions of the press bed not covered by paper. When the next sheet was fed through, it received the correct impression plus it acquired a partial offset transfer by contacting this wet area of the press bed. Just as with #3, the first sheet going through the press following an accident of this kind will receive the strongest transfer, and it will become gradually less noticeable on succeeding sheets.

	V. FINE	UNC.
☐ $1 Federal Reserve Note, Series 1969D, Signatures Banuelos-Schultz. Offset of a portion of reverse side on face.		
☐ Dark	18.00	40.00
☐ Light	15.00	30.00

5. PRINTED FOLD

Notes showing printed folds occur as the result of folds in the paper before printing, which probably happen most often when the sheet is being fed into the press. If the sheet is folded in such a manner that a portion of the reverse side is facing upward, as shown here, it will receive a part of the impression intended for its obverse. Naturally the positioning of these misplaced portions of printing is very random, depending on the nature and size of the fold.

	V. FINE	UNC.
☐ $20 Federal Reserve Note, Series 1977, Signatures Morton-Blumenthal. Federal Reserve district seal and district number printed on reverse	90.00	160.00

6. THIRD PRINT ON REVERSE

The cause of this error is obvious, the sheet having been fed through the press on the wrong side (back instead of front) for the third impression or "third print." In the so-called "third print," the note receives the Treasury and Federal Reserve District seals, district numbers, and serial numbers.

	V. FINE	UNC.
☐ $1 Federal Reserve Note. Third print on reverse	120.00	280.00

7. BOARD BREAKS

The terminology of this error is misleading. It suggests that the fern-like unprinted areas were caused by a broken printing plate. Actually they must have resulted from something, probably linty matter, sticking to the printing ink. The assumption reached by the public, when it encounters such a note, is that the blank streaks were caused by the paper being folded in printing. This, however, is not possible, as that would yield an error of a much different kind (see **PRINTED FOLD**).

It should be pointed out that Board Breaks are easily created by counterfeiters by erasing portions of the printed surface, and that the collector ought to examine such specimens closely.

	V. FINE	UNC.
☐ $20 Federal Reserve Note. Board breaks on reverse	40.00	80.00

8. MISSING SECOND PRINT

The "second print" is the front face, or obverse of the note—the "first" print being the reverse or back. A note with a Missing Second Print has not received the primary impression on its obverse, though the back is normal and the front carries the standard "third print" matter (Treasury seal, serial numbers, etc.). These errors, while they probably occur frequently, are so easily spotted by B.E.P. checkers that such notes are very scarce on the market.

	V. FINE	UNC.
☐ $10 Federal Reserve Note. Missing second print	260.00	675.00

9. PRINTED FOLD

This note was folded nearly in half before receiving the Third Print, which fell across the waste margin on the reverse side. Had the note not been folded, this waste margin would have been removed in the cutting process. This note, when unfolded, is grotesque in shape.

	V. FINE	UNC.
☐ $1 Federal Reserve Note. Printed fold with Federal Reserve District seal, district numbers, and serial numbers on reverse. (Naturally, this note lacks the "third print" matter, such as the Treasury seal, that was supposed to appear on the righthand side of the obverse.)	185.00	375.00

	V. FINE	UNC.

☐ $5 Federal Reserve Note. Printed fold with entire Federal Reserve District seal, portion of another Federal Reserve District seal, and portion of two different serial numbers on the reverse. It may be hard to imagine how a freak of this nature occurs. This note was folded diagonally along a line bisecting the Lincoln Memorial building slightly to the right of center. The lefthand portion of the reverse side was thereby drawn down across the lefthand side of the obverse, extending well below the bottom of the note. It reached far enough down to catch the district seal intended for the note beneath it, as well as a bit of the serial number. This is why the two serial numbers are different; they were supposed to go on two different notes. Obviously, when something this dramatic happens in printing, not only one error note is created but several—at least—at the same time. Not all necessarily reach circulation, however 200.00   475.00

10. THIRD PRINT BLACK INK MISSING OR LIGHT

Though the machinery used is ultra-modern, U.S. currency notes are printed by the same basic technique used when printing was first invented more than 500 years ago. Ink is spread on the metal plates and these are pressed on the sheets as they go through the press. Because the inking is manually fed (as is the paper), an even flow is usually achieved. When an under-inked note is found, it is generally merely "light," giving a faded appearance. But sometimes the plate will be very improperly inked, due to mechanical misfunction or some other cause, resulting in whole areas being unprinted or so lightly printed that they cannot be seen without close inspection. These are not especially valuable notes but counterfeit specimens are frequently made.

	V. FINE	UNC.

☐ $1 Federal Reserve Note, Series 1977, Signatures of Morton-Blumenthal. Federal Reserve district seal and district numbers missing from lefthand side, remainder of "third print" material light but distinct. If the lefthand serial number was strong, there might be suspicion of this being a counterfeit 25.00 50.00

11. THIRD PRINT GREEN INK MISSING OR LIGHT

In this case, the green rather than the black ink was applied too lightly to the printing plate.

	V. FINE	UNC.

☐ $5 Federal Reserve Note, Series 1977, Signatures of Morton-Blumenthal .. 25.00 45.00

12. NOTE FOLDED DURING OVERPRINT

This note was folded as it was being overprinted and failed to receive the district seal and district numbers at the left side of its obverse. This kind of error, like all involving missing portions of printing, has been extensively counterfeited.

	V. FINE	UNC.
☐ $2 Federal Reserve Note, Series 1976, Signatures of Neff-Simon	30.00	70.00

13. FAULTY ALIGNMENT

Notes of this kind were formerly called "miscut," and sometimes still are. "Faulty alignment" is a more inclusive term which encompasses not only bad cutting but accidents in printing. If the sheet shifts around in the press, it will not receive the printed impressions exactly where they should be. Even if the cutting is normal, the resulting note will be misaligned; the cutting machine cannot correct botched printing. It is very easy to determine where the fault lies. If one side of the note has its design higher than the opposite side, this is a printing error. If the misalignment occurs equally on both sides, the problem was in cutting. Since the two sides are not printed in the same operation, it would be a one-in-a-million chance for them to become equally misaligned.

The value of such notes depends upon the degree of misalignment. Collectors are especially fond of specimens showing a portion—even if very slight, as with the one pictured of an adjoining note.

	V. FINE	UNC.
☐ $5 Federal Reserve Note. Bottom left of reverse shaved (or "bled"), corresponding portion of adjoining note just visible at top. This ranks as a "dramatic" specimen.		
☐ Slight	16.00	37.00
☐ Dramatic	37.00	160.00

14. INSUFFICIENT PRESSURE

Under-inking of the printing plate is not the only cause of weak or partially missing impressions. If the press is not operating correctly and the inked plate meets the sheet with insufficient pressure, the result is similar to under-inking. This probably happens as a result of a sheet going through just as the press is being turned off for the day, or at other intervals. Supposedly all action ceases at the instant of turn-off, but considering the rapidity of this operation, it is likely that a random sheet could pass through and be insufficiently impressed. The note pictured here received normal "third prints," as is generally the case with notes whose first or second print is made with insufficient pressure.

	V. FINE	UNC.
☐ $20 Federal Reserve Note, Series 1977, Signatures of Morton-Blumenthal	80.00	150.00

15. PRINTED FOLD

This note, along with a large portion of the adjoining note, became folded after the second print. When it passed through the press to receive the third print or overprints (seals, serial numbers, etc.), these naturally failed to appear on the folded area.

	V. FINE	UNC.
☐ $1 Federal Reserve Note. Printed fold with overprints partially missing.		
☐ Small	30.00	87.00
☐ Large	95.00	260.00

16. DOUBLE IMPRESSION

Double impressions have traditionally been traced to the sheet of notes passing through the press twice, which would be the logical explanation. However, in considering the method by which currency is printed, it would seem more likely that double impression notes have not made two trips through the press. They probably result from the automatic paper feed jamming. The sheet just printed fails to be ejected, and the printing plate falls upon it a second time instead of on a fresh sheet. This does not merely create a strong impression, but a twin, or ghost impression, since the sheet is not positioned exactly the same way for the second strike. Though the paper feed may not be operating properly, there will still be some slight movement—enough to prevent the second impression from falling directly atop the first.

	V. FINE	UNC.
☐ $1 Federal Reserve Note, Series 1977A, Signatures of Morton-Miller. Double "second print" impression.		
☐ Partial	150.00	275.00
☐ Complete	400.00	1350.00

17. DOUBLE IMPRESSION OF OVERPRINTS ("DOUBLE THIRD PRINT")

This note is normal as far as the primary obverse and reverse printings are concerned. It received twin impressions of the overprints or "third print." This was not caused by jamming of the paper feed as discussed above. Naturally, the serial numbers are different, as the automatic numbering machine turns with every rise and fall of the press.

	V. FINE	UNC.
☐ $20 Federal Reserve Note, Series 1950. Signatures of Priest-Humphrey. Double impression of overprints.		
☐ Partial	125.00	370.00
☐ Complete	280.00	750.00

18. THIRD PRINT (OR OVERPRINTS) SHIFTED

Whenever the overprints (serial number, seals, etc.) are out of position, vertically or horizontally, this is known as "third print shifted" or "overprints shifted." In the example pictured, shifting is extreme. This is a premium value specimen which would command the higher of the two sums quoted. Normally, the overprinting on a "shifted" note fails to touch the portrait, or touches it only slightly. The cause of this kind of error is a sheet feeding incorrectly into the press for the overprinting operation. As striking and desirable as these notes are to collectors, they often go unnoticed by the public.

	V. FINE	UNC.
☐ $100 Federal Reserve Note, Series 1969C, Signatures of Banuelos-Schultz. Third print shifted.		
☐ Slight	150.00	195.00
☐ Dramatic	190.00	310.00

19. INK SMEARS

Ink smearing is one of the more common abnormalities of currency notes. Generally it can be attributed to malfunction of the automatic inking device which inks the printing plate. When performing properly, ink is applied at a steady, controlled pace to the printing plate. A very minor disorder in the machine can dispense enough extra ink to yield very spectacular "smeared notes," such as the one illustrated. The value of ink smear notes depends upon the area and intensity of the smear. They are quite easily faked, so the buyer should be cautious.

	V. FINE	UNC.
☐ $1 Federal Reserve Note. Ink smear.		
☐ Small	15.00	27.00
☐ Large	32.00	60.00

20. PRINTING FOLD

This note was crumpled along the right side prior to the third printing or application of overprints. Hence the "third print" matter on the lefthand side is normal, but portions of the overprint on the right appear on the note's reverse side.

	V. FINE	UNC.
☐ $20 Federal Reserve Note, Series 1977, Signatures Morton-Blumenthal ...	80.00	170.00

21. BLANK CREASE

It occasionally happens that a note becomes creased prior to the reverse or obverse printing, in such a way that a small fold is created. During the printing procedure this fold hides a portion of the note's surface, which fails to receive the impression. These notes are actually double errors—the cutting machine cuts them without knowledge of the fold, and when the fold is opened out the bill is then of larger than normal size. Since "crease errors" are difficult to spot in the B.E.P.'s checking, they find their way into circulation in rather sizable numbers. It is difficult to place standard values on them because the price depends on the exact nature of the specimen. The wider the crease, the more valuable the note will be. Premium values are attached to notes with multiple creases that cause the blank unprinted area to fall across the portrait.

	V. FINE	UNC.
☐ Blank crease note, any denomination. Value stated is collector premium over and above face value (if note has additional value because of series, signatures, etc., this too must be added).		
☐ Single crease	12.00	25.00
☐ Multiple crease	22.00	42.00

22. MIXED DENOMINATION

The two notes pictured are normal in themselves, and if they were not owned together as a set, no premium value would be attached to them. The error (which may be dubious to term as such) lies with their serial numbers. The $5 note has a serial number one digit higher than the $1, suggesting that it was fed into the printing machine intended to print overprints (or "third prints") on $1 bills. Even when this does happen (probably infrequently), it is very difficult to obtain "matching" notes of the kind illustrated, in which the serial numbers are only a single digit apart. Even if you had a $5 note and $1 note (or other combination of denominations) from sheets that were fed one after the other, the odds on getting one-digit-apart serial numbers are extremely small.

The value is given for an uncirculated set only, as there would be no possibility of finding such matched notes except in a bank pack. Once released into circulation, they can never again be mated.

UNC.

☐ Mixed denomination pair from bank pack, $5 Federal Reserve Note within pack of $1
Federal Reserve notes 2600.00

23. BLANK REVERSE

U.S. currency has its reverse printed before the obverse—in other words, back before front. The only logical explanation for blank reverse notes is that blank paper found its way into the batch of sheets on which reverses had already been printed. They were then fed—without detection—into the press for application of the obverse. They continued to escape notice during printing of the overprints, and miraculously got into circulation.

	V. FINE	UNC.
☐ $100 Federal Reserve Note. Blank reverse	210.00	420.00

	V. FINE	UNC.
☐ $20 Federal Reserve Note, Series 1977, Signatures of Morton-Blumenthal. Blank reverse	110.00	280.00

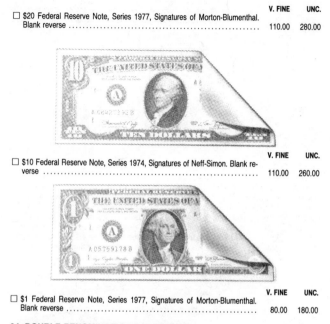

	V. FINE	UNC.
☐ $10 Federal Reserve Note, Series 1974, Signatures of Neff-Simon. Blank reverse	110.00	260.00

	V. FINE	UNC.
☐ $1 Federal Reserve Note, Series 1977, Signatures of Morton-Blumenthal. Blank reverse	80.00	180.00

24. DOUBLE DENOMINATION COUNTERFEIT

This is a counterfeit or faked error. We include it to show the kind of work done by counterfeiters, and how such items can be made to resemble genuine errors. This happens to be a counterfeit of an error note that cannot exist in its genuine state. Thus, there can be no hesitancy in proclaiming it a fake. Anyone who is even slightly familiar with the way currency is printed should instantly recognize this item as a fraud. Nevertheless, fakers succeed in selling (often at high prices) specimens of this kind, probably because some collectors want the impossible for their albums. Genuine double or twin denomination notes have the obverse of one denomination and the reverse of a different denomination. They do not consist of two obverses or two reverses, such as the one pictured. The note illustrated carries four serial numbers. For it to be genuine, it would have had to pass through the "third print" (overprinting) process twice. Obviously it was made by gluing a

$1 and $5 note together. Much more deceptive paste-ups are created with the notes correctly paired so that the obverse of one and reverse of the other shows. Beware!

25. INVERTED OBVERSE

U.S. currency is printed reverse first. Therefore, when the back and front do not face in the same vertical direction (as they should), the note is known as an IN-VERTED OBVERSE. The term ''inverted reverse'' is never used. This, of course, results from the sheet being fed through upside-down for the obverse or second print. Though these specimens are scarce in uncirculated condition, they often pass through many hands in circulation before being spotted. The uninformed public is not even aware that a note with faces in opposite directions is an error and has premium value.

	V. FINE	UNC.
☐ $2 Federal Reserve Note, Series 1976, Signatures of Neff-Simon. Inverted obverse	160.00	350.00

26. MISSING THIRD PRINT

Also known as missing overprint. Note released into circulation without having gone through the ''third print'' operation.

	V. FINE	UNC.
☐ $1 Federal Reserve Note, Series 1977, Signatures Morton-Blumenthal. Missing third print	120.00	260.00

27. FOREIGN MATTER ON OBVERSE

Sometimes foreign matter, usually paper scraps of one kind or another, gets between the printing plate and the sheet. This naturally results in the area covered being blank on the note. Because of the extreme pressure exerted in printing, the foreign matter is occasionally "glued" to the note and travels with it into circulation. If the appendage is paper, it will normally be found to be of the same stock from which the note is made—apparently a shred from one of the sheet margins that worked its way into a batch of sheets awaiting printing. The value of such notes varies greatly, depending on the size of the foreign matter and its placement. It's rare to find notes in which foreign matter became attached before the first or second print. Nearly always, they found their way to the note after the second print and before the third.

	V. FINE	UNC.
☐ $1 Federal Reserve Note, Series 1974, Signatures Neff-Simon. Foreign matter on obverse	90.00	160.00

	V. FINE	UNC.
☐ $1 Silver Certificate, Series 1935E. Signatures of Priest-Humphrey. Foreign matter on obverse. More valuable than the preceding because of the note's age and the foreign matter being larger	250.00	625.00

28. MISSING PORTION OF REVERSE DESIGN
(DUE TO ADHERENCE OF SCRAP PAPER)

In this instance, the foreign matter got in the way of the first print, or reverse printing. It prevented the covered area from being printed, but it later became dislodged and is no longer present. What appears on the illustration to be a strip of paper on the note is really the blank unprinted area once covered by the strip. Obviously a note that merely had a random strip of paper attached, over a normally printed design, would have no collector interest.

	V. FINE	UNC.
☐ $1 Federal Reserve Note. Missing portion of reverse design due to adherence of scrap paper	65.00	125.00

29. OVERPRINT PARTIALLY MISSING

The overprint or third print on this note is normal on the righthand side and missing entirely on the left. This was caused by the note being folded (more or less in half, vertically) immediately before overprinting. Had the lefthand side been folded over the face, this would have interfered with the overprints on the righthand side. Instead, this specimen was folded over the reverse side, or downward, with the result that the missing portion of overprint did not strike the note at all—it simply hit the printing press bed. The reverse side of this note is normal.

	V. FINE	UNC.
☐ $1 Federal Reserve Note, Series 1963A. Overprint partially missing	45.00	90.00

30. THIRD PRINT OFFSET ON REVERSE

This note is normal on the obverse but carries an "offset" of the third print or overprints on its reverse. It would appear that the overprints are showing through to the reverse, as if the note were printed on very thin paper. Actually, this "mirror image" is caused by a malfunction in the printing or paper-feeding machinery. The inked plate for printing the overprints contacted the machine bed without a sheet of paper being in place. Therefore, as the next sheet came through it received the normal overprint on its face and picked up the offset impression on its reverse from the machine bed. Each successive sheet going through the press also received an offset, but it naturally became fainter and fainter as the ink was absorbed. The value of a note of this kind depends on the intensity of the impression.

	V. FINE	UNC.
☐ $5 Federal Reserve Note. Offset impression of overprints on reverse	160.00	410.00

CONFEDERATE MONEY

The Civil War Centennial of 1961–65 has generally been credited with sparking an interest in the collecting and study of Confederate or C.S.A. notes. This, however, is not totally borne out by facts, as C.S.A. currency had advanced steadily in value since the 1940's. It rides a crest of popularity today surpassing the early 1960's. This is due in part to the exhaustive research carried out since that time and numerous books and articles published. Even today, some C.S.A. notes would still appear to be undervalued based on their availability vs. regular U.S. issues.

History. It became apparent upon the outbreak of the Civil War that both sides would experience extreme coinage shortages and each took to the printing of notes that could be exchanged in lieu of bullion or "real money" (which always meant coined money until the 1860's). The South suffered more serious difficulties than the North, as it did not have as many skilled printers or engravers at its command. Also, with the war being fought on its territory rather than the North's, there was an ever-present danger of sabotage to plants printing money or engaging in related activities. The Confederacy tried by all available means to satisfy the currency demand, and succeeded in distributing quite a large quantity of notes. Its shortage was taken up by notes issued by private banks, individual states, counties, railroads, and private merchants. Merchant tokens, to take the place of rapidly disappearing small change, poured forth in abundance during this period. All told, the Confederate Congress authorized the printing of about one and a half billion dollars worth of paper currency. It is impossible to determine the total actually produced but it would appear that this figure was far surpassed. At the war's conclusion, these notes were worthless as the C.S.A. no longer existed and the federal government refused to redeem them. Many were discarded as scrap but a surprising number were held faithfully by their owners, who believed "the South will rise again." The South did indeed rise, industrially and economically, and those old C.S.A. notes rose too. They still aren't spendable but many are worth sums in excess of face value as collectors' pieces. Until about 1900, however, practically no value was placed on Confederate currency—even by collectors.

Designs. Some surprising designs will be observed, including mythological gods and goddesses that seem to relate very little to the Southern artistic or cultural climate of the 1860's. Many scholarly efforts have been made to explain away the use of such motifs but the simple fact is that they appeared not so much by choice as necessity. Southern printers, not having the facilities of their Northern counterparts, were compelled to make do with whatever engravings or "stock cuts" were already on hand, as inappropriate as they might have proved. However, a number of original designs were created reflecting unmistakably regional themes and at times picturing heros or leaders of the Confederacy. Slaves at labor, used as a symbol of the South's economic strength and its supposed advantage over the North, where labor was hired, was a frequent motif. Sailors were also depicted, as well as railroad trains and anything else that appeared symbolic of Southern industry. Probably the most notable single design, not intended to carry the satirical overtones it now possesses, is "General Francis Marion's Sweet Potato Breakfast" on the $10 1861 issue note. In general, the C.S.A. notes are not so badly designed a group as might be anticipated in light of conditions. The designing, was in fact, several leagues improved over the printing, which often left much to be desired. George Washington is depicted—not for being the first U.S. President but as a native son of Virginia. Jefferson Davis, President of the C.S.A., is among the more common portraits. He became even more disliked in the North than he otherwise might have been, because of his picture turning up on currency. But after the war he took a moderate stand and erased the old ill feelings; he even had words of praise for Lincoln. Other individuals whose portraits (not necessarily very faithful) will be encountered are:

John C. Calhoun, U.S. Senator who led the battle for slavery and Southern Rights (later called "states rights").

Alexander H. Stephen, Davis' Vice-President of the C.S.A.

Judah P. Benjamin, holder of various official titles in the Southern government.

C. G. Memminger, Secretary of the Treasury and Secretary of War.

Lucy Pickens, wife of South Carolina's governor and the only woman (aside from mythological types) shown on C.S.A. currency.

John E. Ward.

R. M. T. Hunter.

Printers. The study of printers of C.S.A. notes is complex, made no less so by the fact that some contractors produced only plates, others did only printing (from plates procured elsewhere), while some did both. The principal Southern printer was the lithography firm of Hoyer & Ludwig of Richmond, Virginia. Also located at Richmond were Keatinge & Ball, which did commendable, if not exactly inspired, work, and B. Duncan, who also worked at Columbia, South Carolina. Another firm involved in quite a bit of note printing was J. T. Paterson of Columbia. The so-called "Southern Bank Note Company" was a fictitious name used to disguise the origin of notes prepared in the North. Some early notes were marked "National Bank Note Co., New York," but it was subsequently decided to remove correct identification from the notes of this printer, undoubtedly on the latter's request (fearing prosecution for aiding the enemy).

Cancellations. Two varieties of cancels are commonly found on C.S.A. notes. First is the cut cancel (CC), in which a knife or similar instrument has been used to make piercings in a design or pattern. Unless roughly executed, such cuts do not materially reduce a specimen's value. In the case of some notes, examples without cancellation are almost impossible to find. The COC or Cut-Out Cancel is more objectionable because, instead of merely leaving slits, a portion of the paper was removed. The reduction of value for a Cut-Out Cancel averages around 25 percent. These are considered "space fillers" if the issue is fairly common, but a rare note with a COC may be very desirable. Pen Cancellations (PC) are far less frequently encountered. These show the word "Canceled" written out by hand across the note's face, in ink. Unless the ink is heavy or blotchy, a pen cancel will not have too much bearing on value. As the note is not physically injured, it would seem to be the least offensive of the three varieties. Whenever a note is being sold, presence of a cancel, of whatever type, should be plainly spelled out. Some collectors are not interested in canceled specimens. In time, as the scarce issues become even scarcer, they will probably have to be accepted as a fact of life.

Signatures. There are so many signature combinations on C.S.A. notes that utter confusion would await anyone attempting to collect them on this basis. The names are unknown and in most instances difficult to trace, representing not government officials but employees authorized to sign for the Treasurer and Registrar of the Treasury. Only the first six notes bear the actual signatures of these officials.

Condition Grades. While condition standards are basically the same for Confederate currency as other notes of their age, some allowance must be made for paper quality and deficiencies in printing and cutting. These matters have nothing to do with the preservation or wear and can be observed just as frequently in uncirculated specimens as those in average condition. Without a source of good paper, printers were obliged to use whatever was most easily and quickly obtainable. Often the paper was thin, or stiff, or contained networks of minute wrinkles which interfered with printing. Cutting was generally not done by machine, as in the North, but by hand with a pair of scissors—workers actually took the sheets and cut apart notes individually. When paper-cutting devices were employed, they were apparently not of the best quality. In any case, regular edges on C.S.A. notes are uncommon and their absence does not constitute grounds for classifying an otherwise perfect specimen in a condition grade below Uncirculated. When the occasional gem is located—a well-printed, well preserved note on good paper, decently cut—its value is sure to be higher than those listed. The collector is not advised to confine himself to such specimens, as his activities would become seriously limited.

UNCIRCULATED—UNC. An uncirculated note shows no evidence of handling and is as close to "new condition," as possible. An uncirculated specimen may, however, have pinholes or a finger smudge, which should be mentioned in a sales offering. If these are readily noticeable, the note deserves to be classified as "almost uncirculated." Crispness is hardly a criterion of uncirculation as this quality is expected in notes graded as low as Very Fine.

ALMOST UNCIRCULATED—A.U. Similar to the above grade, but not quite as good as an uncirculated specimen. The note bears no indication of having actually circulated but has minor flaws resulting from accident or mishandling, such as individuals counting crinkles.

EXTREMELY FINE—X.F. An X.F. note is on the borderline between uncirculated and circulated. It has not been heavily handled but may reveal several imperfections: a pinhole, finger smudge, counting crinkles, or a light wallet fold. The fold is not so heavy as to be termed a crease.

VERY FINE—V.F. Has been in circulation but is not worn or seriously creased. It must still be clean and crisp, without stains or tears. Fine to Very Fine condition is considered the equivalent of "average circulated" but not "average condition" (which is another term for poor).

FINE—F. A note that has been in circulation and shows it, but has no physical injuries or just slight ones.

VERY GOOD—V.G. A well-circulated note bearing evidence of numerous foldings. It may possibly have creased corners and wrinkles as well as light staining, smudging, or pinholes, but major defects (such as a missing corner) would place it into an even lower category.

GOOD—G. Good notes heavily circulated, worn, possibly stained or scribbled on edges could be frayed or "dog-eared." There may be holes larger than pin punctures, but not on the central portion of design. This is the lowest grade of condition acceptable to a collector, and only when nothing better is available. Unless very rare, such specimens are considered space-fillers only.

A.B.P.—AVERAGE BUYING PRICES. The average buying prices given here are the approximate sums paid by retail dealers for specimens in good condition. As selling prices vary, so do buying prices, and in fact they usually vary a bit more. A dealer who is overstocked on a certain note is sure to offer less than one who has no specimens on hand. The dealer's location, size of operation, and other circumstances will also influence the buying price. We present these figures merely as approximate guides to what sellers should expect.

CONFEDERATE STATES OF AMERICA—1861 ISSUE
MONTGOMERY, ALABAMA
$1,000,000 Authorized by "Act of March 9th." Written Dates "1861."
"NATIONAL BANK NOTE CO., NY"

T1

Face Design: Green and black, bears "Interest Ten Cents Per Day," 607 issued. John C. Calhoun left, Andrew Jackson right.

CRISWELL	NOTE		A.B.P.	GOOD	UNC.
☐ 1	$1000	....	1600.00	2650.00	10,000.00

"NATIONAL BANK NOTE CO., NY"

T2

Face Design: Green and black, bears "Interest Five Cents Per Day," 607 issued. Cattle crossing a brook.

CRISWELL	NOTE		A.B.P.	GOOD	UNC.
☐ 2	$500	....	1600.00	2700.00	10,000.00

CONFEDERATE STATES OF AMERICA—1861 ISSUE
"NATIONAL BANK NOTE CO., NY"

T3

Face Design: Green and black, bears "Interest One Cent Per Day." Railway train, Minerva left.

CRISWELL	NOTE		A.B.P.	GOOD	UNC.
☐ 3	$100	....	900.00	1600.00	2750.00

"NATIONAL BANK NOTE CO., NY"

T4

Face Design: Green and black, bears "Interest Half A Cent Per Day." Negroes hoeing cotton.

CRISWELL	NOTE		A.B.P.	GOOD	UNC.
☐ 4	$50	....	700.00	1300.00	2200.00

CONFEDERATE STATES OF AMERICA—1861 ISSUE
"AMERICAN BANK NOTE CO., NY"
(Though ostensibly by the "SOUTHERN BANK NOTE CO.")

T5

Face Design: Green and black, red fibre paper, bears "Interest One Cent Per Day." Railway train, Justice left and Minerva right.

CRISWELL	NOTE		A.B.P.	GOOD	UNC.
☐ 5	$100	....	80.00	180.00	500.00

T6

Face Design: Green and black, red fibre paper, bears "Interest Half A Cent Per Day." Pallas and Ceres seated on bale of cotton, Washington at right.

CRISWELL	NOTE		A.B.P.	GOOD	UNC.
☐ 6	$50	....	70.00	130.00	450.00

CONFEDERATE STATES OF AMERICA—1861 ISSUE
$20,000,000 Authorized by "Act of May 16th, 1861"
"HOYER & LUDWIG, RICHMOND, VA"
(All Lithographic Date "July 25th, 1861")

T7

Face Design: Ceres and Proserpina flying, Washington left.

CRISWELL	NOTE	A.B.P.	GOOD	UNC.
☐ 7–13	$100	80.00	165.00	480.00

T8

Face Design: Washington, Tellus left.

CRISWELL	NOTE	A.B.P.	GOOD	UNC.
☐ 14–22	$50	20.00	32.00	70.00

CONFEDERATE STATES OF AMERICA—1861 ISSUE

Face Design: Exists in a variety of colors.

CRISWELL	NOTE	A.B.P.	GOOD	UNC.
☐ 21	$20	20.00	38.00	80.00

NOTE: The above type notes were bogus. For years it was thought they were a regular Confederate issue, and evidence exists that they were circulated as such. No collection of Confederate notes is complete without one. There is no evidence as to who the printer was, but the authors have reason to believe he was located somewhere in Ohio. It is not a product of S. C. Upham, of Philadelphia, the well-known counterfeiter of Confederate notes.

T9

Face Design: Large sailing vessel, "20" at left.

CRISWELL	NOTE	A.B.P.	GOOD	UNC.
☐ 23–33	$20	12.00	25.00	70.00

CONFEDERATE STATES OF AMERICA—1861 ISSUE

T10

Face Design: Liberty seated by Eagle, with shield and flag.

NOTE: There are at least 42 minor varieties of this note, including a supposed 10 or 11 stars on shield. Usually the stars are so indistinct that a note may show from six to 15 stars. The other differences are minute changes in the size of the "10" in the upper corners. We list only the major type.

CRISWELL	NOTE	A.B.P.	GOOD	UNC.
☐ 34–40	$10	22.00	65.00	450.00

T11

Face Design: Liberty seated by Eagle, sailor left.

CRISWELL	NOTE	A.B.P.	GOOD	UNC.
☐ 42–44	$5....................................	110.00	610.00	9500.00

CONFEDERATE STATES OF AMERICA—1861 ISSUE
"J. MANOUVRIER, NEW ORLEANS"
(Written Date "July 25th, 1861")

T12

Face Design: "Confederate States of America" in blue on blue reverse.

CRISWELL	NOTE	A.B.P.	GOOD	UNC.
☐ 46–49	$5	180.00	1850.00	5200.00

$100,000,000 authorized by "Act of Aug. 19th, 1861."
$50,000,000 authorized by "Act of Dec. 24th, 1861."

"HOYER & LUDWIG, RICHMOND, VA"
(Lithographic Date, "September 2nd, 2d, & s, 1861")

T13

Face Design: Negroes loading cotton, sailor left.

CRISWELL	NOTE	A.B.P.	GOOD	UNC.
☐ 50–58	$100	12.00	20.00	60.00

CONFEDERATE STATES OF AMERICA—1861 ISSUE

T14

Face Design: Moneta seated by treasure chests, sailor left.

CRISWELL	NOTE	A.B.P.	GOOD	UNC.
☐ 59–78	$50	9.00	14.00	40.00

"SOUTHERN BANK NOTE CO., NEW ORLEANS"

T15

Face Design: Black and red on red fibre paper. Railway train, Justice right, Hope with anchor left.

CRISWELL	NOTE	A.B.P.	GOOD	UNC.
☐ 79	$50	220.00	520.00	3300.00

CONFEDERATE STATES OF AMERICA—1861 ISSUE
"KEATINGE & BALL, RICHMOND, VA"

T16

Face Design: Black and green, red fibre paper. Portrait of Jefferson Davis.

CRISWELL	NOTE	A.B.P.	GOOD	UNC.
☐ 80–94	$50	11.00	22.00	180.00

"HOYER & LUDWIG, RICHMOND, VA"

T17

Face Design: Black with green ornamentation, plain paper. Ceres seated between Commerce and Navigation, Liberty left.

CRISWELL	NOTE	A.B.P.	GOOD	UNC.
☐ 99–100	$20	42.00	85.00	475.00

CONFEDERATE STATES OF AMERICA—1861 ISSUE
"HOYER & LUDWIG, RICHMOND, VA"

T18

Face Design: Large sailing vessel, sailor at capstan left.

CRISWELL	NOTE		A.B.P.	GOOD	UNC.
☐ 101–136	$20	....	5.00	11.00	30.00

"SOUTHERN BANK NOTE CO., NEW ORLEANS"

T19

Face Design: Black and red on red fibre paper. Navigator seated by charts, Minerva left, blacksmith right.

CRISWELL	NOTE		A.B.P.	GOOD	UNC.
☐ 137	$20	....	130.00	525.00	2200.00

CONFEDERATE STATES OF AMERICA—1861 ISSUE

T20

Face Design: Industry seated between cupid and beehive, bust of A. H. Stevens left.

PRINTED BY "B. DUNCAN, COLUMBIA, SC"

CRISWELL	NOTE	A.B.P.	GOOD	UNC.
☐ 139–140	$20	4.00	10.00	45.00

PRINTED BY "B. DUNCAN, RICHMOND, VA"

CRISWELL	NOTE	A.B.P.	GOOD	UNC.
☐ 141–143	$20	4.00	9.00	45.00

"KEATINGE & BALL, COLUMBIA, SC"

T21

Face Design: Portrait of Alexander H. Stephens.

YELLOW-GREEN ORNAMENTATION

CRISWELL	NOTE	A.B.P.	GOOD	UNC.
☐ 144	$20	11.00	38.00	215.00

DARK-GREEN ORNAMENTATION

CRISWELL	NOTE	A.B.P.	GOOD	UNC.
☐ 145–149	$20	11.00	34.00	215.00

CONFEDERATE STATES OF AMERICA—1861 ISSUE
"SOUTHERN BANK NOTE CO., NEW ORLEANS"

T22

Face Design: Black and red, red fibre paper. Group of Indians, Thetis left, maiden with "X" at right.

CRISWELL	NOTE		A.B.P.	GOOD	UNC.
☐ 150–152	$10.00		60.00	12.00	385.00

"LEGGETT, KEATINGE & BALL, RICHMOND, VA"

T23

Face Design: Black and orange red. Wagonload of cotton, harvesting sugar cane right. John E. Ward left.

CRISWELL	NOTE		A.B.P.	GOOD	UNC.
☐ 153–155	$10		80.00	160.00	825.00

CONFEDERATE STATES OF AMERICA—1861 ISSUE
"LEGGETT, KEATINGE & BALL, RICHMOND, VA"

T24

Face Design: Black and orange red. R. M. T. Hunter left, vignette of child right.

CRISWELL	NOTE	A.B.P.	GOOD	UNC.
☐ 156–160	$10	12.00	34.00	185.00

"KEATINGE & BALL, RICHMOND, VA"

CRISWELL	NOTE	A.B.P.	GOOD	UNC.
☐ 161–167	$10.00	12.00	34.00	165.00

"KEATINGE & BALL, RICHMOND, VA"

T25

Face Design: Hope with anchor, R. M. T. Hunter left, C. G. Memminger, right.

CRISWELL	NOTE	A.B.P.	GOOD	UNC.
☐ 168–171	$10.00	10.00	22.00	170.00

CONFEDERATE STATES OF AMERICA—1861 ISSUE
"KEATINGE & BALL, RICHMOND, VA"

T26

Face Design: Hope with anchor, R. M. T. Hunter left, C. G. Memminger, right.

NOTE: There are three types of red "X" and "X" overprints. That section of the note on which the overprints appear is illustrated in double size.

Face Design: Solid red "X" and "X" overprint.

CRISWELL	NOTE	A.B.P.	GOOD	UNC.
☐ 173–188	$10.00	13.00	26.00	170.00

Face Design: Coarse lace "X" and "X" red overprint.

CRISWELL	NOTE	A.B.P.	GOOD	UNC.
☐ 189–210	$10.00	11.00	28.00	160.00

CONFEDERATE STATES OF AMERICA—1861 ISSUE

Face Design: Fine lace "X" and "X" red overprint.

CRISWELL	NOTE	A.B.P.	GOOD	UNC.
☐ 211–220	$10	12.00	22.00	160.00

T27

Face Design: Liberty seated by shield and eagle.

CRISWELL	NOTE	A.B.P.	GOOD	UNC.
☐ 221–229	$10	660.00	1100.00	V. RARE

CONFEDERATE STATES OF AMERICA—1861 ISSUE
"HOYER & LUDWIG, RICHMOND, VA"

T28

Face Design: Ceres and Commerce with an urn.

CRISWELL	NOTE		A.B.P.	GOOD	UNC.
☐ 230–234	$10		5.00	11.00	60.00

"J. T. PATERSON, COLUMBIA, SC"

CRISWELL	NOTE		A.B.P.	GOOD	UNC.
☐ 235–236	$10		5.00	11.00	75.00

"B. DUNCAN, RICHMOND, VA"

T29

Face Design: Negro picking cotton.

CRISWELL	NOTE		A.B.P.	GOOD	UNC.
☐ 237	$10		13.00	26.00	180.00

CONFEDERATE STATES OF AMERICA—1861 ISSUE
"B. DUNCAN, COLUMBIA, SC"

T30

Face Design: Gen. Francis Marion's "Sweet Potato Dinner." R. M. T. Hunter left, Minerva right.

CRISWELL	NOTE	A.B.P.	GOOD	UNC.
☐ 238	$10	5.00	11.00	65.00

NO ENGRAVER'S NAME

CRISWELL	NOTE	A.B.P.	GOOD	UNC.
☐ 239–241	$10	5.00	11.00	65.00

"SOUTHERN BANK NOTE CO., NEW ORLEANS"

T31

Face Design: Black and red on red fibre paper. Minerva left, Agriculture, Commerce, Industry, Justice and Liberty seated at center, statue of Washington right.

CRISWELL	NOTE	A.B.P.	GOOD	UNC.
☐ 243–245	$5	40.00	80.00	330.00

CONFEDERATE STATES OF AMERICA—1861 ISSUE
"LEGGETT, KEATINGE & BALL, RICHMOND, VA"

T32

Face Design: Black and orange red. Machinist with hammer, boy in oval left.

CRISWELL	NOTE	A.B.P.	GOOD	UNC.
☐ 246–249	$5	65.00	145.00	760.00

"LEGGETT, KEATINGE & BALL, RICHMOND, VA"

T33

Face Design: Black and white note with blue-green ornamentation. C. G. Memminger, Minerva right.

CRISWELL	NOTE	A.B.P.	GOOD	UNC.
☐ 250–253	$5	6.00	11.00	115.00

"KEATINGE & BALL, RICHMOND, VA"

CRISWELL	NOTE	A.B.P.	GOOD	UNC.
☐ 254–257	$5	8.00	22.00	140.00

NO ENGRAVER'S NAME

CRISWELL	NOTE	A.B.P.	GOOD	UNC.
☐ 258–261	$5	8.00	17.00	145.00

CONFEDERATE STATES OF AMERICA—1861 ISSUE
"KEATINGE & BALL, RICHMOND, VA"

T34

Face Design: C. G. Memminger, Minerva right.

CRISWELL	NOTE	A.B.P.	GOOD	UNC.
☐ 262–270	$5	9.00	22.00	130.00

"PRINTED BY HOYER & LUDWIG, RICHMOND, VA"

T35

Face Design: Loading cotton left, "Indian Princess" right.

CRISWELL	NOTE	A.B.P.	GOOD	UNC.
☐ 271	$5	825.00	1600.00	V. RARE

CONFEDERATE STATES OF AMERICA—1861 ISSUE
"HOYER & LUDWIG, RICHMOND, VA"

T36

Face Design: Ceres seated on bale of cotton, sailor left.

CRISWELL	NOTE	A.B.P.	GOOD	UNC.
☐ 272	$5	5.00	10.00	55.00

"J. T. PATERSON & CO., COLUMBIA, SC"

CRISWELL	NOTE	A.B.P.	GOOD	UNC.
☐ 274	$5	5.00	11.00	40.00

"J. T. PATERSON & CO., COLUMBIA, SC"

CRISWELL	NOTE	A.B.P.	GOOD	UNC.
☐ 276–282	$5	5.00	11.00	45.00

CONFEDERATE STATES OF AMERICA—1861 ISSUE
"B. DUNCAN, RICHMOND, VA"

T37

Face Design: Sailor seated beside bales of cotton, C. G. Memminger left, Justice and Ceres right.

CRISWELL	NOTE	A.B.P.	GOOD	UNC.
☐ 284	$5	8.50	21.00	77.00

"B. DUNCAN, COLUMBIA, SC"

CRISWELL	NOTE	A.B.P.	GOOD	UNC.
☐ 285	$5	5.50	11.00	55.00

"B. DUNCAN, COLUMBIA, SC"

T38

Face Design: Personification of South striking down Union, J. P. Benjamin left.

NOTE: Dated "September 2, 1861," through an error. No Confederate note less than $5 was authorized in 1861.

CRISWELL	NOTE	A.B.P.	GOOD	UNC.
☐ 286	$2	76.00	260.00	V. RARE

Col. Grover C. Criswell

Known as the *"Richest Man in the World in Confederate Money,"* Col. Criswell has been a Collector-Dealer for 35 years.

He has authored numerous books and articles on Confederate currency, lectured extensively on the subject, had articles published and illustrated in *Parade Magazine, Life Magazine, People Magazine* and many hobby publications. He has appeared on such National T.V. Shows as *"What's My Line," "To Tell The Truth"* and *"The Today Program."*

A Life Member of the American Numismatic Association, he has served seven terms as a member of the Board of Governors, and President.

He is a member of over 100 Numismatic, Philatelic and Historical Societies, 60 of which are life memberships, and served on the Florida Civil War Centennial Commission and as an advisor to the National Civil War Centennial Commission.

Other Books on Currency:

Confederate and Southern States Currency
This 291-page hard-cover book lists and prices ALL varieties of notes issued by the Confederate Central Government, and the Southern States, from 1821 to 1895. **$25.00**

Confederate and Southern States Bonds
This 374-page hard-cover book lists and prices ALL bonds issued by the Confederate and Southern States from 1861 to 1882. **$24.95**

A Banking History of Louisiana
A complete historical background of banking in the South from 1818 to 1930.
$10.00

Available from: Criswell's Publications
Ft. McCoy, FL. 32637

Criswell's Maintains an
"EXPERTIZING SERVICE" FOR PAPER MONEY AND BONDS

The Certificates are recognized throughout the world by Insurance Companies, Banks, Administrators, Dealers and Individuals.

One Certificate per item is furnished on currency, bonds, stocks, fiscal papers, etc. The fee is $1.00 per item or 10% of its value, but will not exceed $10.00 per item.

Criswell's also specialized in appraisals on collections or large lots. Arrangements should be made in advance before shipping very large lots. When writing please state the number and general type of items to be appraised and an estimate of the fee can be given.

The HOUSE OF COLLECTIBLES Series

☐ Please send me the following price guides—
☐ I would like the most current edition of the books listed below.

THE OFFICIAL PRICE GUIDES TO:

☐	199-3	**American Silver & Silver Plate** 5th Ed.	$11.95
☐	513-1	**Antique Clocks** 3rd Ed.	10.95
☐	283-3	**Antique & Modern Dolls** 3rd Ed.	10.95
☐	287-6	**Antique & Modern Firearms** 6th Ed.	11.95
☐	738-X	**Antiques & Collectibles** 8th Ed.	10.95
☐	289-2	**Antique Jewelry** 5th Ed.	11.95
☐	539-5	**Beer Cans & Collectibles** 4th Ed.	7.95
☐	521-2	**Bottles Old & New** 10th Ed.	10.95
☐	532-8	**Carnival Glass** 2nd Ed.	10.95
☐	295-7	**Collectible Cameras** 2nd Ed.	10.95
☐	548-4	**Collectibles of the '50s & '60s** 1st Ed.	9.95
☐	740-1	**Collectible Toys** 4th Ed.	10.95
☐	531-X	**Collector Cars** 7th Ed.	12.95
☐	538-7	**Collector Handguns** 4th Ed.	14.95
☐	748-7	**Collector Knives** 9th Ed.	12.95
☐	361-9	**Collector Plates** 5th Ed.	11.95
☐	296-5	**Collector Prints** 7th Ed.	12.95
☐	001-6	**Depression Glass** 2nd Ed.	9.95
☐	589-1	**Fine Art** 1st Ed.	19.95
☐	311-2	**Glassware** 3rd Ed.	10.95
☐	243-4	**Hummel Figurines & Plates** 6th Ed.	10.95
☐	523-9	**Kitchen Collectibles** 2nd Ed.	10.95
☐	291-4	**Military Collectibles** 5th Ed.	11.95
☐	525-5	**Music Collectibles** 6th Ed.	11.95
☐	313-9	**Old Books & Autographs** 7th Ed.	11.95
☐	298-1	**Oriental Collectibles** 3rd Ed.	11.95
☐	746-0	**Overstreet Comic Book** 17th Ed.	11.95
☐	522-0	**Paperbacks & Magazines** 1st Ed.	10.95
☐	297-3	**Paper Collectibles** 5th Ed.	10.95
☐	744-4	**Political Memorabilia** 1st Ed.	10.95
☐	529-8	**Pottery & Porcelain** 6th Ed.	11.95
☐	524-7	**Radio, TV & Movie Memorabilia** 3rd Ed.	11.95
☐	288-4	**Records** 7th Ed.	10.95
☐	247-7	**Royal Doulton** 5th Ed.	11.95
☐	280-9	**Science Fiction & Fantasy Collectibles** 2nd Ed.	10.95
☐	747-9	**Sewing Collectibles** 1st Ed.	8.95
☐	358-9	**Star Trek/Star Wars Collectibles** 2nd Ed.	8.95
☐	086-5	**Watches** 8th Ed.	12.95
☐	248-5	**Wicker** 3rd Ed.	10.95

THE OFFICIAL:

☐	445-3	**Collector's Journal** 1st Ed.	4.95
☐	549-2	**Directory to U.S. Flea Markets** 1st Ed.	4.95
☐	365-1	**Encyclopedia of Antiques** 1st Ed.	9.95

☐	369-4	**Guide to Buying and Selling Antiques** 1st Ed.	$9.95
☐	414-3	**Identification Guide to Early American Furniture** 1st Ed.	9.95
☐	413-5	**Identification Guide to Glassware** 1st Ed.	9.95
☐	448-8	**Identification Guide to Gunmarks** 2nd Ed.	9.95
☐	412-7	**Identification Guide to Pottery & Porcelain** 1st Ed.	9.95
☐	415-1	**Identification Guide to Victorian Furniture** 1st Ed.	9.95

THE OFFICIAL (SMALL SIZE) PRICE GUIDES TO:

☐	309-0	**Antiques & Flea Markets** 4th Ed.	4.95
☐	269-8	**Antique Jewelry** 3rd Ed.	4.95
☐	085-7	**Baseball Cards** 8th Ed.	4.95
☐	647-2	**Bottles** 3rd Ed.	4.95
☐	544-1	**Cars & Trucks** 3rd Ed.	5.95
☐	519-0	**Collectible Americana** 2nd Ed.	4.95
☐	294-9	**Collectible Records** 3rd Ed.	4.95
☐	306-6	**Dolls** 4th Ed.	4.95
☐	359-7	**Football Cards** 7th Ed.	4.95
☐	540-9	**Glassware** 3rd Ed.	4.95
☐	526-3	**Hummels** 4th Ed.	4.95
☐	279-5	**Military Collectibles** 3rd Ed.	4.95
☐	745-2	**Overstreet Comic Book Companion** 1st Ed.	4.95
☐	278-7	**Pocket Knives** 3rd Ed.	4.95
☐	527-1	**Scouting Collectibles** 4th Ed.	4.95
☐	494-1	**Star Trek/Star Wars Collectibles** 3rd Ed.	3.95
☐	307-4	**Toys** 4th Ed.	4.95

THE OFFICIAL BLACKBOOK PRICE GUIDES OF:

☐	743-6	**U.S. Coins** 26th Ed.	3.95
☐	742-8	**U.S. Paper Money** 20th Ed.	3.95
☐	741-X	**U.S. Postage Stamps** 10th Ed.	3.95

THE OFFICIAL INVESTORS GUIDE TO BUYING & SELLING:

☐	534-4	**Gold, Silver & Diamonds** 2nd Ed.	12.95
☐	535-2	**Gold Coins** 2nd Ed.	12.95
☐	536-0	**Silver Coins** 2nd Ed.	12.95
☐	537-9	**Silver Dollars** 2nd Ed.	12.95

THE OFFICIAL NUMISMATIC GUIDE SERIES:

☐	254-X	**The Official Guide to Detecting Counterfeit Money** 2nd Ed.	7.95
☐	257-4	**The Official Guide to Mint Errors** 4th Ed.	7.95

SPECIAL INTEREST SERIES:

☐	506-9	**From Hearth to Cookstove** 3rd Ed.	17.95
☐	530-1	**Lucky Number Lottery Guide** 1st Ed.	4.95
☐	504-2	**On Method Acting** 8th Printing	6.95

	TOTAL	

SEE REVERSE SIDE FOR ORDERING INSTRUCTIONS